William Ewart Gladstone

Speeches on the Irish Question in 1886

William Ewart Gladstone

Speeches on the Irish Question in 1886

ISBN/EAN: 9783744717212

Printed in Europe, USA, Canada, Australia, Japan

Cover: Foto ©ninafisch / pixelio.de

More available books at **www.hansebooks.com**

SPEECHES

ON

THE IRISH QUESTION

IN 1886.

BY THE

RIGHT HON. W. E. GLADSTONE, M.P.

With an Appendix

CONTAINING THE FULL TEXT OF THE GOVERNMENT OF IRELAND AND THE SALE AND PURCHASE OF LAND BILLS OF 1886.

Revised Edition.

EDINBURGH: ANDREW ELLIOT.

1886.

PREFACE.

THE present Volume is issued as a continuation of the previous Series containing the Midlothian Speeches of 1879, 1880, 1884, and 1885. The whole has been revised on Mr. Gladstone's behalf; the portion of the Speech on the Second Reading of the Government of Ireland Bill, dealing with the Representation of Irish Interests at Westminister, having been corrected by Mr. Gladstone himself. It is right to state that the revision of the Parliamentary portion of the Speeches has not been so complete as could have been wished. It was conducted somewhat hurriedly amid the pressure of official work, and it is therefore hoped that allowance will be made for any slight inaccuracies which may have escaped notice.

P. W. C.

19 CASTLE STREET,
EDINBURGH, 28*th August* 1886

CONTENTS.

Government of Ireland Bill.

Sale and Purchase of Land (Ireland) Bill.

Government of Ireland Bill.

Addresses to the Midlothian Electors.

Speeches during General Election.

APPENDIX.

I.

FIRST HOUSE OF COMMONS SPEECH.

THURSDAY, APRIL 8, 1886.

GOVERNMENT OF IRELAND BILL.

MR. GLADSTONE, on rising to ask leave to introduce a Bill for the Better Government of Ireland, said:—

I could have wished, Mr. Speaker, on several grounds that *Introduction.* it had been possible for me, on this single occasion, to open to the House the whole of the policy and intentions of the Government with respect to Ireland. The two questions of land and of Irish government are, in our view, closely and inseparably connected, for they are the two channels through which we hope to find access, and effectual access, to that question which is the most vital of all—namely, the question of social order in Ireland. As I have said, those two questions are, in our view—whatever they may be in that of any one else—they are in our view, for reasons which I cannot now explain, inseparable the one from the other. But it is impossible for me to attempt such a task. Even as it is, the mass of materials that I have before me I may, without exaggeration, call enormous. I do not know that at any period a task has been laid upon me involving so large and so diver-

House of Commons, April 8.

sified an exposition, and it would be in vain to attempt more than human strength can, I think, suffice to achieve. I may say that, when contemplating the magnitude of that task, I have been filled with a painful mistrust; but that mistrust, I can assure the House, is absorbed in the yet deeper feeling of the responsibility that would lie upon me, and of the mischief that I should inflict upon the public interest, if I should fail to bring home to the minds of members, as I seem to perceive in my own mind, the magnitude of all the varied aspects of this question. What I wish is that we should no longer fence and skirmish with this question, but that we should come to close quarters with it; that we should get if we can at the root; that we should take measures not merely intended for the wants of to-day and of to-morrow, but if possible that we should look into a more distant future; that we should endeavour to anticipate and realize that future by the force of reflection; that we should if possible unroll it in anticipation before our eyes, and make provision now, while there is yet time, for all the results that may await upon a right or wrong decision of to-day.

Social order in Ireland.

Mr. Speaker, on one point I rejoice to think that we have a material, I would say a vital, agreement. It is felt on both sides of the House, unless I am much mistaken, that we have arrived at a stage in our political transactions with Ireland, where two roads part one from the other, not soon probably to meet again. The late Government—I am not now referring to this as a matter of praise or blame, but simply as a matter of fact—the late Government felt that they had reached the moment for decisive resolution when they made the announcement, on the last day of their Ministerial existence, that their duty compelled them to submit to Parliament proposals for further repressive criminal legislation. We concur entirely in that conclusion, and we think that the time is come when it is the duty of Parliament, when the honour of Parliament and its duty alike require, that it should endeavour to come to some decisive resolution in this matter; and our intention is,

House of Commons, April 8.

sir, to propose to the House of Commons that which, as we think, if happily accepted, will liberate Parliament from the restraints under which of late years it has ineffectually struggled to perform the business of the country; will restore legislation to its natural, ancient, unimpeded course; and will, above all, obtain an answer—a clear, we hope, and definitive answer—to the question whether it is or is not possible to establish good and harmonious relations between Great Britain and Ireland on the footing of those free institutions to which Englishmen, Scotchmen, and Irishmen are alike unalterably attached.

Our imperative duty.

Now, when I say that we are imperatively called upon to deal with the great subject of social order in Ireland, do not let me for a moment either be led myself or lead others into the dangerous fault of exaggeration. The crime of Ireland, the agrarian crime of Ireland, I rejoice to say, is not what it was in other days—days now comparatively distant, days within my own earliest recollection as a member of Parliament. In 1833 the Government of Lord Grey proposed to Parliament a strong Coercion Act. At that time the information at their command did not distinguish between agrarian and ordinary crime as the distinction is now made. As to the present time, it is easy to tell the House that the serious agrarian crimes of Ireland, which in 1881 were 994, in 1885 were 239. But I go back to the period of 1832. The contrast is, perhaps, still more striking. In 1832 the homicides in Ireland were 248, in 1885 they were 65. The cases of attempts to kill, happily unfulfilled, in the first of those years were 209, in 1885 were 37. The serious offences of all other kinds in Ireland in 1832 were 6014, in 1885 they were 1057. The whole criminal offences in Ireland in the former year were 14,000, and in the latter year 2683.

Coercion a failure.

So far, therefore, sir, we are not to suppose that the case with which we have now to deal is one of those cases of extreme disorder which threaten the general peace of society. Notwithstanding that, sir, in order to lay the ground for the

House of Commons, April 8.

important measure we are asking leave to introduce, and well I am aware that it does require broad and solid grounds to be laid in order to justify the introduction of such a measure, in order to lay that ground I must ask the House to enter with me into a brief review of the general features of what has been our course with regard to what is termed coercion, or repressive criminal legislation. And, sir, the first point to which I would call your attention is this, that whereas exceptional legislation—legislation which introduces exceptional provisions into the law—ought itself to be in its own nature essentially and absolutely exceptional, it has become for us not exceptional but habitual. We are like a man who, knowing that medicine may be the means of his restoration to health, endeavours to live upon medicine. Nations, no more than individuals, can find a subsistence in what was meant to be a cure. But has it been a cure? Have we attained the object which we desired, and honestly desired, to attain? No, sir, agrarian crime has become, sometimes upon a larger and sometimes upon a smaller scale, as habitual in Ireland as the legislation which has been intended to repress it, and that agrarian crime, although at the present time it is almost at the low-water mark, yet has a fatal capacity of expansion under stimulating circumstances, and rises from time to time, as it rose in 1879–81, to dimensions and to an exasperation which becomes threatening to general social order and to the peace of private and domestic life. I ought, perhaps, to supply an element which I forgot at the moment in comparing 1832 and 1885, that is, to remind the House that the decrease of crime is not so great as it looks, because the population of Ireland at that time was nearly 8,000,000, whereas it may be taken at present at 5,000,000. But the exact proportion, I believe, is fairly represented by the figure I will now give. The population of Ireland now, compared with that time, is under two-thirds, the crime of Ireland now, as compared with that period, is under one-fifth.

But the agrarian crime in Ireland is not so much a cause

House of Commons, April 8.

as it is a symptom. It is a symptom of a yet deeper mischief of which it is only the external manifestation. That manifestation is mainly threefold. In the first place, with certain exceptions for the case of winter juries, it is impossible to depend in Ireland upon the finding of a jury in a case of agrarian crime according to the facts as they are viewed by the Government, by the Judges, and by the public, I think, at large. That is a most serious mischief, passing down deep into the very groundwork of civil society. It is also, sir, undoubtedly a mischief that in cases where the extreme remedy of eviction is resorted to by the landlord—possibly in some instances unnecessarily resorted to, but in other instances resorted to after long patience has been exhausted—these cases of eviction, good, bad, and indifferent as to their justification, stand pretty much in one and the same discredit with the rural population of Ireland, and become, as we know, the occasion of transactions that we all deeply lament. Finally, sir, it is not to be denied that there is great interference in Ireland with individual liberty in the shape of intimidation. Now, sir, I am not about to assume the tone of the Pharisee on this occasion. There is a great deal of intimidation in England too when people find occasion for it; and if we, the English and the Scotch, were under the conviction that we had such grave cause to warrant irregular action, as is the conviction entertained by a very large part of the population in Ireland, I am not at all sure that we should not, like that part of the population in Ireland, resort to the rude and unjustifiable remedy of intimidation. I am very ambitious on this important and critical occasion to gain one object, that is, not to treat this question controversially. I have this object in view, and I do not despair of attaining it; and in order that I may do nothing to cause me to fail of attaining it I will not enter into the question, if you like, whether there ever is intimidation in England or not. But I will simply record the fact, which I thought it but just to accompany with a confession with regard to ourselves, I will simply record

Agrarian crime a symptom of a deeper mischief.

Intimidation.

House of Commons, April 8.

the fact that intimidation does prevail, not to the extent that is supposed, yet to a material and painful extent in Ireland. The consequence of that is to weaken generally the respect for law, and the respect for contract, and that among a people who, I believe, are as capable of attaining to the very highest moral and social standard as any people on the face of the earth. So much for coercion, if I use the phrase it is for brevity for repressive legislation generally, but there is one circumstance to which I cannot help calling the special attention of the House.

Why coercion has failed.

Nothing has been more painful to me than to observe that in this matter we are not improving, but, on the contrary, we are losing ground. Since the last half century dawned, we have been steadily engaged in extending, as well as in consolidating, free institutions. I divide the period since the Act of Union with Ireland into two, the first from 1800 to 1832, the epoch of what is still justly called the Great Reform Act, and, secondly, from 1833 to 1885. I do not know whether it has been as widely observed as I think it deserves to be, that in the first of those periods, thirty-two years, there were no less than eleven years,—it may seem not much to say, but wait for what is coming,—there were no less than eleven of those thirty-two years in which our Statute-book was free throughout the whole year from repressive legislation of an exceptional kind against Ireland. But in the fifty-three years since we advanced far in the career of Liberal principles and actions—in those fifty-three years, from 1833 to 1885—there were but two years which were entirely free from the action of this special legislation for Ireland. Is not that of itself almost enough to prove that we have arrived at the point where it is necessary that we should take a careful and searching survey of our position? For, sir, I would almost venture, trusting to the indulgent interpretation of the House, to say that the coercion we have heretofore employed has been spurious and ineffectual coercion, and that if there is to be coercion, which God forbid, it ought to be adequate to attain its end. If it is to attain its end it must be different, differently maintained, and maintained with a different spirit, courage, and consistency compared with the coercion with which we have been heretofore familiar.

Coercion morally worn out.

Well, sir, what are the results that have been produced? This result above all—and now I come to what I consider to be the basis of the whole mischief—that rightly or wrongly, yet in point of fact, law is discredited in Ireland, and discredited in Ireland upon this ground especially that it comes to the people of that country with a foreign aspect and in a foreign garb. These coercion Bills of ours, of course, for it has become a matter of course, I am speaking of the facts and not of the merits, these coercion Bills are stiffly resisted by the members who represent Ireland in Parliament. The English mind, by cases of this kind and by the tone of the press towards them, is estranged from the Irish people, and the Irish mind is estranged from the people of England and Scotland. I will not speak of other circumstances attending the present state of Ireland, but I do think that I am not assuming too much when I say that I have shown enough in this comparatively brief review, and I wish it could have been briefer still, to prove that if coercion is to be the basis for legislation we must no longer be seeking, as we are always laudably seeking, to whittle it down almost to nothing at the very first moment we begin, but we must, like men, adopt it, hold by it, sternly enforce it till its end has been completely attained, with what results to peace, goodwill, and freedom I do not now stop to inquire. Our ineffectual and spurious coercion is morally worn out. I give credit to the late Government for their conception of the fact. They must have realized it when they came to the conclusion in 1885 that they would not propose the renewal or continuance of repressive legislation. They were in a position in which it would have been comparatively easy for them to have proposed it, as a Conservative Government following in the footsteps of a Liberal Administration. But they

House of Commons, April 8.

determined not to propose it. I wish I could be assured that they and the party by whom they are supported were fully aware of the immense historic weight of that determination. I have sometimes heard language used which appears to betoken an idea on the part of those who use it that this is a very simple matter—that, in one state of facts, they judged one way in July, and that, in another state of facts, they judged another way in January; and that consequently the whole ought to be effaced from the minds and memories of men. Depend upon it, the effect of that decision of July never can be effaced; it will weigh, it will tell upon the fortunes and circumstances both of England and of Ireland.

Effectual coercion.

The return to the ordinary law, I am afraid, cannot be said to have succeeded. Almost immediately after the lapse of the Crimes Act boycotting increased fourfold. Since that time it has been about stationary; but in October it had increased fourfold compared with what it was in the month of May. Well, now, if it be true that resolute coercion ought to take the place of irresolute coercion, if it be true that our system, such as I have exhibited it, has been—we may hide it from ourselves, we cannot hide it from the world—a failure in regard to repressive legislation, will that other coercion, which it is possible to conceive, be more successful? I can, indeed, conceive, and in history we may point to circumstances in which coercion of that kind, stern, resolute, consistent, might be, and has been, successful. But it requires, in my judgment, two essential conditions, and these are the autocracy of Government and the secrecy of public transactions. With those conditions that kind of coercion to which I am referring might possibly succeed. But will it succeed in the light of day, and can it be administered by the people of England and Scotland against the people of Ireland, by the two nations which, perhaps, above all others upon earth —I need hardly except America—best understand and are most fondly attached to the essential principles of liberty?

House of Commons, April 8.

An alternative remains. Stripping the law of its foreign garb.

Now I enter upon another proposition, to which I hardly expect broad exception can be taken. I will not assume, I will not beg the question, whether the people of England and Scotland will ever administer that sort of effectual coercion which I have placed in contrast with our timid and hesitating repressive measures; but this I will say, that the people of England and Scotland will never resort to that alternative until they have tried every other. Have they tried every other? Well, some we have tried, to which I will refer. I have been concerned with some of them myself. But we have not yet tried every alternative, because there is one, not unknown to human experience, on the contrary widely known to various countries in the world, where this dark and difficult problem has been solved by the comparatively natural and simple, though not always easy, expedient of stripping law of its foreign garb and investing it with a domestic character. I am not saying that this will succeed; I by no means beg the question at this moment; but this I will say, that Ireland, as far as I know, and speaking of the great majority of the people of Ireland, believes it will succeed, and that experience elsewhere supports that conclusion. The case of Ireland, though she is represented here not less fully than England or Scotland, is not the same as that of England or Scotland. England, by her own strength and by her vast majority in this House, makes her own laws just as independently as if she were not combined with two other countries. Scotland, a small country, smaller than Ireland, but a country endowed with a spirit so masculine that never in the long course of history, excepting for two brief periods, each of a few years, was the superior strength of England such as to enable her to put down the national freedom beyond the border, Scotland, wisely recognized by England, has been allowed and encouraged in this House to make her own laws as freely and as effectually as if she had a representation six times as strong. The consequence is that the mainspring of law in England is felt by

House of Commons, April 8.

the people to be English; the mainspring of law in Scotland is felt by the people to be Scotch; but the mainspring of law in Ireland is not felt by the people to be Irish, and I am bound to say—truth extorts from me the avowal—that it cannot be felt to be Irish in the same sense as it is English and Scotch.

The net results of this statement which I have laid before the House, because it was necessary as the groundwork of my argument, are these. In the first place, it amounts to little less than a mockery to hold that the state of law and of facts conjointly, which I have endeavoured to describe, conduces to the real unity of this great, noble, and world-wide Empire. In the second place, something must be done, something is imperatively demanded from us, to restore to Ireland the first conditions of civil life, the free course of law, the liberty of every individual in the exercise of every legal right, the confidence of the people in the law and their sympathy with the law, apart from which no country can be called, in the full sense of the word, a civilized country, nor can there be given to that country the blessings which it is the object of civilized society to attain. Well, this is my introduction to the task I have to perform; and now I ask attention to the problem we have before us.

Imperial unity and separate legislatures.

It is a problem not unknown in the history of the world; it is really this, there can be no secret about it as far as we are concerned, how to reconcile Imperial unity with diversity of legislation. Mr. Grattan not only held these purposes to be reconcilable, but he did not scruple to go the length of saying this,—"I demand the continued severance of the Parliaments with a view to the continued and everlasting unity of the Empire." Was that a flight of rhetoric, an audacious paradox? No, it was the statement of a problem which other countries have solved, and under circumstances much more difficult than ours. We ourselves may be said to have solved it, for I do not think that any one will question the fact that, out of the six last centuries, for five centuries at least Ireland has had a Parliament separate from ours. That is a fact undeniable. Did that separation of Parliament destroy the unity of the British Empire? Did it destroy it in the eighteenth century? Do not suppose that I mean that harmony always prevailed between Ireland and England. We know very well there were causes quite sufficient to account for a recurrence of discord. But I take the eighteenth century alone. Can I be told that there was no unity of empire in the eighteenth century? Why, sir, it was the century which saw our navy come to its supremacy. It was the century which witnessed the foundation of that great, gigantic manufacturing industry which now overshadows the whole world. It was, in a pre-eminent sense, the century of empire, and it was, in a sense but too conspicuous, the century of wars. Those wars were carried on, that empire was maintained and enormously enlarged, that trade was established, that navy was brought to supremacy, when England and Ireland had separate Parliaments. Am I to be told that there was no unity of empire in that state of things?

House of Commons, April 8.

Examples from other countries.

Well, sir, what has happened elsewhere? Have any other countries had to look this problem in the face? The last half-century, the last sixty or seventy years since the great war, has been particularly rich in its experience of this subject and in the lessons which it has afforded to us. There are many cases to which I might refer to show how practicable it is, or how practicable it has been found by others whom we are not accustomed to look upon as our political superiors, to bring into existence what is termed local autonomy, and yet not to sacrifice, but to confirm Imperial unity.

Sweden and Norway.

Let us look to those two countries, neither of them very large, but yet countries with which every Englishman and every Scotchman must rejoice to claim his kin—I mean the Scandinavian countries of Sweden and Norway. Immediately after the great war the Norwegians were ready to take sword in hand to prevent their coming under the domination of Sweden. But the Powers of Europe undertook the settlement of that

House of Commons, April 8.

question, and they united those countries upon a footing of strict legislative independence and co-equality. Now, I am not quoting this as an exact precedent for us, but I am quoting it as a precedent, and as an argument *a fortiori*, because I say they confronted much greater difficulties, and they had to put a far greater strain upon the unity of their country, than we can ever be called upon to put upon the unity of ours. The Legislatures of Sweden and of Norway are absolutely independent. The law even forbids, what I hope never will happen between England and Ireland, that a Swede, if I am correct in my impression, should bear office ot any kind in the Norwegian Ministry. There is no sort of supremacy or superiority in the Legislature of Sweden over the Legislature of Norway. The Legislature of Norway has had serious controversies, not with Sweden, but with the King of Sweden, and it has fought out those controversies successfully upon the strictest constitutional and Parliamentary grounds. And yet, with two countries so united, what has been the effect? Not discord, not convulsions, not danger to peace, not hatred, not aversion, but a constantly-growing sympathy; and every man who knows their condition knows that I speak the truth when I say that, in every year that passes, the Norwegians and the Swedes are more and more feeling themselves to be the children of a common country, united by a tie which is never to be broken.

Austria and Hungary.

I will take another case—the case of Austria and Hungary. In Austria and Hungary there is a complete duality of power. I will not enter upon the general condition of the Austrian Empire, or upon the other divisions and diversities which it includes, but I will take simply this case. At Vienna sits the Parliament of the Austrian Monarchy; at Buda-Pesth sits the Parliament of the Hungarian Crown; and that is the state of things which was established, I think, nearly twenty years ago. I ask all those who hear me whether there is one among them who doubts that, whether or not the condition of Austria be at this moment, or be

House of Commons, April 8.

not, perfectly solid, secure, and harmonious, after the enormous difficulties she has had to confront, on account of the boundless diversity of race, whether or not that condition be perfectly normal in every minute particular, this, at least, cannot be questioned, that it is a condition of solidity and of safety compared with the time when Hungary made war on her, war which she was unable to quell when she owed the cohesion of the body politic to the interference of Russian arms, or in the interval that followed, when there existed a perfect legislative union and a supreme Imperial Council sat in Vienna.

Our immense advantages.

Now, I have quoted these illustrations as illustrations which show, not that what we are called upon to consider can be done, but that infinitely more can be done, has been done, under circumstances far less favourable. What was the state of Sweden and Norway, two small countries, Norway undoubtedly inferior in population, but still unassailable in her mountain fastnesses, what was the case of Sweden and Norway for bringing about a union by physical and material means? There were no means to be used but moral means, and those moral means have been completely successful. What, again, was the case of Austria, where the seat of empire in the Archduchy was associated not with the majority, but with the minority of the population, and where she had to face Hungary with numbers far greater than her own? Even there, while having to attempt what was infinitely more complex and more dangerous than even prejudice can suppose to be that which I am about to suggest, it is not to be denied that a great relative good and relative success have been attained. Our advantages are immense in a question of this kind. I do not know how many gentlemen who hear me have read the valuable work of Professor Dicey on the Law of the Constitution. No work that I have ever read brings out in a more distinct and emphatic manner the peculiarity of the British Constitution in one point to which, perhaps, we seldom have occasion to refer, namely,

House of Commons, April 8.

the absolute supremacy of Parliament. We have a Parliament to the power of which there are no limits whatever, except such as human nature, in a Divinely-ordained condition of things, imposes. We are faced by no co-ordinate Legislatures, and are bound by no statutory conditions. There is nothing that controls us, and nothing that compels us, except our convictions of law, of right, and of justice. Surely that is a favourable point of departure in considering a question such as this.

Ireland's former Parliament.

I have referred to the eighteenth century. During that century you had beside you a co-ordinate Legislature. The Legislature of Ireland before the Union had the same title as that of Great Britain. There was no juridical distinction to be drawn between them. Even in point of antiquity they were as nearly as possible on a par, for the Parliament of Ireland had subsisted for five hundred years. It had asserted its exclusive right to make laws for the people of Ireland. That right was never denied, for gentlemen ought to recollect, but all do not perhaps remember, that Poynings' Law was an Irish law imposed by Ireland on herself. That claim of the Parliament of Ireland never was denied until the reign of George II.; and that claim denied in the reign of George II. was admitted in the reign of George III. The Parliament, the great Parliament of Great Britain, had to retract its words and to withdraw its claim, and the Legislature which goes by the name of Grattan's Parliament was as independent in point of authority as any Legislature over the wide world. We are not called upon to constitute another co-ordinate Legislature. While I think it is right to modify the Union in some particulars, we are not about to propose its repeal.

"Dismemberment" a misnomer.

What is the essence of the Union? That is the question. It is impossible to determine what is and what is not the repeal of the Union, until you settle what is the essence of the Union. Well, I define the essence of the Union to be this, that before the Act of Union there were two independent, separate, co-ordinate Parliaments, after the Act of Union there was but one. A supreme statutory authority of the Imperial Parliament over Great Britain, Scotland, and Ireland as one United Kingdom was established by the Act of Union. That supreme statutory authority it is not asked, so far as I am aware, and certainly it is not intended, in the slightest degree to impair. When I heard the hon. member for Cork, in a very striking speech at the commencement of the Session, ask for what I think he termed local autonomy or Irish autonomy, I felt that something was gained in the conduct of this great question. If he speaks, as I believe he speaks, the mind of the vast majority of the representatives of Ireland, I feel that we have no right to question for a moment, in this free country, under a representative system, that the vast majority of the representatives speak the mind of a decided majority of the people. I felt, sir, that something had been gained. Ireland had come a great way to meet us, and it was more than ever our duty to consider whether we could not go some way to meet her. The term "Dismemberment of the Empire," as applied to anything that is now before us, is, in my judgment, I will not argue it at any length now—simply a misnomer. To speak, in connection with any meditated or possible plan, of the dismemberment of the Empire or the disintegration of the Empire is, in the face of the history of the eighteenth century, not merely a misnomer, but an absurdity. Some phrases have been used which I will not refer to, simply because I do not think that they quite accurately describe the case, and because they might open a door to new debate. We hear of national independence, we hear of legislative independence, we hear of an independent Parliament, and we hear of federal arrangements. These are not descriptions which I adopt or which I find it necessary to discuss.

House of Commons, April 8.

Proposed solutions.

Then again, under a sense of the real necessities of the case, there are gentlemen who have their own philanthropic, well-intended plans for meeting this emergency. There are those

House of Commons, April 8.

who say, "Let us abolish the Castle"; and I think that gentlemen of very high authority, who are strongly opposed to giving Ireland a domestic Legislature, have said, nevertheless, that they think there ought to be a general reconstruction of the administrative Government in Ireland. Well, sir, I have considered that question much, and what I want to know is this—how, without a change in the Legislature, without giving to Ireland a domestic Legislature, there is to be, or there even can possibly be, a reconstruction of the Administration. We have sent to Ireland to administer the actual system the best men we could find. When Lord Spencer undertook that office, he represented, not in our belief merely, but in our knowledge, for we had known him long, the flower of the British aristocracy, that portion of the British aristocracy which to high birth and great influence of station unites a love of liberty and of the people as genuine as that which breathes within any cottage in the land. And yet, sir, what is the result? The result is that, after a life of almost unexampled devotion to the public service in Ireland, Lord Spencer's administration not only does not command, which is easily understood, the adhesion and the commendation of the hon. member for Cork and his colleagues, but it is made the subject of cavil and of censure in this House of Parliament, and from the spot where I now stand, by members of the late Conservative Government. I want to know, for we have not come to our conclusions without making careful examination of the conclusions of other people, I want to know how it is possible to construct an administrative system in Ireland without legislative change, and what gentlemen mean when they speak of the administrative system of Ireland. The fault of the administrative system of Ireland, if it has a fault, is simply this, that its spring and source of action, or, if I can use an anatomical illustration without a blunder, what is called the motor muscle, is English and not Irish. Without providing a domestic Legislature for Ireland, without having an Irish

House of Commons, April 8.

Parliament, I want to know how you will bring about this wonderful, superhuman, and, I believe, in this condition, impossible result, that your administrative system shall be Irish and not English.

Limited boons without finality.

There have been several plans liberally devised for granting to Ireland the management of her education, the management of her public works, and the management of one subject and another, boons very important in themselves, under a central elective body; boons any of which I do not hesitate to say I should have been glad to see accepted, or I should have been glad to see a trial given to a system which might have been constructed under them, had it been the desire and the demand of Ireland. I do not think such a scheme would have possessed the advantage of finality. If it had been accepted, and especially if it had been freely suggested from that quarter, by the Irish representatives, it might have furnished a useful *modus vivendi.* But it is absurd, in my opinion, to talk of the adoption of such a scheme in the face of two obstacles, first of all, that those whom it is intended to benefit do not want it, do not ask it, and refuse it; and, secondly, the obstacle, not less important, that all those who are fearful of giving a domestic Legislature to Ireland would naturally and emphatically, and rather justly, say: "We will not create your central board and palter with this question, because we feel certain that it will afford nothing in this world except a stage from which to agitate for a further concession, and because we see that by the proposal you make you will not even attain the advantage of settling the question that is raised."

A domestic Legislature for Ireland.

Well, sir, [what we seek is the settlement of that question; and [we think that we find that settlement in the establishment, by the authority of Parliament, of a legislative body sitting in Dublin for the conduct of both legislation and administration, under the conditions which may be prescribed by the Act, defining Irish, as distinct from Imperial, affairs.] There is the head and front of our offending. Let us pro-

House of Commons, April 8.

ceed to examine the matter a little further. The essential conditions of any plan that Parliament can be asked or could be expected to entertain are, in my opinion, these. The unity of the Empire must not be placed in jeopardy. The safety and welfare of the whole—if there is an unfortunate conflict, which I do not believe—the welfare and security of the whole must be preferred to the security and advantage of the part. The political equality of the three countries must be maintained. They stand by statute on a footing of absolute equality, and that footing ought not to be altered or brought into question. There should be what I will at present term an equitable distribution of Imperial burdens.

Safeguards for the minority.

Next I introduce a provision which may seem to be exceptional, but which, in the peculiar circumstances of Ireland, whose history unhappily has been one long chain of internal controversies as well as of external difficulties, is necessary, in order that there may be reasonable safeguards for the minority. I am asked why there should be safeguards for the minority. Will not the minority in Ireland, as in other countries, be able to take care of itself? Are not free institutions, with absolute publicity, the best security that can be given to any minority? I know, sir, that in the long run our experience shows they are. After we have passed through the present critical period, and obviated and disarmed, if we can, the jealousies with which any change is attended, I believe, as most gentlemen in this House may probably believe, that there is nothing comparable to the healthy action of free discussion, and that a minority asserting in the face of day its natural rights is the best security and guarantee for its retaining them. We have not reached that state of things. I may say, not entering into detail, there are three classes to whom we must look in this case. We must consider, I will not say more on that subject to-day, the class immediately connected with the land. A second question, not, I think, offering any great difficulty, relates to the Civil Service and the offices of the Executive Government in Ireland. The third question relates to what is commonly called the Protestant minority, and especially that important part of the community which inhabits the province of Ulster, or which predominates in a considerable portion of the province of Ulster.

House of Commons, April 8.

Opinion in Ulster.

I will deviate from my path for a moment to say a word upon the state of opinion in that wealthy, intelligent, and energetic portion of the Irish community which, as I have said, predominates in a certain portion of Ulster. Our duty is to adhere to sound general principles, and to give the utmost consideration we can to the opinions of that energetic minority. The first thing of all, I should say, is that if, upon any occasion, by any individual or section, violent measures have been threatened in certain emergencies, I think the best compliment I can pay to those who have threatened us is to take no notice whatever of the threats, but to treat them as momentary ebullitions, which will pass away with the fears from which they spring, and at the same time to adopt on our part every reasonable measure for disarming those fears. I cannot conceal the conviction that the voice of Ireland, as a whole, is at this moment clearly and constitutionally spoken. I cannot say it is otherwise when five-sixths of its lawfully-chosen representatives are of one mind in this matter. There is a counter voice; and I wish to know what is the claim of those by whom that counter voice is spoken, and how much is the scope and allowance we can give them. Certainly, sir, I cannot allow it to be said that a Protestant minority in Ulster, or elsewhere, is to rule the question at large for Ireland. I am aware of no constitutional doctrine tolerable on which such a conclusion could be adopted or justified. But I think that the Protestant minority should have its wishes considered to the utmost practicable extent in any form which they may assume.

Schemes for Ulster.

Various schemes, short of refusing the demand of Ireland at large, have been proposed on behalf of Ulster. One scheme is that Ulster itself, or, perhaps with more appearance of reason, a portion of Ulster, should be excluded from the operation of the Bill we are about to introduce. Another

House of Commons, April 8.

scheme is that a separate autonomy should be provided for Ulster, or for a portion of Ulster. Another scheme is that certain rights with regard to certain subjects—such, for example, as education and some other subjects—should be reserved and should be placed to a certain extent under the control of Provincial Councils. These, I think, are the suggestions which have reached me in different shapes; there may be others. But what I wish to say of them is this,—there is no one of them which has appeared to us to be so completely justified, either upon its merits or by the weight of opinion supporting and recommending it, as to warrant our including it in the Bill and proposing it to Parliament upon our responsibility. What we think is that such suggestions deserve careful and unprejudiced consideration. It may be that that free discussion, which I have no doubt will largely take place after a Bill such as we propose shall have been laid on the table of the House, may give to one of these proposals, or to some other proposals, a practicable form, and that some such plan may be found to be recommended by a general or predominating approval. If it should be so, it will, at our hands, have the most favourable consideration, with every disposition to do what equity may appear to recommend. That is what I have to say on the subject of Ulster.

A real settlement.

I have spoken now of the essential conditions of a good plan for Ireland, and I add only this, that in order to be a good plan it must be a plan promising to be a real settlement of Ireland. To show that without a good plan you can have no real settlement, I may point to the fact that the great settlement of 1782 was not a real settlement. Most unhappily, sir, it was not a real settlement; and why was it not a real settlement? Was it Ireland that prevented it from being a real settlement? No, sir, it was the mistaken policy of England, listening to the pernicious voice and claims of ascendency. It is impossible, however, not to say this word for the Protestant Parliament of Ireland. Founded as it was upon narrow suffrage, exclusive in religion, crowded with

House of Commons, April 8.

pensioners and place-holders, holding every advantage, it yet had in it the spark, at least, and the spirit of true patriotism. It emancipated the Roman Catholics of Ireland when the Roman Catholics of England were not yet emancipated. It received Lord Fitzwilliam with open arms; and when Lord Fitzwilliam promoted to the best of his ability the introduction of Roman Catholics into Parliament, and when his brief career was unhappily intercepted by a peremptory recall from England, what happened? Why, sir, in both Houses of the Irish Parliament votes were at once passed by those Protestants, by those men, mixed as they were, with so large an infusion of pensioners and of place-men, registering their confidence in that nobleman, and desiring that he should still be left to administer the government of Ireland. What the Irish Parliament did when Lord Fitzwilliam was promoting the admission of Roman Catholics into Parliament justifies me in saying there was a spirit there which, if free scope had been left to it, would in all probability have been enabled to work out a happy solution for every Irish problem and difficulty, and would have saved to the coming generation an infinity of controversy and trouble.

Irish Members at Westminster.

I pass on to ask, How are we to set about the giving effect to the proposition I have made, to the purpose I have defined, of establishing in Ireland a domestic Legislature to deal with Irish as contradistinguished from Imperial affairs? And here, sir, I am confronted at the outset by what we have felt to be a formidable dilemma. I will endeavour to state and to explain it to the House as well as I can. Ireland is to have a domestic Legislature for Irish affairs. That is my postulate from which I set out. Are Irish members in this House, are Irish representative peers in the other House, still to continue to form part of the respective Assemblies? That is the first question which meets us in consideration of the ground I have opened. Now I think it will be perfectly clear that, if Ireland is to have a domestic Legislature, Irish peers and Irish representatives cannot come here to control English and Scotch

House of Commons, April 8.

affairs. That I understand to be admitted freely. I never heard of their urging the contrary, and I am inclined to believe that it would be universally admitted. The one thing follows from the other. There cannot be a domestic Legislature in Ireland dealing with Irish affairs, and Irish peers and Irish representatives sitting in Parliament at Westminster to take part in English and Scotch affairs. My next question is, Is it practicable for Irish representatives to come here for the settlement, not of English and Scotch, but of Imperial affairs? In principle it would be very difficult, I think, to object to that proposition. But then its acceptance depends entirely upon our arriving at the conclusion that in this House we can draw for practical purposes a distinction between affairs which are Imperial and affairs which are not Imperial. It would not be difficult to say in principle that, as the Irish Legislature will have nothing to do with Imperial concerns, let Irish members come here and vote on Imperial concerns. All depends on the practicability of the distinction. Well, sir, I have thought much, reasoned much, and inquired much, with regard to that distinction. I had hoped it might be possible to draw a distinction, and I have arrived at the conclusion that it cannot be drawn. I believe it passes the wit of man; at any rate it passes not my wit alone, but the wit of many with whom I have communicated. It would be easy to exhibit a case; but the difficulty, I may say, in my opinion, arises from this. If this were a merely legislative House, or if the House of Lords were merely a legislative House—this House, of course, affords the best illustration—I do not think it would be difficult to draw a distinction. We are going to draw the distinction, we have drawn the distinction, in the Bill which I ask leave to lay on the table, for legislative purposes with reference to what I hope will be the domestic Legislature of Ireland. But this House is not merely a legislative House; it is a House controlling the Executive; and when you come to the control of the Executive, then your distinction between Imperial subjects and non-Imperial subjects totally breaks down, they are totally insufficient to cover the whole case.

House of Commons, April 8.

For example, suppose it to be a question of foreign policy. Suppose the Irish members in this House coming here to vote on a question of foreign policy. Is it possible to deny that they would be entitled to take part in discussing an Address to the Crown for the dismissal of the Foreign Minister? It is totally impossible to deny, it is totally impossible to separate, the right of impugning the policy and the right of action against the Minister. Well, sir, if on that account members might take part in an Address dismissing the Foreign Minister, I want to know, considering the collective responsibility of Government—a principle, I hope, which will always be maintained at the very highest level that circumstances will permit, for I am satisfied that the public honour and the public welfare are closely associated with it—if that be so, what will be the effect of the dismissal of the Foreign Minister on the existence and action of the Government to which he belongs? Why, sir, the Government in nineteen cases out of twenty will break down with the Foreign Minister; and when these gentlemen, coming here for the purpose of discussing Imperial questions alone, could dislodge the Government which is charged with the entire interests of England and Scotland, I ask you what becomes of the distinction between Imperial and non-Imperial affairs? I believe the distinction to be impossible, and therefore I arrive at the next conclusion, that Irish members and Irish peers cannot, if a domestic Legislature be given to Ireland, justly retain a seat in the Parliament at Westminster.

The distinction between Imperial and non-Imperial affairs.

If Irish members do not sit in this House and Irish peers do not sit in the other House, how is Ireland to be taxed? I shall assume, as a matter of course, that we should propose that a general power of taxation should pass to the domestic Legislature of Ireland. But there is one very important branch of taxation, involving, indeed, a second branch, which is susceptible of being viewed in a very different aspect from

Fiscal unity.

House of Commons, April 8.

the taxes of Ireland generally. I mean the duties of customs and duties of excise relatively to customs. One thing I take to be absolutely certain. Great Britain will never force upon Ireland taxation without representation. Well, sir, if we are never to force upon Ireland taxation without representation, then comes another question of the deepest practical interest: Are we to give up the fiscal unity of the Empire? I sometimes see it argued that, in giving up the fiscal unity of the Empire, we should give up the unity of the Empire. To that argument I do not subscribe. The unity of the Empire rests upon the supremacy of Parliament and on considerations much higher than considerations merely fiscal. But I must admit that, while I cannot stand on the high ground of principle, yet on the very substantial ground of practice to give up the fiscal unity of the Empire would be a very great public inconvenience and a very great public misfortune—a very great public misfortune for Great Britain; and I believe it would be a still greater misfortune for Ireland were the fiscal unity of the Empire to be put to hazard and practically abandoned. I may say also, looking as I do with hope to the success of the measure I now propose, I, at any rate, feel the highest obligation not to do anything, not to propose anything without necessity, that would greatly endanger the right comprehension of this subject by the people of England and Scotland, which might be the case were the fiscal unity of the Empire to be broken.

Customs and Excise.

There is the dilemma. I conceive that there is but one escape from it, and that is, if there were conditions upon which Ireland consented to such arrangements as would leave the authority of levying customs duties, and such excise duties as are immediately connected with customs, in the hands of Parliament here, and would by her will consent to set our hands free to take the course that the general exigencies of the case appear to require. These conditions I take to be three: in the first place, that a general power of taxation over and above these particular duties should pass unequivocally

House of Commons, April 8.

into the hands of the domestic Legislature of Ireland; in the second place, that the entire proceeds of the customs and excise should be held for the benefit of Ireland, for the discharge of the obligations of Ireland, and for the payment of the balance after discharging those obligations into an Irish Exchequer, to remain at the free disposal of the Irish legislative body.

Provision as to alteration of our proposed Act.

But there is another point which I think ought to engage, and may justly engage, the anxious attention in particular of the representatives of Ireland; and it is this. The proposal which I have now sketched is, that we should pass an Act giving to Ireland what she considers an enormous boon, under the name of a statutory Parliament for the control of Irish affairs, both legislative and administrative. But one of the provisions of that Act is the withdrawal of Irish representative peers from the House of Lords and Irish members from the House of Commons. Well, then, I think it will naturally occur to the Irish, as it would in parallel circumstances to the Scotch or the English, and more especially to the Scotch mind, what would become of the privileges conveyed by the Act after the Scotch members, who were their natural guardians, were withdrawn from Parliament. (A Voice: The Irish members.) I was speaking of the Scotch members in order to bring it very distinctly to the minds of hon. members, supposing that Scotland had entertained, what she has never had reason to entertain, the desire for a domestic Legislature. I must confess I think that Ireland ought to have security on that subject, security that advantage would not be taken, so far as we can preclude the possibility of it, of the absence of Irish representatives from Parliament for the purpose of tampering with any portion of the boon which we propose to confer on Ireland by this Act. I think we have found a method for dealing with that difficulty. I may be very sanguine, but I hope that the day may come when Ireland will have reason to look on this Act, if adopted by Parliament, as for practical purposes her Magna Charta. A Magna Charta

House of Commons, April 8.

for Ireland ought to be most jealously and effectively assured, and it will be assured, against unhallowed and unlawful interference.

Future alterations on Act only with consent of both Legislatures.

Two cases at once occur to the mind. There might be alterations of detail in a law of this kind on which everybody might be agreed. We think it would be very absurd to require either the construction or reconstruction of a cumbrous and difficult machinery for the purpose of disposing of cases of this kind, and therefore we propose that the provisions of this Act might be modified with the concurrence of the Irish Legislature, or in conformity with an Address from the Irish Legislature. That is intended for cases where there is a general agreement. I hope it will not happen, but I admit it might happen, that in some point or other the foresight and sagacity now brought to bear on this subject might prove insufficient. It is possible, though I trust it is not probable, that material alterations might be found requisite, that on these amendments there might be differences of opinion; and yet, however improbable the case may be, it is a case which it might be proper to provide for beforehand. What we then should propose is, that the provisions of this Act should not be altered, except either on an Address from the Irish Legislature to the Crown such as I have described, or else after replacing and recalling into action the full machinery under which Irish representatives now sit here and Irish peers sit in the House of Lords, so that when their case again came to be tried they might have the very same means of defending their constitutional rights as they have now. Now, we believe that is one of those cases which are often best averted by making a good provision against them.

The removal of the Irish Members.

Now, upon the footing which I have endeavoured to describe, we propose to relieve Irish peers and representatives from attendance at Westminster, and at the same time to preserve absolutely the fiscal unity of the Empire. Let me say that there are several reasons that occur to me which might well incline the prudence of Irishmen to adopt an arrange-

House of Commons, April 8.

ment of this kind. If there were Irish representatives in this House at the same time that a domestic Legislature sat in Ireland, I think that the presence of those Irish representatives would have some tendency to disparage the domestic Legislature. I think there would be serious difficulties that would arise, besides the insurmountable difficulty that I have pointed out as to the division of subjects. Even if it were possible to divide the subjects, what an anomaly it would be, what a mutilation of all our elementary ideas about the absolute equality of members in this House, were we to have ordinarily among us two classes of members, one of them qualified to vote on all kinds of business, and another qualified only to vote here and there on particular kinds of business, and obliged to submit to some criterion or other, say the authority of the Chair, novel for such a purpose and difficult to exercise, in order to determine what kinds of business they could vote upon, and what kinds of business they must abstain from voting on! There would, I think, be another difficulty in determining what the number of those members should be. My opinion is that there would be great jealousy of the habitual presence of 103 Irish members in this House, even for limited purposes, after a legislative body had been constructed in Ireland; and on the other hand I can very well conceive that Ireland would exceedingly object to the reduction, the material reduction, of those members. I am sorry to have to mention another difficulty, which is this: Ireland has not had the practice in local self-government that has been given to England and Scotland. We have unfortunately shut her out from that experience. In some respects we have been jealous, in others niggardly towards Ireland. It might be very difficult for Ireland in the present state of things to man a legislative chamber in Dublin, and at the same time to present in this House an array of so much distinguished ability as I think all parties will admit has been exhibited on the part of Ireland during recent Parliaments on the benches of this House.

House of Commons, April 8.

Powers of the Irish legislative body.

But I pass on from this portion of the question, having referred to these two initiatory propositions as principal parts of the foundation of the Bill—namely, first, that it is proposed that the Irish representation in Parliament at Westminster should cease, unless in the contingent, and I hope hardly possible, case to which I have alluded, and next that the fiscal unity of the Empire shall be absolutely maintained. My next duty is to state what the powers of the proposed legislative body will be.

The Control of the Executive.

The capital article of that legislative body will be, that it should have the control of the executive Government of Ireland as well as of legislative business. Evidently, I think, it was a flaw in the system of 1782 that adequate provision was not made for that purpose, and we should not like to leave a flaw of such a nature in the work we are now undertaking. In 1782 there were difficulties that we have not now before us. At that time it might have been very fairly said that no one could tell how a separate Legislature would work unless it had under its control what is termed a responsible Government. We have no such difficulty and no such excuse now. The problem of responsible government has been solved for us in our Colonies. It works very well there; and in perhaps a dozen cases in different quarters of the globe it works to our perfect satisfaction. It may be interesting to the House if I recount the fact that that responsible government in the Colonies was, I think, first established by one of our most distinguished statesmen, Earl Russell, when he held the office of Colonial Secretary in the Government of Lord Melbourne. But it was a complete departure from established tradition, and, if I remember right, not more than two or three years before that generous and wise experiment was tried, Lord Russell had himself written a most able despatch to show that it could not be done, that with responsible government in the Colonies you would have two centres of gravity and two sources of motion in the Empire, while a united Empire absolutely required that there should be but

House of Commons, April 8.

one, and that consequently the proposition could not be entertained. Such was the view of the question while it was yet at a distance, and such perhaps may have been our view on the subject I am now discussing while it was yet at a distance. But it has been brought near to us by the circumstances of the late election, and I believe that if we look closely at its particulars we should find that many of the fears with which we may have regarded it are perfectly unreal, and especially so that great panic, that great apprehension of all, the fear lest it should prove injurious to what it is our first duty to maintain, namely, the absolute unity and integrity of the Empire.

Exceptions to be specified.

There is another point in regard to the powers of the legislative body of which I wish to make specific mention. Two courses might have been followed. One would be to endow this legislative body with particular legislative powers. The other is to except from the sphere of its action those subjects which we think ought to be excepted, and to leave it everything else which is the consequence of the plans before us. There will be an enumeration of disabilities, and everything not included in that enumeration will be left open to the domestic Legislature. As I have already said, the administrative power by a responsible Government would pass under our proposals with the legislative power. Then, sir, the legislative body would be subject to the provisions of the Act in the first place as to its own composition. But we propose to introduce into it what I would generally explain as two orders, though not two Houses; and we suggest that, with regard to the popular order, which will be the more numerous, the provisions of the Act may be altered at any period after the first dissolution; but, with regard to the other and less numerous order, the provisions of the Act can only be altered after the assent of the Crown to an address from the legislative body for that purpose. We should provide generally, and on that I conceive there would be no difference of opinion, that this body should be subject

House of Commons, April 8.

to all the prerogatives of the Crown, but we should insert a particular provision to the effect that its *maximum* duration, without dissolution, should not exceed five years.

Its limitations.

I will now tell the House, and I would beg particular attention to this, what are the functions that we propose to withdraw from the cognizance of this legislative body. The three grand and principal functions are, first, everything that relates to the Crown—succession, prerogatives, and the mode of administering powers during incapacity, regency, and, in fact, all that belongs to the Crown. The next would be all that belongs to defence—the Army, the Navy, the entire organization of armed force. I do not say the police force, which I will touch upon by-and-by, but everything belonging to defence. And the third would be the entire subject of Foreign and Colonial relations. Those are the subjects most properly Imperial, and I will say belonging as a principle to the Legislature established under the Act of Union and sitting at Westminster. There are some other subjects which I will briefly touch upon. In the first place, it would not be competent to the domestic Legislature in Ireland to alter the provisions of the Act which we are now about to pass, as I hope, and which I ask that we should pass with the consent of the three countries—it would not be competent to the Irish legislative body to alter those provisions, excepting in points where they are designedly left open as part of the original contract and settlement. We do not propose universal disability as to contracts, but there are certain contracts made in Ireland under circumstances so peculiar that we think we ought to except them from the action of the legislative body. There are also some analogous provisions made in respect to charters anterior to the Act, which in our opinion ought only to be alterable after the assent of the Crown to an address from the legislative body for that purpose. There is another disability that we propose to lay upon the legislative body; and it is one of those with respect to which I am bound to say, in my belief there is no real

(1) The Crown.

(2) Army and Navy.

(3) Foreign and Colonial relations.

(4) Alterations on this Act when passed.

(5) Exceptional contracts.

apprehension that the thing would be done, but at the same time, though there may not be a warranted apprehension, there are many honest apprehensions which it is our duty to consider as far as we can. We propose to provide that the legislative body should not be competent to pass a law for the establishment or the endowment of any particular religion. Those I may call exceptions of principle. Then there are exceptions of what I may call practical necessity for ordinary purposes. The first of those is the law of trade and navigation. I assume that, as to trade and navigation at large, it would be a great calamity to Ireland to be separated from Great Britain. The question of taxation in relation to trade and navigation I have already mentioned. The same observation applies to the subject of coinage and legal tender, but we do not propose to use the term 'currency,' simply because there is an ambiguity about it. Ireland might think fit to pass a law providing for the extinction of private issues in Ireland, and that no bank notes should be issued in Ireland except under the authority and for the advantage of the State. I own it is my opinion that Ireland would do an extremely sensible thing if she passed such a law. It is my most strong and decided opinion that we ought to have the same law ourselves, but the block of business has prevented that and many other good things towards the attainment of which I hope we are now going to open and clear the way. I only use that as an illustration to show that I should be very sorry if we were needlessly to limit the free action of the Irish Legislature upon Irish matters. There are other subjects on which I will not dwell. One of them is the subject of weights and measures; another is the subject of copyright. These are not matters for discussion at the present moment.

House of Commons, April 8.

(6) *Endowment of religion.*

(7) *Trade and Navigation.*

(8) *Coinage.*

(9) *Weights and Measures.*

(10) *Copyright.*

There is, however, one other important subject, with regard to which we propose to leave it entirely open to the judgment of Ireland—that subject is the Post Office. Our opinion is that it would be for the convenience of both countries if the

Post Office.

House of Commons, April 8.

Post Office were to remain under the control of the Postmaster-General; but the Post Office requires an army of servants, and I think that Ireland might not wish to see all the regulations connected with that unarmed army left to an English authority. We have therefore placed the Post Office in the Bill under circumstances which would enable the legislative body in Ireland to claim for itself authority on this subject if it should see fit. There are some other matters, such as the quarantine laws, and one or two others, which stand in the same category. Now, sir, that I believe I may give as a sufficient description of the exceptions from the legislative action of the proposed Irish Legislature, bearing in mind the proposition that everything which is not excepted is conferred.

Composition of the new Irish legislative body.

I have dealt with the powers of the legislative body. I come next to the composition of the legislative body. We propose to provide for it as follows. I have referred to the protection of minorities. We might constitute a legislative body in Ireland by a very brief enactment, if we were to say that the 103 members now representing Ireland and 103 more members, perhaps elected by the same constituencies, should constitute the one and only legislative House in Ireland without the introduction of what I may call the dual element. But, sir, we are of opinion that, if a proposition of that kind were made, in the first place it would be stated that it did not afford legitimate protection for minorities. And, in the second place, it might be thought by many of those who would be less sensitive on the subject of minorities that some greater provision was required for stability and consistency in the conduct of the complex work of legislation than could possibly be supplied by a single set of men elected under an absolutely single influence. Upon that account, sir, we propose to introduce into this legislative body what we have termed two orders. These orders would sit and deliberate together. There would be a power on the demand of either order for separate voting. The effect of that

House of Commons, April 8.

separate voting would be that while the veto was in force, while it sufficed to bar the enactment of a Bill, there would be an absolute veto of one order upon the other. Such veto, in our view, might be salutary and useful for the purpose of insuring deliberation and consistency with adequate consideration in the business of making laws. But it ought not to be perpetual. If it were perpetual, a block would arise, as it might arise conceivably, and as really, we may almost say, we have seen it arise in certain cases in the Colonies, particularly in one, where there were two perfectly independent orders. What we therefore propose is that this veto can only be operative for a limited time, say until a dissolution, or for a period of three years, whichever might be the longer of the two.

So much, sir, for the relation of these two orders, the one to the other. I may observe that that distinction of orders would be available, and is almost necessary, with a view to maintaining the only form of control over the judicial body known to us in this country, viz. the concurrence of two authorities, chosen under somewhat different influences, in one common conclusion with regard to the propriety of removing a judge from his office.

The First Order and the Irish Peers.

Now, sir, I will just describe very briefly the composition of these orders. It may not have occurred to many gentlemen that, if we succeed in the path we are now opening, with respect to the twenty-eight distinguished individuals who now occupy the place of representative peers of Ireland, it will not be possible, we think, for them to continue to hold their places in the House of Lords after the Irish representatives have been removed from attending the House of Commons. I do not say that the precedent is an exact one; but the House may remember that, in the case of the disestablishment of the Irish Church, we did disable the bishops who were entitled to sit for life from continuing, I mean disable them personally from continuing, to sit in the House of Lords after the disestablishment of the Irish Church. We do not

House of Commons, April 8.

wish, sir, to inflict this personal disability. We propose that these twenty-eight peers shall have the option of sitting, if they think fit, as a portion of the first order in the Irish legislative assembly, and that they shall have the power, that they shall personally have the power, of sitting there, as they sit in the House of Lords, for life. There may, sir, be those who think this option will not be largely used. I am not one of that number. I believe that the Irish peers have an Irish as well as an Imperial patriotism. In the eighteenth century Irish peers were not ashamed of the part they played in the Irish Parliament. It was, I think, the Duke of Leinster who moved the Address in the Irish House of Peers, which he carried, expressing the confidence of that House in Lord Fitzwilliam. I may be too sanguine, but I say boldly that if this measure pass under happy circumstances, especially if it pass without political exasperation, one of its effects will be a great revival of the local as well as a great confirmation and extension of Imperial patriotism. At any rate, it is our duty, I think, to provide that the Irish peers, the twenty-eight representative Irish peers, may form part of the Irish legislative body. There will be no disability entailed upon any Irish peer from being at once a member of the Irish legislative body and likewise of the House of Lords. In the last century many distinguished men sat in both, and in the circumstances we certainly see no cause for putting an end to the double qualification which was thus enjoyed, and which, I think, worked beneficially. There is a difficulty, however, to which I will just advert for one moment, in combining the connection or place of these twenty-eight peers who are to sit for life with the rest of the first order of the Chamber. We propose as to the remainder of the first order that it shall consist of seventy-five members to be elected by the Irish people, under conditions which we propose to specify in the schedule to the Act, not yet filled up as to its details. But I mention at once the two provisions which would apply to the election of seventy-five members. First of all, the constituency would be

House of Commons, April 8.

a constituency composed of persons occupying to the value of £25 and upwards; and, secondly, they would be elected for a period, as a general rule, of ten years, with a little exception I need not now refer to. Thirdly, they will be elected subject to a property qualification of realty to the extent of £200 a-year, or of personalty to the extent of £200 a-year, or a capital value of £4000. The peers would ultimately be replaced by twenty-eight members, elected under the above conditions. We cannot ensure that all these twenty-eight peers shall die at the same time: it would, consequently, be extremely difficult to devise an electoral machinery for the purpose of supplying their places by election. We therefore propose to grant to the Crown power, limited to a term which we think may fairly well exhaust the present generation, of filling their places by nomination, not for life, but down to the date to be fixed by the Act. After the system had ceased to operate, and the representative peers had ceased to be in that first order, the first order of the legislative body would be elected entirely upon the basis I have described.

The Second Order to consist of 204 Members.

With regard to the second order, its composition would be simple. Of course, it would be proposed to the 103 gentlemen who now represent Ireland in this House from county districts, from citizen towns, and from the University of Dublin, that they should take their places in the Irish Legislative Chamber in Dublin. We should likewise propose as nearly as possible to duplicate that body. Another 101 members, not 103, we propose should be elected by the county districts and the citizen towns in exactly the same manner as that in which the present 101 members for counties and towns have been elected. We shall also propose that in the event of any refusal to sit, refusals to accept the option given, the place shall be filled up by election under the machinery now existing. I ought to say a word about Dublin University. We do not propose to interfere by any action of ours with the existing arrangements of Dublin University in one way or another. But certainly we could

House of Commons, April 8.

not ask the House to adopt a plan at our suggestion which would double the representation of Dublin University. We propose to leave it as it is, but at the same time to empower the legislative body, if it should think fit, to appoint a corresponding representation by two members in favour of the Royal University of Ireland. There would be no compulsion to exercise that power, but it would be left to the discretion of the legislative body. The effect of that would be to give to the first order of the proposed Legislative Chamber or body a number making 103, to give to the second order the number of 206 at the outside, or 204 if the power of the Royal University were not exercised, and to leave the relations of the two orders upon the footing which I have described.

The Irish Executive.

I must now say a few words upon the subject of the Executive; and what we think most requisite with regard to the Executive is that our Act should be as elastic as possible. It is quite evident that, though the legislative transition can be made, and ought to be made, *per saltum*, by a single stroke, the Executive transition must necessarily be gradual. We propose, therefore, sir, to leave everything as it is, until it is altered in the regular course; so that there shall be no breach of continuity in the government of the country, but that by degrees, as may be arranged by persons who, we feel convinced, will meet together in a spirit of co-operation, and will find no great, much less insurmountable, difficulty in their way, the old state of things shall be adjusted to the new. On the one hand, the representatives of the old system will remain on the ground; on the other hand, the principle of responsible government is freely and fully conceded. That principle of responsible government will work itself out in every necessary detail. It has often, sir, been proposed to abolish the Viceroyalty, and some gentlemen have even been sanguine enough to believe that to abolish the Viceroyalty was to solve the whole Irish problem. I must say that I think that that involves a faculty of belief far beyond any power either of the understanding or imagination to which

House of Commons, April 8.

I have ever been able to aspire. We propose to leave the Viceroyalty without interference by the Act, except in the particulars which I am about to name. The office of the Viceroy will only be altered by statute. He would not be the representative of a party. He would not quit office with the outgoing Government. He would have round him, as he has now, in a certain form, a Privy Council, to aid and to advise him. Within that Privy Council the executive body would form itself under the action of the principal responsible Government, for the purpose of administering the various offices of the State. The Queen would be empowered to delegate to him, in case his office should be permanently continued, which I am far from believing to be unlikely, any of the prerogatives which she now enjoys or which she would exercise under this Act. And, finally, we have not forgotten that his office almost alone is still affected by one solitary outstanding religious disability, a kind of Lot's wife when everything else has been destroyed, and that religious disability we propose by our Bill to remove.

Judges.

The next point is with regard to the judges of the superior courts, and here I draw a partial distinction between the present and the future judges. As regards the judges of the superior courts now holding office, we desire to secure to them their position and their emoluments in the same absolute form as that in which they now exist. Although they would become chargeable upon the Consolidated Fund of Ireland, which we propose to constitute by the Act, still they would retain their lien, so to call it, on the Consolidated Fund of Great Britain. Under the peculiar circumstances of Ireland, we cannot forget that some of these judges, by no fault of their own, have been placed in relations more or less uneasy with popular influences, and with what under the new Constitution will in all probability be the dominating influence in that country. We cannot overlook the peculiarities of Irish history in framing the provisions of this Bill, and we therefore propose, both with regard to the judges now holding office and with regard to

House of Commons, April 8.

other persons who, in what they deemed loyal service to the Empire, have been concerned in the administration and conduct of the criminal law in Ireland, that Her Majesty may, not lightly or wholesale, but if she should see cause on any particular occasion, by Order in Council antedate the pensions of these particular persons. With regard to the future judges we hold the matter to be more simple. We propose to provide that they should hold office during good behaviour, that their salaries, these are the superior judges alone, should be charged on the Irish Consolidated Fund, that they shall be removable only on a joint address from the two orders of the legislative body, and that they should be appointed under the influence, as a general rule, of the responsible Irish Government. There is an exception which we propose to make in regard to the Court of Exchequer, which is a Court of Revenue Pleas. I will not enter into any details now, but the enormous financial relations which will subsist between Great Britain and Ireland, if our measure be carried, make us feel, for reasons which I shall perhaps on another occasion more fully explain, that it is necessary for us to keep a certain amount of hold on the Court of Exchequer, or at least on two of its members; but the general rule of our measure will be that the action of the judges will pass under the new Irish Executive, and will rest with them, just as it rested in former times with the old Irish Executive.

The Police.

I must now say a few words on the important subject of the Irish constabulary. The substance of those words really amounts to this, that I think there remains much for consideration in order to devise the details of a good and prudent system; but we think it our first duty to give a distinct assurance to the present members of that distinguished and admirable force that their condition will not be put to prejudice by this Act, either in respect of their terms of office, their terms of service, or with regard to the authority under which they are employed. The case of the Dublin police is not quite the same, but we propose the same conditions with regard to the Dublin police, as far, at least, as the terms of service are concerned. With regard to the local police I will say nothing, because I do not want at present to anticipate what may be matter hereafter for free consideration or discussion, or for the action of the Irish legislative body. There will be no breach of continuity in the administration with regard to the police. One thing I cannot omit to say. The constabulary, as I have said, is an admirable force, and I do not intend to qualify in the smallest degree what I have already said, but the constabulary on its present footing exhibits one of the most remarkable instances of waste of treasure and of enormous expense, not with good results, but with unhappy results, with which and under which the civil government and the general government of Ireland have hitherto been carried on. The total charge of the constabulary amounts to a million and a half, including the Dublin police. Now, Ireland is a cheaper country than England, and if the service were founded on the same principle and organized in the same manner it ought, per thousand of the population, to be cheaper in Ireland than in England, assuming Ireland to be in a normal condition; and our object is to bring it into a normal condition.

House of Commons, April 8.

Present cost of Irish Police.

Now the House will perhaps be surprised when I tell them this. The present constabulary of Ireland costs £1,500,000 a-year, every penny of it now paid out of the British Exchequer. If the police of Ireland were organized upon the same principles and on the same terms as the police in England, instead of costing £1,500,000, it would cost £600,000 a-year. That will convey to the House an idea, first, of the enormous charge at which we have been governing Ireland under our present system; and, secondly, of the vast field for judicious reductions which the system I am now proposing ought to offer to the Irish people. I anticipate a vast reduction, both in the force and in the expenditure. The charge is now a million and a half. We propose that the Consolidated Fund of Great Britain, this subject I shall

House of Commons, April 8.

revert to in the financial statement which I shall have to put before the House, shall for a time relieve the Irish legislative body of all expenditure in excess of a million. I am bound to say that I do not look upon a million as the proper charge to be imposed on Ireland. I am perfectly convinced, however, that the charge will be reduced to a much smaller sum, of which Ireland, of course, will reap the benefit. After two years the legislative body may fix the charge for the whole police and for the constabulary of Ireland, with a saving of existing rights. One thing I must say. We have no desire to exempt the police of Ireland in its final form from the ultimate control of the legislative body. We have no jealousies on the subject; and I own I have a strong personal opinion that, when once the recollection of the old antipathies has been effectually abated, the care of providing for the ordinary security of life and property of the citizens will be regarded as the very first duty of any good local Government in Ireland. I think it will be understood from what I have stated that the constabulary would remain under the present terms of service and under the present authority, although I do not say that this is to be so for ever. Assuming control over the constabulary, that control will be prospective, and will not import any injury to existing rights.

Civil Service.

With respect to the Civil Service, of course the future Civil Service of the country generally will be absolutely under the legislative body. With respect to the present Civil Service, we have not thought that their case was exactly analogous either to the constabulary or the judicial offices, and yet it is a great transition; and moreover it will without doubt be the desire of the legislative body of Ireland forthwith, or very early, to effect a great economy in its establishment. We have therefore considered to some extent in what way we can at once provide what is just for the civil servants of Ireland, and at the same time set free the hands of the legislative body to proceed with this salutary work of economy and retrenchment. Our opinion is that, upon the whole, it will be wise in the joint interests of both to authorize the civil servants now serving to claim the gratuity or pension which would be due to them upon the abolition of their offices, provided they shall serve not less than two years, to prevent an inconvenient lapse in the practical business of the country, and at the close of those two years both parties would be free to negotiate afresh, the civil servants not being bound to remain, and the legislative body not being in any way bound to continue to employ them. That is all I have to say upon the subject of the new Irish Constitution.

House of Commons, April 8.

Imperial charges.

I am afraid I have still many subjects on which I have some details to show, and I fear I have already detained the House too long. I have now, sir, to give a practical exposition of the phrase which I have used, that we looked upon it as an essential condition of our plan that there should be an equitable distribution of Imperial charges. The meaning of that is, What proportion shall Ireland pay? I must remind gentlemen before I enter upon the next explanation that the proportion to be paid is not the only thing to be considered; you have to consider the basis upon which that proportionate payment is to be applied. Looking upon the proportionate payment we now stand thus. At the time of the Union it was intended that Ireland should pay 2-17ths, or in the relation of 1 to 7½ out of the total charge of the United Kingdom. The actual true payment now made by the Irish taxpayer is not 1 to 7½, but something under 1 to 12, or about 1 to 11½—that is the total expenditure. The proposal I make is that the proportion chargeable to Ireland shall be 1 to 14, or 1-15th, but that will not be understood until I come to join it with other particulars. I will look, however, sir, a little to the question what are the best tests of capacity to pay. Many of these tests have been suggested; one of them is the income-tax, which I conceive to be a very imperfect indication. The income-tax, I believe, would give a proportion not of 1 to 14, but of 1 to 19. This is to be borne in mind, if you have

House of Commons, April 8.

regard to the income-tax, that while, on the one hand, it is paid in Ireland upon a lower valuation than in England or in Scotland, because, as we all know, in England Schedule A is levied on the full rent, it is also unquestionable that many Irishmen also hold securities upon which dividends are received in London and pay income-tax, I hope, before the dividends come into the hands of the persons entitled to them. Therefore it is almost a certainty that a considerable sum ought to be added to the Irish income-tax, which would raise it from the proportion of 1 to 19 to perhaps 1 to 17. But there are two other tests which I consider far superior to the income-tax. One is the test afforded us by the death duties, not by the amount levied, because the amounts levied vary capriciously according to the consanguinity scale, but by the property passing under the death duties. The amount of property on which, on an average of three years, the death duties fell was for Great Britain £170,000,000, and for Ireland £12,908,000, or 1 to 13. I have taken three years, because they represent the period since we entered upon a somewhat new administration of the death duties, and that is by far the best basis of comparison. When we come to the valuation, inasmuch as Ireland is valued much lower in proportion to the real value than England and Scotland, the valuation in the latest year for which we have returns is in Great Britain £166,000,000, and for Ireland £13,833,000, giving a proportion of 1 to 12, or 1-13th.

What proportion Ireland should pay.

Under these circumstances, what ought we to do? In my opinion we ought to make for Ireland an equitable arrangement, and I think that, when I propose to assume the proportion of 1-15th, it will be seen that that is an equitable or even generous arrangement, after I have mentioned three considerations. The first of these considerations is that, if we start an Irish legislative body, we must start it with some balance to its credit. But if we are to start it with a balance to its credit, I know of no way except the solitary £20,000

House of Commons, April 8.

a-year which still remains to be worked out of the Church surplus after all the demands made upon it. I know of no way of honestly manufacturing that balance except by carving it out of the Budget for the coming year, and providing for the sum at the expense, as it will then be, not of the Irish Exchequer exclusively, but at the expense of the English and Scotch taxpayers. That is one consideration; the second consideration is this. I take this 1 to 14 or 1-15th for the purpose of ascertaining what share Ireland is to pay to the Imperial expenditure. But when I said that Ireland now pays 1 to 11½ or 1 to 12½ of the Imperial expenditure, I meant the amount of the whole gross Imperial expenditure; and when I say that we shall ask her to pay 1-15th of the Imperial expenditure in the future, that is an Imperial expenditure very materially cut down. For, upon consideration, it has been thought right, in computing the military expenditure, to exclude from it altogether what ought strictly to be called war charges. We do not propose to assume, in fixing the future Imperial contribution of Ireland, to base that calculation on the supposition of her sharing in charges analogous, for example, to the vote of credit for 11 millions last year. Therefore this proportion of 1-15th is to be applied to a scale of Imperial expenditure materially reduced.

How Ireland's share is to be paid.

But, sir, there is another consideration which I think it right to mention. It is this, that this Imperial contribution would be paid by Ireland out of a fund composed in the first instance of the entire receipts paid into the Irish Exchequer; but that is not a true test of the amount of taxation paid by Ireland. There are goods which pay duty in England, and which are exported, duty paid, to Ireland, which are consumed in Ireland, and upon which, therefore, the duty is really paid by Irishmen, while the receipts go into the Imperial Exchequer. But there is not only a corresponding movement the other way, but there is a movement very much larger and more important. More than one million of duty, I think £1,030,000, is paid upon spirits in Ireland that are

House of Commons, April 8.

exported to Great Britain. Every shilling of that duty is really paid by the Englishman and the Scotchman; but at the same time the whole receipts go into the Irish Exchequer. The same thing holds with respect to the porter brewed in Ireland. The same thing holds with regard to the very considerable manufacture of tobacco carried on in Ireland. We have made it the object of our best efforts to ascertain how much money Ireland loses to England by the process which I have described, and which I have no doubt is accurately understood by all members of the House; how much money Ireland loses to Great Britain by the flow of duty-paid commodities from Great Britain to Ireland; and how much Great Britain loses to Ireland from the flow of such commodities from Ireland to Great Britain. The result of this investigation is—I state it with confidence, not actually as if it were to be demonstrated in every point by Parliamentary returns, but I state it as a matter of certainty with regard to the far greater portion of the sum, and as a matter certainly subject to very little doubt—that the Irish receipt gains from Great Britain by the process I have described more than Great Britain gains from Ireland, and more, to no less an amount than £1,400,000, paid by the British taxpayer and forming part of the Irish receipt. If you maintain the fiscal unity of the Empire, if you do not erect, which I trust you will not erect, custom-houses between Great Britain and Ireland, if you let things take their natural course, according to the ordinary and natural movement of trade, £1,400,000 will be paid to the benefit of Ireland as a charge upon the English and Scotch taxpayer, and will form a portion of the fund out of which Ireland will defray the Imperial contribution which we propose to levy upon her.

Financial benefit to Ireland.

If this amount of Imperial contribution to be paid by Ireland, which I have described as 1-14th, comes to be reduced by subtracting this sum of £1,400,000, the portion which Ireland will have to pay will be, not 1-14th, but a fraction under 1-26th. That is a very great

House of Commons, April 8.

change. It is a benefit she gets, not only in the state of the law, but owing to the course of trade. We cannot take it away without breaking up the present absolute freedom between the two countries. I hope this will be borne in mind by those who think this charge of 1-15th a heavy charge to be thrown upon Ireland, and by those who think, as I certainly do, that in a case of this kind, after all that has occurred, when two countries are very strong and very rich compared with a third of far more restricted means, the pecuniary arrangement ought to be equitable and even bountiful in some moderate degree. It will be interesting to the House to know what payment *per capita* the plan I have described will allot to the Irishman and to the Briton respectively—(I use the word " Briton," because I know that it will gratify my friends from Scotland). The incidence of this plan *per capita* I will state as follows. In the first place, if I were to take the present contribution of Ireland to the entire expenditure of the country according to the receipt into the two Exchequers, the inhabitant in Great Britain pays £2, 10s. *per capita* and the inhabitant in Ireland £1, 13s. 7d. That is obviously and inequitably high for Ireland. But if I take the real payment of the Irish taxpayer and compare that with the real payment of the English taxpayer, it will follow that the English payment is £2, 10s. 11d. as against £1, 7s. 10d. of Ireland, which is certainly a more equitable proportion.

Now I pass to the basis of 1-14th or 1-15th. This is not founded upon the total expenditure of the country, but upon what we are about to reckon as Imperial expenditure and the respective contribution to the Imperial Exchequer. The respective contribution *per capita* will be for Great Britain £1, 10s. 11d., and for Ireland 13s. 5d., and I do not think that that is an inequitable arrangement. I wish to exhibit exactly what alterations we propose to make. Under the proportion now proposed Ireland will pay 13s. 5d., while, if the present proportion were main-

House of Commons, April 8.

tained, she would pay 16s. 10d., which will be a very considerable diminution in the amount of her contribution *per capita*.

Present system extravagant.

I will state only one other striking fact with regard to the Irish expenditure. The House would like to know what an amount has been going on, and at this moment is going on, of what I must call not only a waste of public money, but a demoralizing waste of public money, demoralizing in its influence upon both countries. The civil charges *per capita* at this moment are in Great Britain 8s. 2d., and in Ireland 16s. They have increased in Ireland in the last fifteen years by 63 per cent., and my belief is that, if the present legislative and administrative systems be maintained, you must make up your minds to a continued, never-ending, and never-to-be-limited augmentation. The amount of the Irish contribution upon the basis I have described would be as follows. One-fifteenth of the annual debt charge of £22,000,000 would be £1,466,000; 1-15th of the Army and Navy charge, after excluding what we call war votes, and also excluding the charges for Volunteers and Yeomanry, would be £1,666,000; and the amount of the civil charges which are properly considered Imperial would entail upon Ireland £110,000, or a total charge properly Imperial of £3,242,000. I am now ready to present what I may call an Irish Budget, a debtor and creditor account for the Irish Exchequer. The customs produce in Ireland a gross sum of £1,880,000, the excise £4,300,000, the stamps £600,000, the income-tax £550,000, and non-tax revenue, including the Post Office, £1,020,000. And, perhaps, here again I ought to mention, as an instance of the demoralizing waste which now attends Irish administration, that which will perhaps surprise the House to know—namely, that, while in England and Scotland we levy from the Post Office and Telegraph system a large surplus income, in Ireland the Post Office and the Telegraphs just pay their expenses, or leave a surplus so small as not to be worth mentioning. I

House of Commons, April 8.

call that a very demoralizing way of spending money. Although I believe that there is no purer department in the country than the Post Office, yet the practical effect of our method of administrating Ireland by influences known to be English and not Irish leads to a vast amount of unnecessary expenditure.

Ireland's assets and liabilities.

The total receipts of the Irish Exchequer are thus shown to amount to £8,350,000, and against that I have to place an Imperial contribution which I may call permanent, because it will last for a great number of years, of £3,242,000. I put down £1,000,000 for the constabulary, because that would be a first charge, although I hope that it will soon come under very effective reduction. I put down £2,510,000 for the other civil charges in Ireland, and there, again, I have not the smallest doubt that that charge will likewise be very effectually reduced by an Irish Government. Finally, the collection of revenue is £834,000, making a total charge thus far of £7,586,000. Then we have thought it essential to include in this arrangement, not only for our own sakes, but for the sake of Ireland also, a payment on account of the Sinking Fund against the Irish portion of the National Debt. The Sinking Fund is now paid for the whole National Debt. We have now got to allot a certain portion of that debt to Ireland. We think it necessary to maintain that Sinking Fund, and especially for the interest of Ireland. When Ireland gets the management of her own affairs, I venture to prophesy that she will want, for useful purposes, to borrow money. But the difficulty of that operation will be enormously higher or lower according to the condition of her public credit. Her public credit is not yet born. It has yet to lie like an infant in the cradle, and it may require a good deal of nursing, but no nursing would be effectual unless it were plain and palpable to the eye of the whole world that Ireland had provision in actual working order for discharging her old obligations so as make it safe for her to contract new obligations more nearly allied to her own immediate wants.

House of Commons, April 8.

I therefore put down three-quarters of a million for Sinking Fund. That makes the total charge £7,946,000, against a total income of £8,350,000, or a surplus of £404,000. But I can state to the House that that £404,000 is a part only of the Fund which, under the present state of things, it would be the duty of the Chancellor of the Exchequer of the three countries to present to you for the discharge of our collective expenditure.

Irish legislation since 1829.

Sir, the House has heard me with astonishing patience while I have endeavoured to perform what I knew must prove an almost interminable task. There is only one subject more on which I feel it still necessary to detain the House. It is commonly said in England and Scotland—and in the main it is, I think, truly said—that we have for a great number of years been struggling to pass good laws for Ireland. We have sacrificed our time, we have neglected our own business, we have advanced our money, which I do not think at all a great favour conferred on her, and all this in the endeavour to give Ireland good laws. That is quite true in regard to the general course of legislation since 1829. But many of those laws have been passed under influences which can hardly be described otherwise than as influences of fear. Some of our laws have been passed in a spirit of grudging and of jealousy. It is most painful for me to consider that when, after four or five years of Parliamentary battle, a Municipal Corporation Act was passed for Ireland it was a very different measure to that which in England and Scotland created complete and absolute municipal life. Were I to come to the history of the land question, I could tell a still sadder tale. Let no man assume that he fully knows that history until he has followed it from year to year, beginning with the Devon Commission or with the efforts of Mr. Sharman Crawford. The appointment of the Devon Commission does, in my opinion, the highest honour to the memory of Sir Robert Peel. Then notice the mode in which the whole labours of that Commission were frustrated by the domination of selfish interests in the British Parliament. Our first effort at land legislation was delayed until so late a period as the year 1870. I take this opportunity of remarking that sound views on the land question were not always confined to Irish members, nor to the Liberal side of this House. The late Mr. Napier, who became Lord Chancellor of Ireland, when he sat in this House for the academical constituency of Dublin, developed with great earnestness truly liberal views on the subject of Irish land, and made generous efforts in that direction, efforts which were, however, intercepted.

House of Commons, April 8.

Legislation from an uncongenial source.

But, sir, I do not deny the general good intentions of Parliament on a variety of great and conspicuous occasions, and its desire to pass good laws for Ireland. But let me say that in order to work out the purposes of government there is something more in this world occasionally required than even the passing of good laws. It is sometimes requisite not only that good laws should be passed, but also that they should be passed by the proper persons. The passing of many good laws is not enough in cases where the strong permanent instincts of the people, their distinctive marks of character, the situation and history of the country, require not only that these laws should be good, but that they should proceed from a congenial and native source, and besides being good laws should be their own laws. In former times it might have been doubted, I have myself doubted, whether this instinct had been thus developed in Ireland. If such doubts could be entertained before the last general election, they can be entertained no longer.

Colonial experience.

The principle that I am laying down I am not laying down exceptionally for Ireland. It is the very principle upon which within my recollection, to the immense advantage of the country, we have not only altered but revolutionized our method of governing the Colonies. I had the honour to hold office in the Colonial Department, perhaps I ought to be ashamed to confess it, fifty-one years ago. At that time

House of Commons, April 8.

the Colonies were governed from Downing Street. It is true that some of them had legislative assemblies, but with these we were always in conflict. We were always fed with information by what was termed the British party in those Colonies. A clique of gentlemen constituted themselves the British party; and the non-British party, which was sometimes called the "disloyal party," was composed of the enormous majority of the population. We had continual shocks, continual debates, and continual conflicts. All that has changed. England tried to pass good laws for the Colonies at that period, but the Colonies said, "We do not want your good laws; we want our own." We admitted the reasonableness of that principle, and it is now coming home to us from across the seas. We have to consider whether it is applicable to the case of Ireland. Do not let us disguise this from ourselves. We stand face to face with what is termed Irish nationality. Irish nationality vents itself in the demand for local autonomy or separate and complete self-government in Irish, not in Imperial, affairs. Is this an evil in itself? Is it a thing that we should view with horror or apprehension? Is it a thing which we ought to reject or accept only with a wry face, or ought we to wait until some painful and sad necessity is incumbent upon the country, like the necessity of 1780 or the necessity of 1793? Sir, I hold that it is not. There is a saying of Mr. Grattan, who was indeed a fiery and fervid orator, but he was more than that, he was a statesman, his aphorisms are in my opinion weighty, and even profound, and I commend them to the careful reflection and examination of the country, when he was deprecating the surrender of the Irish Parliament and pointing out that its existence did not prevent the perfect union of the two countries, he remarked: "The Channel forbids union, the ocean forbids separation." Is that Channel nothing? Do what you will with your steamers and your telegraphs, can you make that Channel cease to exist, or to be as if it were not? These sixty miles may appear a little thing, but I ask you what are the twenty miles between England and France? These few miles of water have exercised a vital influence upon the whole history, the whole development, and the whole national character of our people.

House of Commons, April 8.

Local and Imperial patriotism

These, sir, are great facts. I hold that there is such a thing as local patriotism, which in itself is not bad, but good. The Welshman is full of local patriotism, the Scotchman is full of local patriotism; the Scotch nationality is as strong as it ever was, and should the occasion arise, which I believe it never can, it will be as ready to assert itself as in the days of Bannockburn. I do not believe that such local patriotism is an evil. I believe it is stronger in Ireland even than in Scotland. Englishmen are eminently English, Scotchmen are profoundly Scotch, and, if I read Irish history aright, misfortune and calamity have wedded her sons to her soil. The Irishman is more profoundly Irish, but it does not follow that because his local patriotism is keen he is incapable of Imperial patriotism. There are two modes of presenting the subject. The one is to present what we now recommend as good, and the other to recommend it as a choice of evils. Well, sir, I have argued the matter as if it were a choice of evils; I have recognized as facts entitled to attention the jealousies which I do not share or feel, and I have argued it on that ground as the only ground on which it can be argued, not only in a mixed auditory, but in the public mind and to the country, which cannot give a minute investigation to the operations of that complicated question. But in my own heart I cherish the hope that this is not merely the choice of the lesser evil, but may prove to be rather a good in itself. What is the answer to this? It is only to be found in the view which rests upon the basis of despair and of absolute condemnation of Ireland and Irishmen as exceptions to the beneficent provisions which enable men in general, and Europeans in particular, and Americans, to be capable of performing civil duties, and which considers an Irishman either as a *lusus naturæ* or one for whom justice, common sense, moderation,

House of Commons, April 8.

and national prosperity have no meaning, and who can only understand and appreciate perpetual strife and dissension. Well, sir, I am not going to argue that view, which to my mind is founded on a monstrous misconception. I say that the Irishman is as capable of loyalty as any other man. I say, if his loyalty has been checked in its development, why is it? Because the laws by which he is governed do not present themselves to him, as they do to us in England and Scotland, with a native and congenial aspect, and I think I can refer to two illustrations which go strongly to support the doctrine I have advanced. Take the case of the Irish soldier, and of the Irish constabulary. Have you a braver or a more loyal man in your army than the Irishman, who has shared every danger with his Scotch and English comrades, and who has never been behind them when confronted by peril, for the sake of the honour and safety of his Empire? Compare this case with that of an ordinary Irishman in Ireland. The Irish soldier has voluntarily placed himself under military law, which is to him a self-chosen law, and he is exempted from that difficulty which works upon the population in Ireland—namely, that they are governed by a law which they do not feel has sprung from the soil. Consider how common it is to hear the observation, in discussing the circumstances of Ireland, that, while the constabulary are largely taken from the Roman Catholic population, and from the very class most open to disaffection, where disaffection exists, they form a splendid model of obedience, discipline, and devotion such as the world can hardly match. How is this? It is because they have undertaken a voluntary service which takes them completely out of the category of the ordinary Irishman. They are placed under an authority which is to them congenial because freely accepted. Their loyalty is not checked by the causes that operate on the agricultural population of Ireland. It has grown as freely in the constabulary and in the army as if every man in the constabulary and every Irish soldier had been an Englishman or a Scotchman.

House of Commons, April 8.

Real unity.

However this may be, we are sensible that we have taken an important decision; our choice has been made. It has not been made without thought; it has been made in the full knowledge that trial and difficulty may confront us on our path. We have no right to say that Ireland, through her constitutionally-chosen representatives, will accept the plan I offer. Whether it will be so I do not know,—I have no title to assume it,—but if Ireland does not cheerfully accept it, it is impossible for us to attempt to force upon her what is intended to be a boon; nor can we possibly press England and Scotland to accord to Ireland what she does not heartily welcome and embrace. There are difficulties, but I rely upon the patriotism and sagacity of this House; I rely on the effects of free and full discussion; and I rely more than all upon the just and generous sentiments of the two British nations. Looking forward, I ask the House to assist us in the work which we have undertaken, and to believe that no trivial motive can have driven us to it—to assist us in this work which we believe will restore Parliament to its dignity, and legislation to its free and unimpeded course. I ask you to stay that waste of public treasure which is involved in the present system of government and legislation in Ireland, and which is not a waste only, but which demoralizes while it exhausts. I ask you to show to Europe and to America that we too can face political problems which America twenty years ago faced, and which many countries in Europe have been called upon to face, and have not feared to deal with. I ask that in our own case we should practise with firm and fearless hand what we have so often preached, the doctrine which we have so often inculcated upon others—namely, that the concession of local self-government is not the way to sap or impair, but the way to strengthen and consolidate unity. I ask that we should learn to rely less upon merely written stipulations, and more upon those better stipulations which are written on the heart and mind of man. I ask that we should apply to Ireland that happy experience which we have gained in

House of Commons, April 8.

England and in Scotland, where the course of generations has now taught us, not as a dream or a theory, but as practice and as life, that the best and surest foundation we can find to build upon is the foundation afforded by the affections, the convictions, and the will of the nation; and it is thus, by the decree of the Almighty, that we may be enabled to secure at once the social peace, the fame, the power, and the permanence of the Empire.

II.

SECOND HOUSE OF COMMONS SPEECH.

TUESDAY, APRIL 13, 1886.

GOVERNMENT OF IRELAND BILL.

Mr. Gladstone, on rising to reply at the close of the debate on the motion for leave to introduce the Bill, said:—

Introduction. Position of matters in 1871.

I will make at the outset one or two very brief remarks upon the speech of the right hon. gentleman (Sir M. Hicks-Beach). He has quoted words from me with an extension given to them that they do not carry in the original document. The argument which I made upon the proposal of 1871 was this, that no case had at that time been made to justify any radical change in any of the institutions of the country generally, or any interference with the constitution of the Imperial Parliament; and I own that at that time, after the Church Act of 1869, and after the Land Act of 1870, I did cherish the hope that we might be able, by legislation from this House, to meet the wants and the wishes of Ireland. I cherished that hope at that time; but at that time, if the right hon. gentleman has done me the justice to make himself completely acquainted with the sentiments expressed in that speech, he will find that it contains none of the apprehensions with which the minds of hon. members opposite are filled, and that, on the contrary, I then stated in the most explicit manner that I had heard with joy, and I accepted with the utmost satisfaction, the assurance that the demand which was begin-

House of Commons, April 13.

ning to be made by Mr. Butt for Home Rule did not involve in any way the disintegration of the Empire. But I certainly will not enter into a discussion on the Transvaal Convention, with regard to which I may make the observation that I think that the topics we have to deal with relevant to the matter are sufficient, and I do not consider that any observation from me is wanted on an act, which I believe has been recognized by this country as a great act of justice, and as the undoing, perhaps that is the more accurate description of it, of the great act of injustice which stains the memory of our legislation on this subject.

Mistrust of Ireland.

The right hon. gentleman says that I have shown mistrust of the Irish Legislature by providing safeguards for minorities. I have already stated in the most distinct terms that the safeguards provided, as far as I am concerned, are not in consequence of mistrust entertained by me, but they are in consequence of mistrust entertained by others. They are reasonable precautions by way of contribution on our part to disarm honest though unfounded jealousy; and however little it may appear that they are likely to attain their end, yet I cannot regret that we have made them. One more observation with respect to the foreign garb of English laws. The right hon. gentleman must understand that I have used those words not with respect to the beneficial acts which have been done on many occasions by this Parliament for the purpose of meeting the wants of Ireland, but with regard to the ordinary operations of the criminal law in that country, especially in association, as it has constantly been, with the provisions of special repressive or coercive legislation.

Lastly, I must express the astonishment with which I heard the right hon. gentleman refer to the Roman Catholic Association. He spoke of the disappearance of that association from the scene as a great triumph obtained by the vigour and firmness of the Government and the Parliament over unruly elements in Ireland. Why, sir, on the contrary, the disappearance of the Roman Catholic Association was due entirely to the introduction of the Roman Catholic Relief Bill, as unhappily the introduction of that Relief Bill was due, as the Duke of Wellington himself declared, to his apprehension of civil war, and as the alternative to it. The right hon. gentleman could not have afforded a more unhappy instance of that which has been a too common feature of the relations of this House to Ireland, and of those combinations the recurrence of which we are striving to avoid. I was told by my noble friend the member for the Rossendale Division that I had not a formulated demand from Ireland. No, sir, but the Duke of Wellington had a pretty well formulated demand; and we now know, and I am glad that the observations of the right hon. gentleman gave the Irish members below the gangway an opportunity of bearing testimony, we now know in substance what is demanded by Ireland through her constitutionally chosen representatives; and therefore I say, if it be a just and reasonable demand, we cannot hasten too soon to meet it; and we will not wait until the day of disaster, the day of difficulty, and I will add the day of dishonour, to yield, as we have so often yielded, to necessity that which we were unwilling to yield to justice.

Essential conditions of the Bill.

Sir, I desire to avoid details in this stage of the debate and at this hour of the night, and I will endeavour to make this sacrifice, at any rate, that I will neither defend myself nor censure anybody else; but I will deal as far as I can with some of the arguments that have recently been laid before us.

One detail I must notice which has been largely introduced into this debate, and in so striking a manner by many members of the House—it is that which relates to the presence of Irish members, or the cessation of their presence, at Westminster. When I spoke on Thursday last, I laid down—and now I am going to answer an appeal of the right hon. gentleman who asked me what were the essential conditions of this Bill—I laid down, I say, five essential conditions, from which it appeared to me we could under no circumstances depart, and under which the grant of a domestic

House of Commons, April 13.

Legislature to Ireland would be justifiable and wise. These were the essential conditions under which, in our opinion, the granting of a domestic Legislature to Ireland would be justifiable and wise: first, that it must be consistent with Imperial unity; secondly, that it must be founded upon the political equality of the three nations; thirdly, that there must be an equitable distribution of Imperial burdens; fourthly, that there should be safeguards for the minority; and fifthly, that it should be in the nature of a settlement, and not of a mere provocation for the revival of fresh demands. These, I stated, were the only conditions.

A correction.

I find I have been reported as having stated that the retention of customs and excise by this country and the absence of Irish members from this House were likewise vital and essential conditions. I do not think I used those epithets. If I did, it was probably an inadvertence, for which I apologize, and unquestionably it was in entire contradiction to what I had just stated before, when I laid down the only essential conditions. Sir, what I think with regard to the Irish members, although the question is much too large for me to attempt to enter fully into it at present, what I thought clear with regard to the Irish members was in the first place this—that the 103 Irish members could not possibly continue as now to come here and vote upon all matters, English, Scotch, Irish, and Imperial alike. That I conceived to be wholly indisputable. I stated that I had hoped, that I had long tried to find, some practicable means of distinction between Imperial and British matters, and that my efforts had entirely failed, nor could I see my way to such a distinction. I also stated that in my opinion it was impossible for England, and that no doubt England would never desire or dream of inflicting or forcing upon Ireland taxation without representation; that if Irish members were to disappear either permanently or for a time, I do not say I used these epithets, were to disappear from this House, it must be by the consent of Ireland herself.

House of Commons, April 13.

Irish members at Westminster.

Since that time a variety of suggestions have been made in many speeches, which have shown how much interest is felt in this question. It has been suggested that Irish members might come here with limited powers. But I have certainly failed to discover means of drawing the line. It has been stated that they might come in limited numbers, and it has been suggested in a wise and weighty speech delivered by my hon. friend the member for Bedford last night that an interval of absence from this House was eminently desirable, and perhaps almost of vital necessity for Ireland herself with a view to her own purposes. Then, says my hon. friend, if I understood him right, after such an interval of years has passed, during which, God knows, there will be enough to do for any Parliament, any representative body, that Ireland can be supplied with, after such an interval, if it is desired that Irish members in any number, or any proportion, or under any conditions should reappear in this House, that is a problem which, however difficult, British statesmanship may be found adequate to solve. There was great force in what my hon. friend said. I cannot, however, bind myself with regard to these observations or to any of the propositions which I have just cited. I cannot bind myself, still less any of my colleagues; but I think, bearing in mind the importance of the subject, and the vast and immeasurable importance of the purposes we have in view, I do not think we should be right, it would be even presumptuous, were we to take upon ourselves in the face of the House at this early stage of the discussion on the Bill, entirely to close the doors against any consideration of this kind.

The position, therefore, remains exactly as it was; but I have thought that that reference which I have made to the speech of my hon. friend is no more than that, and other portions of that speech, eminently deserve.

The voice of Ireland.

Now, sir, my right hon. friend the member for East Edinburgh has addressed the House very fully to-night, and has raised a great number of questions connected with this Bill.

House of Commons, April 13.

My right hon. friend is terribly alarmed at the argument drawn from the presence of eighty-six Nationalist members, eighty-five of them from Ireland, in this Parliament. He is perfectly alarmed at this argument. I do not know whether he did me the honour to refer to my view of it. If he did, he is entirely mistaken. He treated it as if a statement had been made by me to the effect that because there are eighty-five Nationalist members in this House, you must do whatever they demand; and, treating it in that way and having created this phantom, it is easy enough to show that it is a most formidable proposition. He spent a long time in showing the most portentous consequences to which it would lead. Yes, sir, but that is not the argument so far as I used it; it was not the argument so far as I have heard it. What I ventured to say was this, that the deliberate and constitutional expression of the wishes of Ireland through the vast majority of her members entails upon this House the duty and the obligation of a respectful and a favourable consideration of every wish that Ireland may entertain, consistently with the interests and the integrity of the Empire. My right hon. friend said there was a parity in principle between Ireland and Scotland. I entirely agree with him. His experience as a Scotch member is short. If the vast majority of Scotchmen demand something on the ground that Scotch feeling and opinion show that it is essentially required in order to satisfy the just wishes of Scotland, I would advise my right hon. friend, if he wishes to be consistent with regard to the integrity of the Empire, not to put himself in conflict with those expressions of opinion.

Faith in the people.

Then, sir, my right hon. friend said that no analogy could be drawn, and so said my noble friend the member for Rossendale, from the proceedings of the Protestant Parliament of Grattan. What was the meaning of all this? I have been arguing, and others have argued, that Grattan's Parliament showed no tendency and no disposition towards a

House of Commons, April 13.

separation of the kingdoms, and that Grattan himself looked upon the separation of the Parliaments as a means of uniting the hearts of the people. That has been met by the statement now that that was a Protestant Parliament and a landlords' Parliament. Sir, if that is the way to make a Parliament safe and sound, if to re-introduce religious disabilities, if to narrow the franchise, if to centre power in the hands of the landlords, or if you are to go further and fill more than half the benches of Parliament with pensioners and placemen, then if these are the elements of safety in a Parliament, in what gross and woeful error have we been in this Parliament for half a century! We have been breaking down the exclusive power of class; we have been widening the franchise over the whole kingdom and effacing from the statute-book one by one, until the very last perhaps is contained in this Bill, every vestige of religious disability. There is no faith in the people with those who make these declarations. Their faith seems to be in shutting out the people, and in regarding popular influence as a source of danger. In this happy country we have found it a source of strength; and the enterprise we are now engaged in is to see whether we cannot also find security for it in Ireland that it shall be to her a similar source of strength under circumstances happier than those of her history heretofore.

Ireland's misdeeds and sufferings.

My right hon. friend seems to sum up the misdeeds of the Irish people in an emphatic question—"In what country except Ireland would a no-rent manifesto have been produced?" That is the inquiry which he puts. My first observation upon it is this: in what country except Ireland can you show so lamentable, so deplorable a history,—a history so disgraceful to those who had any hand in bringing it about, and relations so deplorable between those who owned the land and those who occupied it? The speech of my right hon. friend appeared to proceed upon the assumption that there were ineradicable and incurable vices in Irishmen which placed them in a category different from the

House of Commons, April 13.

people of other nations, that they had a sort of double dose of original sin. Is it to be wondered at that the notions of Irishmen should to some extent be gone awry upon the subject of land and the relations connected with it, when you bear in mind that the Devon Commission, appointed by a Tory Government, reported that the agricultural population of Ireland were called upon to bear, and that they did bear, with admirable and exemplary patience, sufferings greater than those which fell to the lot of any other people in Europe? Are you so ignorant as to suppose, when these sufferings had been borne for generations, I may say for centuries, as disclosed to the world on the highest authority, and when attempt after attempt to apply something like a remedy to the miseries that existed from the operation of the land laws in Ireland had failed through the narrow jealousy and selfishness of a class—that these things could pass without leaving a mark in history? Does my right hon. friend think that these things can pass and set their mark upon history, and yet leave no mark in the nature and disposition and habits of men who have been sufferers under such abominations?

Examples from abroad.

My right hon. friend thinks my analogy with foreign countries is bad—that Austria and Hungary, Norway and Sweden, have nothing to do with these things. But my statement has been entirely misapprehended. I will recall the terms of it for the benefit of the right hon. gentleman. I never said that the analogy was exact, that the circumstances were exactly parallel. What I said was that the circumstances were such as would show that we are called upon, in this country, to do, with infinitely greater advantages, what they have done in the face of infinitely greater difficulties. My right hon. friend appears to think it a difficulty in our way that we have got an Imperial Parliament and a greater number of subordinate local Parliaments related to the British Empire. My point is that there is not in Sweden a supremacy of the Swedish Parliament over

Norway, that there is not in Austria a supremacy of the Austrian Parliament over Hungary, and that, even without the advantage of such supremacy, the problem has in those countries been solved in substance, and that, in the case of Norway and Sweden particularly, by the adoption of the simple expedient of granting a domestic Legislature and practical local independence, the union of the two countries, which at one time seemed hopeless and impossible, has become close, and is growing closer from day to day. Then how is it that these illustrations have no bearing upon the great problem that we have before us?

House of Commons, April 13.

The interests of England and Ireland inseparable.

Again, my right hon. friend states as a difficulty that our interests are so interlaced with Ireland. I am astonished to hear that observation called upon to pass muster and do duty among the arguments against this Bill. Why, if our interests are so interlaced, and I thank God it is true that they are so interlaced, is not that in itself a strong presumption of the extreme unlikelihood that Irishmen will overlook that interlacing and proceed as if they were perfectly independent, as if they had nothing to do with us, no benefit to derive from us, and no injury to suffer from injury to us? No! the truth is this. It is assumed—and this is the basis of the speech of my right hon. friend—that the Irishman will do wrong, and that there is no way of making him listen to the dictates of prudence, of kindness, of justice, of good sense, except by taking into your own hands the reins by which you can govern him and teaching him how he shall walk. On that principle it is that my right hon. friend went over all the different classes of subjects, and described the dreadful changes that everything was to undergo: legislation was to be changed, administration was to be changed, the Civil Service was to be changed, the face of nature itself was to be changed. Such is the terrible picture. And why? Is there no common sense among that portion of our fellow-countrymen?

The speech of my right hon. friend recalled to my memory a striking sentence of Lord Russell's fifty years ago, which

House of Commons, April 13.

imprinted itself deeply on my memory at the time, and which I have never forgotten, and I hope never shall forget. It was at the time when, under the administration of the Melbourne Government, Mr. Thomas Drummond was Under-Secretary for Ireland, and when with singular success he was endeavouring to conduct the Irish Administration, so far as he could, in sympathy with the feelings of the people. His misdeeds, as I suppose I must call them, found their climax in the utterance of the portentous doctrine which shocked Conservatism from Land's End to John O'Groat's—he had the audacity to say that "property had its duties as well as its rights." The corresponding misdeeds of Mr. Drummond, and in some sense of the Lord-Lieutenant, caused many debates in this House, in which I am thankful to say I took no part, but to which I was an attentive listener. Every sort of objection and accusation was brought forward against the proceedings of the Irish Government of that day; and Lord Russell, in his quiet way, rising to take part in a debate, said:—"It appears to me that all these objections, all these difficulties, and all these accusations"—I may not be quoting every word accurately, but I am very near the mark—"may be summed up in one single sentence. It comes, sir, to this, that, as England is inhabited by Englishmen, and Scotland by Scotchmen, so Ireland is inhabited by Irishmen." Lord Russell knew very well that Irishmen did not come here to conquer us seven hundred years ago, but that we went to Ireland to conquer—we favoured Irishmen with our company, we have been all along the stronger party of the two, and it is one of the uniform and unfailing rules that guide human judgment, if not of the moment yet of history, that when a long relation has existed between a nation of superior strength and one of inferior strength, and when that relation has gone wrong, the responsibility and the guilt rests in the main upon the strong rather than upon the weak.

Power of veto.

My right hon. friend asked me questions as to the provisions of this Bill, and I must confess my surprise at some

House of Commons, April 13.

of them, coming as they do from one who is an old official hand. They were questions most proper to be asked, perhaps on the second reading of a Bill, certainly in Committee, but I have never heard of such questions upon the motion for leave to introduce a Bill. If questions of that kind are to be asked, why, sir, this House ought to alter its rules and give an hon. member applying for leave to introduce a Bill the power of laying it upon the table of the House before it is read a first time. For example, my right hon. friend asked a question about the veto. Well, sir, we have stated with regard to that point that there is no limitation to the veto in the Bill, and, if the right hon. gentleman asked my opinion, my opinion is the principle upon which the veto is now worked—if the right hon. gentleman will take the trouble to read the valuable work of Professor Dicey, to which I have before referred, he will find a most careful and interesting elucidation of the subject—the principle upon which the veto is now worked in the great Colonial dependencies of this country, though I do not admit that Ireland will be reduced to the *status* of a colony, I believe that principle to be applicable for all practical purposes to Ireland with a domestic Legislature.

Income-tax.

Then my right hon. friend asked a question about the levying of the Income-tax. He did not seem to have even an elementary idea of what the Irish Income-tax would be, and he asked where the dividends would be payable, whether the dividends would be payable in London or in Dublin. Why, sir, no such questions can possibly arise under this Bill as the Bill stands. The Irish Income-tax will be just as distinct from the Income-tax of England and Scotland as if it were a French income-tax. Well, I will give you another illustration, as if it were an Indian Income-tax. From time to time they have in India the blessing of an Income-tax; but in India the whole machinery, the incidence of the tax, the liability to pay it, are all as totally distinct from the tax in this country as if the Income-tax there were laid in another planet.

House of Commons, April 13.

American Civil War.

My right hon. friend finally laid very much stress on the case of the United States of America. He pointed out that insidious advisers recommended the Northern States not to insist upon the maintenance of the Union, but that they did insist on the maintenance of the Union and carried their point. Why, true, sir; but, having carried their point, what did they do? Having the Southern States at their feet, being in a position in which they were entitled to treat them as conquered countries, they invested every one of them with that full autonomy, a measure of which we are now asking for Ireland. I say a measure of which autonomy, because I believe that their autonomy is much fuller than that which we are now asking for Ireland.

A final settlement.

Well, sir, I may say some words more. My right hon. friend said, I am not quite sure whether my right hon. friend said so, but certainly my noble friend the member for Rossendale did, that these enactments if carried would lead to further demands from Ireland. That is a favourite objection. The right hon. gentleman who has just sat down has been extremely cautious in this matter, and he has promised Ireland, I hope I am not misrepresenting him, almost nothing except a reasonable allowance of repressive criminal legislation. The phantom of local government and a little control over education and public works, and such things, find no place whatever in the speech of the leader of the Opposition, but they find a place in the speech of my right hon. friend behind me and of my noble friend the member for Rossendale. Well, sir, we are going to give to the Irish people, if we are permitted, that which we believe to be in substantial accordance with their full, possible, and reasonable demands. In our opinion, that is the way to stop further demands.

Mr. Burke's wisdom.

I should like to quote Mr. Burke, and I hope we shall hear much of Mr. Burke in the course of this discussion, for the writings of Mr. Burke upon Ireland, and still more upon America, are a mine of gold for the political wisdom with which they are charged, applicable to the circumstances of to-day, full of the deepest and most valuable lessons to guide the policy of a country. He was speaking for conciliation with America, and those to whom he was preaching in vain met him with this idle cavil, that his conciliation would tend to further demands. They refused this conciliation, but further demands came, and they were granted, but with hands dyed in blood, and after hundreds of millions had been added to our National Debt, and when disparagement, at the very least, of England's fame had gone through the length and breadth of the world in connection with that wretched consummation. They were granted, and they left behind them in America an inheritance, not of good-will or affection such as now prevails, but of rancour and resentment which for generations were not effaced, and which were the happy consequences of a boastful resistance. I am not afraid, sir, of the same consequences in the same form. There is no question of war with Ireland, but it is a question of what I care for more than anything else, the character, the honour, and the fair fame of my country; it is a question of humanity, of justice, and of a desire to make atonement for a long, a too long, series of former, and not yet wholly forgotten wrongs. Now, sir, what did Mr. Burke say on that occasion when he was advocating conciliation with America? He said that the more and the better state of liberty any people possessed, the less would they hazard in the vain attempt to make it more.

House of Commons, April 13.

Alternatives—Is Ireland to be restricted to what England and Scotland may demand?

What are the proposals of my noble friend? They are: First a little dose of coercion, and next a grudging gift to Ireland of such self-government as England and Scotland may be pleased to choose for themselves. Now I deny the justice of the principle that self-government in Ireland is necessarily to be limited by the wishes of England and Scotland for themselves. Upon what basis of justice does that argument rest? Why may not Ireland have specialities in her case which England and Scotland may not have? We have no

House of Commons, April 13.

right to say that what England wants and Scotland wants Ireland may have, but nothing else. You must show that what Ireland wants is mischievous before you are justified in refusing her. I am speaking now of the favourite topic of "further demands." Was there ever a device more certain to prolong all the troubles of Parliament, was there ever a system of policy less hopeful of attaining any solid standing ground, than this proposal to dole out to Ireland from year to year with grudging and misgiving, and with a frank statement that it is a dangerous business, that which she does not want, and which if she accepts at all she will only accept for the purpose of making further demands? It was denied in very clear language by the Irish representatives that they sought to press forward from this measure to other measures. They claim, and very fairly and reasonably claim, because no member of Parliament could divest himself of the right, to examine in Committee the provisions of the Bill, and to demand this or that amendment. But they have expressly disclaimed the intention to make what my noble friend calls further demands. Let him put to them the same question, and ask them for the same assurances, as to the proposals made in this debate by a most distinguished person, one who, unfortunately, I know only three years ago declared that there should be no extension of local government until the Irish members made a total change in their methods of speech and action. No doubt measures doled out in the shape of municipal corporations here and there would be certain to be used for the purpose of making further demands. I commend the consistency and caution of the right hon. gentleman the leader of the Opposition, because he fairly told us at the commencement of the session, when he was asked what boons would be given to Ireland in the way of local government, that no enlargement of the powers of local government should be given which might be used as a lever to weaken and destroy the legislative Union, or (as he went on to say) enable the political majority to tyrannize over the minority. A very

House of Commons, April 13.

sensible, a very consistent course. If you grant some small modicum of local government, it would simply be a device for securing perpetual disturbance of this Parliament from year to year by Irish members, and they would strengthen the leverage with which they would urge those demands and advance them to their natural consummation.

Has Parliament any mandate on this subject?

My noble friend complains that this was a question which has not been referred to the people. I should like to know what is the upshot of that observation? What does it mean? I think it can hardly mean anything else than this, that the Government had committed a fault in bringing forward this question at the present time because it had not brought the matter under public consideration at the general election. It seems to me that that is an extraordinary doctrine. I want to know where it is to be found laid down by any Constitutional authority. My hon. friend the Attorney-General asked whether there was any mandate for coercion. No, sir, there was no mandate for coercion, and you cannot want a mandate for any measures necessary to maintain the law. Very well, sir; but if you do not want a mandate for the measures of force and repression, intended to maintain the law, much less do you want a mandate for measures intended to maintain and strengthen the law by laying hold of the hearts of the people, and which aim at no force and no repression, but at a union far closer and more durable than that which now exists on the Statute Book.

I do not know whether my noble friend has given much attention to the case of the Reform Act, but it is a rather curious one from this point of view. The election of 1830 was conducted almost entirely without reference to the subject of reform. At that time the election extended over very many weeks, and it was only just before it had quite finished, and the Yorkshire election, if I recollect rightly, was about the last, that those great events occurred in Paris which produced a sympathetic effect here, and roused a cry

House of Commons, April 13.

for reform in England; but in the main the Parliament was elected without the least reference to reform. Yes, sir; but when that Parliament met, and when it was found that the wants of the country required reform, although it was denounced as revolution, and I can assure hon. gentlemen opposite that all their invectives are weak and ineffective in comparison, Parliament set about its work manfully; the Government proposed to Parliament, and Parliament entertained, the great proposal then laid before it. It would be a very different thing indeed if my colleagues who have spoken in the debate had evaded the real issue, or had declared that the question was unfit to come before us. I never uttered an opinion, nor shall I utter an opinion, that it is a subject unfit to come before the people; I think we who propose this Bill should be the last persons who should be jealous of any reference to the people.

Mr. Chamberlain's proposals.

Coming now to the proposals of my right hon. friend the member for West Birmingham, in the first place, let me say that I at once accord to him, what, however, he cannot want according by me, that is, his perfect and entire good faith in the representations that he made, upon which a misapprehension prevailed between us as to his title to enter upon certain matters. If anything further is required upon that point, it certainly can keep until Friday next, when the Bill on the land question is brought forward. Quite irrespective of the land law, my right hon. friend stated four points, any one of which was an ample justification of the step which he felt himself called upon to take. But he, at any rate, gave no countenance to coercive legislation. He looks into the future, and he sees how light and trivial is the talk about coercive legislation. But my right hon. friend went a great deal further, and suggested a Commission or Committee, to be formed of all parties, to deal with this subject. I will not criticize that proposal. I venture the opinion that no solution of the question will ever proceed from a Royal Commission or a Committee composed of all parties, much less pass through Parliament. Then my right hon. friend spoke of federation. If you are to have federation there must be some body to federate, and there will be no body unless a legislative body is entitled to act for the people. It appears to me that my right hon. friend goes further than we do, because he is in favour of not only giving a domestic Legislature, but of appending to it that rather formidable postscript of some arrangement under which this Parliament is to part with some of its powers and throw them into the common stock along with powers coming from other portions of the Empire. I cannot, therefore, say that he has remained behind us in this matter.

House of Commons, April 13.

Divided hostility.

What is really material to observe is the mutual relations of harmony and concord subsisting between the plans of those who think they ought to sink differences and unite together for the purpose of finding a solution for the Irish problem. The Chancellor of the Exchequer, in his masterly statement, exhibited in full detail the relations actually subsisting among those most distinguished gentlemen and great Parliamentary authorities. He has shown that the Border Burghs does not agree with Birmingham, and that Birmingham does not agree with Rossendale, and that Rossendale does not agree with Paddington, and again Edinburgh is distinct in shade from them all. There is a decided want of common feature, common action, common purpose, common principle; there is no united basis of action except the basis of hostility to this Bill.

The Government plan holds the field.

When I speak of this plan, I speak of it as a plan in its essence and not in its detail. It may derive much advantage from the wisdom of Parliament. It has been produced and brought to light under a degree of pressure such as I believe never was applied by circumstances to any Government; such, at least, I will venture to say, as there is no case of in the half-century to which my recollection extends. It may be improved by the wisdom of this House, but, speaking of it as a plan, I say it holds the field. It has many enemies; it has not a single rival. No one has been bold

House of Commons, April 13.

enough to propose an intelligible system of what, in my opening statement, I called effectual coercion—the only kind of coercion that can be adequate to the end you have in view. And, sir, as the plan holds the field, so the subject holds the field. Never, I think, have I witnessed such signs of public absorption in this House and out of this House. Moreover, it is safe to prophesy that the subject will continue to hold the field. Many who are here advocate important reforms; many think, and I am one of them, that legislation is in arrear. The demands upon your time and thought are beyond your capacity, even with your best exertions, to meet. But, sir, you may dismiss all these subjects from your mind, until this matter is disposed of, until the Irish problem is solved. I am not speaking of what gentlemen opposite may threaten or say; I am looking at the nature of the case; I am looking at the profound interest of the whole English and Scotch people, ay, and of the whole civilized world. Until this problem is solved it is idle to think of making real progress with the business of this country in respect to the important subjects which are perfectly ripe for the handling of Parliament. We have come to the time for decisive action; we have come to the time for throwing aside not only private interests and partial affections but private devices and partial remedies. We have come to the time for looking at the whole breadth of this subject and endeavouring to compass it in our minds. We have come to the time when we must answer this question—whether we will make one bold attempt to free Parliament for its great and necessary work, and to establish harmony by Irish laws for Ireland, or whether we will continue, on the other hand, to struggle on as we have done before, living from hand to mouth, leaving England and Scotland to a famine of needful and useful legislation, and Ireland to a continuance of social disease, the depth of which we have never understated, of social disease that you do not know how to deal with, and of angry discord with Great Britain which you make no attempt to cure.

III.

THIRD HOUSE OF COMMONS SPEECH.

FRIDAY, APRIL 16, 1886.

SALE AND PURCHASE OF LAND (IRELAND) BILL.

MR. GLADSTONE, on rising to ask leave to introduce a Bill to make amended Provision for the Sale and Purchase of Land in Ireland, said:—

I have now to ask the permission of the House to bring in *Introduction.* a Bill to make amended provision for the sale and purchase of land in Ireland, and in doing so to complete the speech I began on Thursday last, which, inordinately long though it may have been, still remains unfinished. I use that language to describe, not any power that I know of binding on Parliament to treat these two questions as united questions, that must be a matter for the deliberation of Parliament, but to describe their union in my own mind and in the minds of my colleagues.

Now, sir, I stand rather peculiarly on the present occasion *Our opponents.* in the face of several sections of this House and of the people. As regards the Irish tenants, the proposal I have to make is one which, I think, undoubtedly may confer upon them a very great benefit. As regards the people of Ireland, distinct from the tenants, and considered in the mass, I think that will also be found to be the case. But the principal and the most immediate objects of the measure are the landlords, and I am going to ask the House of Commons to make a great effort—

House of Commons, April 16.

if I may say so, a serious and considerable effort, on behalf of the landlords of Ireland, whom I know to be generally most hostile to the policy which Her Majesty's Government is pursuing.

And I have likewise to take into view the fact that many of those who, far from being hostile, are most friendly to that policy are likewise inclined to give a jealous reception, and I do not make that a matter of complaint, to the proposals I have to lay before the House. In entertaining a jealousy of that kind, in my opinion, they are only fulfilling their duty to the people at large. They have learnt that an effort is to be made in which either the money or the credit of the British Exchequer is to be made available on behalf of the Irish landlords, should the Irish landlords be disposed to accept that boon. I shall never draw a distinction, on the contrary, I would resist the drawing of any such distinction, between the money of the nation and the credit of the nation. The credit of the nation is just as precious as the money of the nation, and the same discretion should be exercised by the representatives of the people in regard to the use of the one as to the expenditure of the other. I will explain, and I think I can make intelligible, the aspect in which we regard this great subject.

Our aim. Social order.

The aim and end of all our endeavours is not, in the first place, for its own sake, simply the contentment of the people in Ireland, it is the social order of the country. That is the first, the greatest, the most sacred, and the most necessary aim of every Government that knows its duty. We have sought, sir, to come at that social order by means different from those hitherto employed, and we distinguish our course broadly from previous courses. The measures by which we hope to administer to what is lacking in social order something in the nature of a permanent and effectual remedy are twofold. In the first place, our petition, our request to the House is that it will make arrangements for governing Ireland, in Irish matters, by Irish laws; and, in the second place, that it will undertake, not a partial, tentative, and timid touching of the land question, but a serious endeavour to settle it; for, sir, as I have said, these questions are at the present moment, in our view, not to be separated one from the other, and of course, when I speak of these questions, I speak of the plan generally which the Government have formed, and I do not include, or attempt to press upon the House, every minute particular of that rather comprehensive and complex plan.

House of Commons, April 16.

The Land Question.

Now, sir, I think that the argument that I have to make, and also the objections that I have to meet, divide themselves into these three heads. It would be demanded of me, in the first place, Must the land system of Ireland be settled? why can you not leave it to be dealt with by the organ which you are asking Parliament to call into existence? This is the first question. Supposing that I am able to prove that an affirmative answer should be given to that inquiry, the next and not less natural question to be put by the representatives of the people, and, moreover, to be put to a certain extent in the tone and with the aspect of rejection, is, Must Great Britain be cumbered with this question? Well, sir, I hope to show that it is an obligation of honour and of policy that Great Britain should undertake it. But I ask no assent to that proposition at present. Then, thirdly, I shall justly be asked, and I shall not attempt to shirk the inquiry, Are we to run pecuniary risks on the part of the English and Scottish people for the purpose of meeting this Irish want? I hope, sir, as I meet the two former inquiries confidently with an affirmative answer, so I hope, in regard to the third, to establish not less strongly and clearly a negative reply. But I admit, without reservation, that upon my proof or non-proof of what I have now asserted, with regard to these three points, all depends as regards the case that I seek to make, and as regards the reception which the House, in my humble judgment, ought to give to that case.

It must be dealt with.

The first question, then, is, Must the land question be dealt with? It is impossible for me, even if I draw largely on

House of Commons, April 16.

the indulgence of the House, to answer that question fully. It can only be answered fully by a careful study of the whole history of Ireland. I shall state the *minimum* of what appears to me to be necessary, and shall trust to the knowledge of hon. members to fill up what may be lacking in my statement. Even the little that I shall state will probably be treated, and may possibly appear, as an indictment against the Irish landlords. Upon that subject I shall say, in a few and summary words, it is an indictment against Irish landlords, against many in the past, against few, I hope, in the present. But, although those upon whom censure ought to be pronounced may be few, they have been the heirs of a sad inheritance. They have taken up, and been compelled to take up, dismal and deplorable traditions, and when oppression has wrought its very painful experience into the heart and mind of the people, it is not in a moment, not in a year, not in a generation, that the traces of that painful, of that dreadful process can be effaced.

Negro emancipation.

I may perhaps refer to a case which, I think, is in point. In 1833 this House, to its great honour, its lasting fame, passed the Act for the emancipation of the negroes in the West Indies. It established a system which is known as apprenticeship, and which was intended to invest the negro population with all the rights of freedom, except the liability to render a certain carefully limited amount of labour for a carefully limited time. That law was, in general, peacefully received and faithfully obeyed; but a great philanthropist in this country, whose name should ever be held in honour—Mr. Joseph Sturge, of Birmingham—paid a visit to Jamaica, made inquiries for himself, by his own eyes and ears satisfied himself that in the case of certain estates in that island there was a deliberate attempt to keep alive the spirit and the institutions of slavery under the guise of apprenticeship. He brought back the statement of that case to this country. It was never, I believe, asserted that this represented the general state of things in the West Indies or probably even in

House of Commons, April 16.

Jamaica. But such was the impression produced by those few cases of horrible abuse and contumacious resistance to the will of Parliament, as well as to the dictates of humanity, that, after a struggle in this House, it was felt that the apprenticeship must at once, against the Parliamentary covenant of 1833, be put an end to; and, accordingly, it reached an unexpected and immediate consummation. That I quote as an instance of the way in which the offences of the few may be visited upon the many. I have the honour of knowing myself many Irish landlords who are an honour to the class to which they belong. I hope that what I have said will show that, in quoting the mournful testimony of history, I do not seek to make them personally responsible for difficulties and for evils of which they are the victims rather than the cause.

Agrarian crime.

I must go back to the origin of agrarian crime. Agrarian crime is the index of the difficulty with which I call upon the House to deal. Agrarian crime had an origin in Ireland. Speaking generally of the Celtic race as they live in Ireland, I believe a great and an almost inexhaustible patience has been one of their most remarkable characteristics. It was not among the Celts of Ireland that agrarian crime began. It was in a population, the population of Tipperary, dashed with a stronger and more vivacious blood, that the spirit of resistance arose. I will take my description of the state of things in that crisis from a source which, if suspected of prepossession at all, cannot be suspected of prepossession, either too favourable to myself personally, or too favourable to the policy which we recommend. I am going to quote from the historical work of Mr. Froude known as "The English in Ireland."

I think, when I refer to the mere name of that distinguished man, it shows that I am not seeking to avail myself unduly of the evidence of a witness who has prejudiced the case in my favour. On that subject I may remind the House that it is the opinion of Mr. Froude that the right course for the

House of Commons, April 16.

British Government to have pursued in the last century would have been to drop the Irish Parliament—that is, never to have summoned it; to appropriate what he terms the hereditary revenues, and to supply the annual deficit in the Irish Exchequer at the cost of the Treasury of England. Therefore you cannot say that the man who proposes such an extinction of representative institutions in Ireland, and the substitution of what he meant to be a benevolent absolutism, is a man prepossessed in favour of the policy which we recommend. But Mr. Froude, although perhaps a man of prepossessions, on that I give no opinion, is certainly a man of truth and honour, and a man who, if he sees what he believes to be injustice, will not allow his heart and his conscience to tamper with the principles involved in exposing it.

Mr. Froude's opinion.

What says Mr. Froude as to the condition of the Irish peasantry before the outbreak of agrarian crime? In the second volume of that work, and on page 20, he compares the condition of the Irish cultivator, as it had then become, with what it had been under his own native chiefs; and Mr. Froude says:—

"To four-fifths of the Irish peasantry the change of masters meant only a grinding tyranny, and tyranny the more unbearable because inflicted by aliens in blood and creed. Under their own chiefs they had been miserable, but they were suffering at least at the hands of their natural Sovereigns"—and here I may say I believe that of his natural Sovereign the Irishman is by nature inclined to think much—"and the clansman who bore his lord's name, and, if harshly used by his own master, was protected by him against others, could not feel himself utterly without a friend. But the oppression of the peasantry in the last century was not even the oppression of a living man—it was the oppression of a system. The peasant of Tipperary was in the grasp of a dead hand. The will of a master whom he never saw was enforced against him by a law irresistible as destiny. The absentee landlords of Ireland had neither community of interest with the people nor sympathy of race. They had no fear of provoking their resentment, for they lived beyond their reach. They had no desire for their welfare, for as individuals they were ignorant of their existence. They regarded their Irish estates as the sources of their income; their only desire was to extract the most out of them which the soil could be made to yield; and they cared no more for the souls and the bodies of those who were in fact committed to their charge, than the owners of a West Indian plantation for the herds of slaves whose backs were blistering in the cane fields."

That was the state of things which attended the origin of agrarian crime in 1760; and from that date its continuance has been uninterrupted, with a terrible facility, from time to time, of expansion to alarming dimensions—nay, more, with a facility and a power of developing itself to the harm of England. I will read a few more words from Mr. Froude on this subject. He shows with what fatal force there came upon Ireland at that period a combination of symptoms grouped together for the misery of the land. In the first place, owing to the increased demand of England for animal food, there was the conversion of the small holdings into large grazing farms. In the second place, owing to the same cause, there was the withdrawal, from the tenants, of the hill pastures, which were traditionally enjoyed by them as accompaniments of their small arable possessions and holdings. There was the constant raising of the rents, and there was a progressive and rapid increase of absenteeism. And Mr. Froude says on this subject, in a passage shorter than that which I have just read:—

"Many causes had combined at that moment to exasperate the normal irritation of the southern peasantry."

And presently he goes on to show that that irritation was not confined to the southern peasantry:—

"With the growth of what was called civilization, absenteeism, the worst disorder of the country, had increased. In Charles II.'s time the absentees were few or none. But the better Irish gentlemen were educated, and the more they knew of

House of Commons, April 16.

the rest of the world, the less agreeable they found Ireland and Irish manners; while the more they separated themselves from their own estates, the more they increased their rents to support the cost of living elsewhere."

Sir, that is the account given by Mr. Froude. I leave the House to appreciate its weight.

The Irish Parliament.

What else have we to take into account? The Irish Parliament, although at that time its independence had not been acknowledged, was alive and active, and was displaying, in numerous controversies between Ireland and England, a real if a narrow patriotism. But I must distinguish broadly between the Irish Parliament—which I rejoice to commend where that can be done—between the Irish Parliament on questions of nationality and the Irish Parliament on questions of class. The Irish Parliament was hostile to absenteeism, for absentees were essentially anti-national. The Irish Parliament did not struggle to do justice to the tenant. It was a Parliament partly of pensioners, partly of placemen, and the rest of landlords. The Irish Parliament did nothing to mitigate the evil, and if it be true that there were fresh Coercion Acts passed from year to year, that deplorable fact only strengthens the statement I make, and shows how the sad and dread mischief of agrarian crime took root in the country.

The offspring of oppression and misery.

Sir, in the varied incidents of social life there are unhappily many marriages which are barren, and many families which die out; but there is one marriage that is never without issue. When oppression on the one hand is married to misery on the other, then there springs from the union a fatal and a hideous progeny of crime; and that crime is endowed with a vitality that perpetuates itself, and hands on the baleful and miserable inheritance from generation to generation. That is the case of absenteeism in Ireland—that is the case of the rooted tendency to crime which springs from causes most disgraceful to those who were charged with the government of Ireland and the care of its population—most disgraceful to them, and

House of Commons, April 16.

most perplexing and embarrassing to us. One other circumstance, tending further to complicate the case, has to be added to those that I have already enumerated. The struggle connected with the agrarian relations between landlord and tenant has continued, and has even been, until very lately, seriously aggravated. The differences of religion down to the year 1829 were the basis of an odious political system, and traces of them, unfortunately, survived that period. The one point of union that there was between the Irish landlord and his tenant, that sentiment of nationality which the old Irish Parliament never lost, has, I am sorry to say, since the Union greatly ceased to operate, ceased to form a bond of connection between those classes, ceased to have a mitigating and beneficial influence on Irish life.

The Land Question an obligation of policy and of honour.

Now, after what I have said, after the fearful exasperation which has been introduced into these agrarian relations, into agrarian relations which are the determining elements of Irish society and Irish life, after the long continuance of the mischief, so that it has become chronic in the system, and forms part of the habits of the people, we arrive at the conclusion that it would be an ill-intended and an ill-shapen kindness to any class in Ireland to hand over to an Irish Legislature, as its first introduction to the work that it may have to perform, the business of dealing with the question of the land. It would be like giving over to Ireland the worse part of her feuds, and confronting her with the necessity for efforts which would possibly be hopeless, but which, at any rate, would be attended with the most fearful risks.

And now I come to my second question. I have shown you how terrible the subject of the land is in itself. I come to my second question, Why is Great Britain to be cumbered with this subject? Are we bound to cumber ourselves with it? Is it an obligation of policy and a dictate of honour? I am satisfied that the House, however reluctant,—it cannot be more reluctant than we are,—if it be an obligation of policy, if it be a dictate of honour, and, still more, if it be partly the

House of Commons, April 16.

one and partly the other, will not shrink from any duty which these considerations may entail. Must we then cumber Great Britain with an endeavour to settle this question, which is no slight task?

The obligation admitted.

Well, sir, I wish to point out that the obligation on our part has been admitted already, admitted in a partial form, but in a form which I believe this House, certainly the party opposite, and perhaps many gentlemen on this side, have shown a disposition to enlarge—namely, the form of our existing Land Purchase Acts. I consider that these Acts present an extremely bad and dangerous form of dealing with this obligation, and I do so on this ground, that their basis is to place the British Treasury in contact with the individual occupier and farmer in Ireland. In our opinion, sir, that is not a wise policy. I do not entertain a mistrust of the Irishman's disposition to liquidate his pecuniary engagements. I believe that he may very well, excepting under circumstances of peculiar exasperation, bear comparison with his competitors in other countries in that matter. But it is a dangerous thing for a State, which the course of policy and the condition of legislation have led the people to regard as essentially a foreign State, to make those people in great numbers individually its debtors; dangerous because tempting the debtor, dangerous because extremely unsafe for the State considered as the creditor.

Safeguards for the minority.

I may name another consideration, which is not one of honour but of prudence. We have struggled to introduce into the Irish Government Bill what are called safeguards for the minority, without, I admit, obtaining the smallest mitigation from our adversaries of their opposition. Acting on the same principle,—and, if I may allow myself to use hallowed words in no jesting spirit, "walking by faith and not by sight,"—we desire, by exhibiting the utmost consideration for the imperilled class, or, at any rate, for the class impressed deeply with fear and apprehension, the Irish landlords, to do everything on their behalf which duty will allow us to do.

If such proposals should produce a mitigating effect, it might lead to an easier and speedier concession to Ireland of what we know to be her demand, and what we believe to be her rights; and, if not, still we have done our best, and we must leave the issue to a higher power.

House of Commons, April 16.

England's responsibility.

Now, sir, what are the substantial reasons, those that I have mentioned are collateral considerations, what are the substantial reasons why, as we think, it is the absolute duty of Great Britain to make herself a party in this matter to the extent, at least, of a just offer and a fair opportunity to be given to Irish landlords? Well, I sum them up in one word. We cannot wash ourselves clean and clear of the responsibility. The deeds of the Irish landlords are to a great extent our deeds. We are *participes criminis;* we, with power in our hands, looked on; we not only looked on, but we encouraged and sustained.

I think it is a hard case, if I may be permitted to say so, for my fellow-representatives of Scotland. The hardest case in this matter is the case of the Scotch people, for England had the blessing in the eighteenth century of a representative system, which, if not perfect, yet, as we know from great occasions like that of 1783, and like that of 1831, did suffice to bring to the front a strong national sentiment. Scotland had no such system. I think that four or five thousand persons had in their hands as voters the entire representation of the whole of Scotland, and they had in their hands the representation of the Scotch people. The Scotch people had, therefore, no responsibility for the dreadful history of the relations between Great Britain and Ireland.

Our "garrison" in Ireland.

I must speak of this Imperial Parliament in which Scotland was not allowed to exercise any national or popular influence. I have said that the landlords were our garrison in Ireland. Let me a little unfold that sentence. We planted them there, and we replanted them. In 1641, in 1688, and again in 1798, we reconquered the country for them. I heard a gallant gentleman speak a few nights ago in this House, who

House of Commons, April 16.

seemed to be under the pious impression that rebellion in Ireland had been put down by the superhuman action of a certain regiment of militia—I really forget which. I beg pardon of my old supporter, but, speaking with all respect for his ability as a speaker, his frankness, uprightness, and the integrity of his whole intention, if he has read the history of the rebellion of 1641, he will find that it was effectually and finally put down, and only put down, by Cromwell, who, whatever he may have been, was not an Irish Protestant. The rebellion of 1688–89 was put down, not by the Protestants of the North, but by the introduction mainly of foreign hosts; and the rebellion of 1798, to which I think the hon. member specially referred, was unquestionably put down, not by the action of what is termed the loyal minority, which undoubtedly, I do not say from its own fault, had not at that period earned the name, but, when the Irish Government in Dublin was in despair, the rebellion was put down by their inducing the British Government in London to equip and send to Ireland a large and adequate force of British soldiers.—(LORD R. CHURCHILL: They had the Yeomanry.)—No doubt they had the Yeomanry, but the Yeomanry could not do it.

The Union.

Well, sir, we have more responsibility than that. We used the whole civil government of Ireland as an engine of wholesale corruption, and we extended that corruption to what ought to have been a sacred thing, namely, the Church which we maintained and supported in the land. We did everything in our power to irritate and to exasperate the Irish people by the whole of that policy. Then came 1795, the brightest period of the history of the Irish Parliament under the Lord-Lieutenancy of Lord Fitzwilliam, when, through the sentiment of nationality, that Parliament was about to do for Ireland what would have given to it the seed of every promise of happiness and prosperity, beginning with the emancipation of the Roman Catholics, a measure that would have led by a chain of links that could not have been broken to Parliamentary reform and the admission of the people to political power. But we took Lord Fitzwilliam away. They strove to keep him, but England would not let them. What then? We brought about the Union. I have avoided that subject because I did not want to enter into the details of it. It is dreadful to read the language of Lord Cornwallis and the disgust of an honourable mind at the transactions in which he found himself under the painful necessity of engaging. I will only say that we obtained that Union, against the sense of every class of the community, by wholesale bribery and unblushing intimidation.

House of Commons, April 16.

Then came the more direct responsibility of the British Parliament. Did things greatly mend under that? Have hon. members considered the Act of 1816 and its effect upon the Irish tenant? Notwithstanding all other changes, there had lingered in Ireland a state of law determining the condition of the tenure of the soil which was of such a nature as practically to protect the tenant in something like a real fixity of tenure. The inefficiency of the remedies had been such that they had allowed the tenants still to dream of something of the old tribal usages, and that something of the old tribal permanence remained. But in the united Parliament was brought in an Act, introduced, as Mr. Leslie Foster, a first-rate authority, said, because, by the law as it then stood, the tenant was enabled to set his landlord absolutely at defiance. All these protections were swept away. I do not enter into the merits of the proceedings. All I am now saying is that they were not likely to reconcile the Irish occupier to his lot, or to root out agrarian crime from the soil. Such was 1816. There is, in my judgment, worse to come. We lingered until 1843, when we come to the time of the Devon Report—a Conservative Report issued under the auspices of a Conservative Ministry. I might read many passages from that Report, but I will read only one, and that not a long one. It is as follows:—"A reference to the evidence of most of the witnesses will show that the agricultural labourer of Ireland

Irish labourers and tenants after the Union.

House of Commons, April 16.

continues to suffer the greatest privations and hardships; that he continues to depend upon casual and precarious employments for his subsistence; that he is still badly housed, badly fed, badly clothed, and badly paid for his labour. Our personal experience and observations during our inquiry have afforded us a melancholy confirmation of these statements: and we cannot forbear expressing our strong sense of the patient endurance"—now, mind that; as I have stated, the Devon Commission was a Conservative Commission, yet still it is most struck by the patient endurance by which the Irish tenant and occupier sustained his lot. (A Voice: Labourer.) I believe that is possible. I have not the Report here. The phrase is "labouring classes"; I believe it means the man who labours upon his land.—(LORD J. MANNERS: And who works for wages?)—Yes, undoubtedly, because the great bulk of these people, half the Irish population, are partly dependent upon wages. However, for fear there should be anything in that objection, on the next occasion I will bring down a stronger passage. This Commission, then, expresses its strong sense "of the patient endurance which the labouring classes," that is, not the labourers alone—the enormous majority at that time of the Irish agricultural tenants belonged to the labouring classes—"have generally exhibited under sufferings, greater, we believe, than the people of any other country of Europe have to sustain."

Bad made worse.

That is the description given at a period when we were maintaining a corn law, for which we boasted that the justification was to be found in the higher level at which it kept our labouring population. That is the Report of the Devon Commission. It does not end there. Passages like this were not overlooked by men of the stamp of Sir R. Peel; and the late Lord Derby in the House of Lords introduced a Bill to give effect to the most important recommendations of the Devon Commission. Had that Bill been passed, much of the subsequent history might have been modified or changed. The House of Lords, as we know, usually accepts with great facility the recommendations of a Tory Government; but this recommendation of a Tory Government, for the improvement of the condition of the occupiers and the agricultural population of Ireland, was too much for the patience and political loyalty of the House of Lords. The next effort was that of Mr. Napier, a gentleman sitting on that side of the House. That Bill was lost also. The mischief did not stop there; we produced the Encumbered Estates Bill, with a general, lazy, uninformed, and irreflective good intention of taking capital to Ireland. What did we do by that Bill? We sold the improvements of the tenants. The tenant lost his old landlord, who was in many cases an easy-going personage, and had oftentimes established a *modus vivendi* with his tenant, who was handed over to a horde of new proprietors, who were told that they might exact a greater rental from the tenant, and who took, in the form of rent, that which was the produce of the tenant's labour. That Bill took away the last mitigation of the case of the Irish peasant; it took it away through a deplorable error of uninformed, and, I must say, irreflective benevolence.—(LORD R. CHURCHILL: It was taken away by Lord Russell.)—I beg pardon. The noble lord's information is always interesting, but sometimes partial. I would say that the Act was suggested to Lord Russell.—(LORD R. CHURCHILL: It was passed by Lord Russell.)—But, sir, I am speaking of this House. I have not said a word against the noble lord's party, or the noble lord's principles, if I knew what his principles were. I am speaking of this House, and I claim no exemption for any great party in this House. Many distinctions may be drawn in respect to the treatment of the land question at that period; I am not aware that any distinction can be drawn in respect of party. It is the fact that this was not the action of a party, but the action of a Parliament, and that is why I ask this House whether, after even such a summary recital as I have given, it is possible to deny that the landlords have been our garrison, and our representatives; that we have

House of Commons, April 16.

House of Commons, April 16.

relied upon them as they have relied upon us; and that we cannot wash our hands of responsibility for their doings, or for the consequences of those doings.

The rights of Irish landlords under Acts of 1870 and 1881.

We acknowledged, I admit in a different way, our concern in the case of the landlords by the Acts of 1870 and 1881. Lord Russell, who was alive at the passing of the first of these Acts, was among its cordial supporters. But I will not dwell upon that subject; it is beside my argument. At that time we modified most essentially the condition of the landlords, and as we did so there arises an obligation from different sources, but tending to the same point—namely, that, in my opinion, Great Britain, within the limits of reason, cannot refuse to be cumbered with this important question of the Irish landlords.

The Government plan.

Having proceeded so far, I have still one important matter to argue, namely, the third of the questions which I put. It is an important inquiry,—whether I am proposing to inflict a pecuniary risk upon the people of England and Scotland. But I think I have now reached a point at which, before dealing with the third question, I ought to explain to the House the scheme which we are about to submit.

I shall have a great number of points to mention; I will therefore mention them in the most summary manner, and I will beforehand endeavour to impress upon hon. members that, although I will do my best under circumstances which have been those of some haste and difficulty, yet I am strongly impressed with the belief that it will not be possible for them to acquire any adequate idea of this measure except by a close inspection of the Bill itself, which we are using every effort to place at the earliest moment in their hands. Even as single provisions, some of them perhaps may be difficult to understand; but, bearing as these provisions do one upon the other, I am confident it would be impossible to appreciate them except in the manner I have suggested.

The Act will take effect on the same day with the Irish Government Act. As we think it our duty to press for the

House of Commons, April 16.

passing of this Bill with the Irish Government Bill, so undoubtedly we provide in the Bill itself that it is not to pass without the Irish Government Act. Secondly, the legislative body in Dublin may appoint any person or body to be what is called under the Bill the State authority. I shall refer again to that phrase, which is used in the Bill in various important relations. Thirdly, the purchases under the Bill are to be made in a Three per Cent. stock, issued on the application, probably, of the Land Commission to the Treasury, and under regulations to be made by the Treasury.

New Three per Cent. stock.

This Three per Cent. stock will, in all likelihood, be what is termed the New Three per Cents. The most obvious name that occurs to every one is the name of Consols. But the amount of the New Three per Cent. stock is £180,000,000, quite sufficient to insure extensive dealings; and it so happens that the mass of Irish dealings in the stocks is in the denomination of Three per Cents. I think the comparison is between £5,000,000 or £6,000,000 for Consols, and £25,000,000 or £27,000,000, I forget which, for the New Three per Cents., and therefore it is probable that that stock will be most convenient for Irish holders. The stock, of course, is to be issued at par; it may suit the convenience of parties and the Treasury to commute it to a stock of a lower denomination, and that may be done with the consent of the Treasury. If it so happen that, under the necessary limitations of the Bill, stock cannot be issued to vendors forthwith, scrip, at the same rate of interest, will be given to them in anticipation. These are general, but still not unimportant, provisions.

The object of the Bill.

Now, sir, I will describe in a very few words what I may term the substance and purpose of the Bill. I will avoid that trap into which it seems I fell the other night about "essential" and "vital" points. It is not difficult to say what are the principal enactments; it is extremely difficult, especially in the early stage of discussion, to say what is vital and what is

House of Commons, April 16.

not. It is very difficult indeed, and in consequence, I suppose, of its being so difficult it is never done. I am not aware that I ever heard of a great measure introduced with a thoroughgoing attempt to separate its enactments into two classes, and to say one of them is vital and you cannot touch them, and the other is non-vital, and you may do with them what you please. I will not attempt that; but I think I will use words which will give to hon. members a sufficient idea of the sense and spirit of the measure, and enable them to judge what are really its main provisions.

The object of this Bill is to give to all Irish landowners the option of being bought out on the terms of the Bill; to give to all Irish landowners an opening towards the exercise of that option. I will show later on what portion of them can exercise it, if they like, under the terms of this particular Bill; but the policy is a policy which is to be distinctly understood as the policy of giving this option to all Irish landowners as regards their rented land, and such lands, with certain exceptions which I will state more particularly, as may be described by the word agricultural. As a general description, please to take that for the present moment. I wish it to be understood that the Bill has no concern whatever with mansions, demesnes, or with woods as commonly understood; and I, for my part—I may be very, very sanguine, but I am in hopes that many a nobleman and many a gentleman in Ireland will long continue to inhabit his mansion and his demesne in a new and happier state of things—yes, I believe it may be possible that even the Irish Nationalists may desire that those marked out by leisure, wealth, and station for attention to public duties, and for the exercise of influence, may become, in no small degree, the natural, and effective, and safe leaders of the people.

The spirit of the Bill.

Sir, the spirit in which we have drawn this Bill I wish also to be understood. You may construe enactments perhaps in different ways; but the spirit in which we have drawn the present measure is that of making on this great occasion—the use or the rejection of which evidently must have important influences on the future course of the question—the spirit in which we have drawn it is that of making the most liberal offer to the Irish landlords that we believe our obligations to them demand, or even justify, or that we can expect the representatives of the people to accept. I come one step nearer to my point, and I will endeavour to give a threefold indication which will be useful in following the leading provisions of the Bill.

House of Commons, April 16.

The groundwork of the Bill is an option to the landlords. Upon that I will only say that we have considered much with regard to an option to the tenants, and, again, with regard to including in the Bill provisions, like those of the present Land Purchase Acts, contemplating voluntary arrangements. I do not say that these are necessarily to be rejected, but we have not seen our way to incorporating them with this measure. The measure, as we have found it our duty to present it, is founded on the landlord's option to sell. The State authority, as I have described it, that is, an organ representing the Irish legislative bodies, is to be the middle term, instead of the Treasury, between the vendor and the occupier. It is through that medium that the transaction is to take place. And lastly, as a general rule, what we propose is that upon the sale the peasant is to become the proprietor. He is not to be, in our view, as a general rule, an occupier subject to rent-charge, or subject to be dealt with by any one as such until the expiration of a certain term when he is to become the proprietor; but he is to become the proprietor at once, except that he is to be subject to a burden which I will presently describe.

The parties to the transaction.

As to the nature of the transaction, the State authority is to be the purchaser, and the occupier is to become the proprietor. There are exceptions. It has appeared that it might not be well in all cases to force the very smallest occupiers to become proprietors, if, for any particular reasons, it did not suit their condition. At any rate, we do not

"Purchaser," "proprietor," and "occupier."

House of Commons, April 16.

compel the tenant at £4 and under to become a proprietor unless he wishes it.

There is another more important exception. Every one knows the great importance in Ireland of what are called congested districts. These congested districts we propose to deal with in a manner which forms an exception to the general rule. In the congested districts we propose that the State authority should be not merely the vehicle through which the purchase is to be effected and carried on to the tenant; but in these congested districts, which we propose to schedule at a certain time in the Bill, the State authority is to be the proprietor.

I am bound to say that we reserve for further consideration the question whether in these districts, and these only, there should be introduced the power of compulsory expropriation of landlords—voluntary expropriation with regard to the landlords being the general basis of this Bill.

Encumbrances and public burdens.

What are commonly known as encumbrances, and what are commonly known in Ireland as public burdens, in which phrase, if I am rightly informed, rates are not usually comprehended, are to be taken over from the selling landlord, and he is entirely discharged from them as a matter of arrangement in the transaction. The mortgages, of course, constitute a very easy portion of the transaction. The more difficult part of the transaction is in the quit-rent and the head-rent, the jointures and miscellaneous payments. But we feel it necessary, for many reasons, to disembarrass the estate of these, and likewise of public burdens, such as the tithes commutation, because otherwise we should be in the difficulty of having the tithes commutation liability divided among a multitude of small holdings, which would be highly inconvenient, if not impracticable. The State authority will take over encumbrances of this character—I do not mean encumbrances in capital sums, but, speaking generally, encumbrances in the form of annual charge—will take them over either with the option of continuing to pay them, or to redeem them upon the terms which are stated in the Bill.

Then comes a rather important provision. No one, as a general rule, will have the option to sell except the immediate landlord, our object being a political and social object, dealing with the heart and root of the difficulty. It is to him that we give this option, in order to bring about relief from the dilemma. But his encumbrancer, that is, the mortgagee, will not, by foreclosing, be able to acquire the option for himself. There are certain provisions which provide for cases where the interest of the immediate landlord is extremely small, and the principal interest in the property is in the superior landlord. I only mention this as an exception, which I will not attempt to explain at present. So much for the general nature of the transaction.

House of Commons, April 16.

What may be sold.

Now we come to the application which is to be made. The first condition is this, the application must, as a general rule, be for the whole of the tenanted estate. I can conceive nothing more grossly unjust to the landlord than to tear his property into rags by arbitrary provisions, and therefore the rule is that the application must be for an integral estate, and the Land Court or Commission will determine what is one estate. But there are two exceptions to which I ought to refer. One is the case of the grazings. The great grazings in Ireland appear to stand in a very different condition from that of most agricultural property. We leave it open to either party to apply the definition of an agricultural holding contained in the Act of 1881, and exclude these grazings from the transaction. The other is that it is impossible to define in the Bill what sort of villages ought, and what ought not, to be included under it. In cases where the village is purely subservient to the agricultural purposes of the estate, it ought to be included in the expropriation. In many cases there may be a village which has other shades of character, or is even essentially different, and that question we treat as exceptional, and leave to be determined by the Land Commission. Now, sir, the next proposition is that town parks will not be included in the Bill. So far as we

House of Commons, April 16.

can judge, they do not belong to the same category. All the applications received are to be registered, and are to rank according to priority. The persons making the application must give security to pay the costs if it be not completed into a binding transaction; and in certain cases the Land Commission is to be intrusted with the power of refusing to entertain the application.

Computing the value of an estate.

Now, sir, I speak to gentlemen many of whom are better acquainted, more minutely acquainted, than I am with the agricultural circumstances of Ireland, and I believe I am right in saying that there is a certain class of estates in Ireland—I will not go the whole length with that eminent authority, Sir James Caird, on a recent occasion—that there is a certain class of estates of which the real, substantial, natural value is from various circumstances so depressed that it would be impossible to put a scale of years in the Bill which would really reach them. We should have to go so low that it might introduce great uncertainty in the general character of the Bill. With regard to these we thought the best thing we could do was to empower the Land Commission to refuse an application in these exceptional cases if it deems it inequitable that the State authority should be required to buy an estate at the price laid down in the Bill.

Finding the net rental.

Now, sir, I come still nearer to the centre of gravity of the Bill. The basis on which we compute the price to be paid to the outgoing landlord is twofold. First of all, it must be taken on the rental at a certain time, subject to certain conditions, and secondly it must be taken in a certain number of years' purchase on that rental. Our basis is to be the net rental; and the net rental is to be ascertained—I have spoken already of the public burdens—by deducting the rates and the outgoings. In the outgoings I include law charges, bad debts, and management. These are the great heads. There are minor heads where particular arrangements have been made, and to these I need not refer. The time upon which the calculation is to be based must be a recent

House of Commons, April 16.

one. We have therefore thought it best to take a year the selection of which would give no encouragement to any artificial action or agitation with a view to illegitimately influencing the standard of rental. The general idea, therefore, would be that it would be for a rental due in the year ending November 1885; the judicial rental, where there is one, to be adopted as the standard of gross rental. Where there is no judicial rental, we are in greater difficulty, and we introduce a provision which enables the Land Court, if it shall see cause, to take a given district of Ireland—probably an electoral division—to take the judicial rents within that division, to take Griffith's valuation within that division, to see the relation between the judicial rents and Griffith's valuation, and to use that relation as a guide in determining what shall be the standard rental which is to be the basis of the transaction.

We have also provided, sir, in order to get over the difficulties connected with the great fluctuations in payments and prices, that the Land Court shall examine the books of the estate. That may sound to gentlemen not conversant with Irish transactions a cumbrous arrangement. But we have extremely able public servants in Ireland conversant with these transactions affecting the land, and we are assured by them, without the least doubt or hesitation, that the examination of the books will be not only a practicable, but the best and by far the most practicable, method of deciding the important question of amount. Those books ought to be examined over a considerable time in order to meet the difficulty which arises out of agricultural fluctuations, and we propose to fix the time at ten years. So much as to the rental.

Number of years' purchase.

Now as to the years' purchase. We propose, sir, that the normal rate, if I may so call it—that is, the rate which we conceive will be applicable on a fairly well-conditioned estate in Ireland, setting apart exceptional cases, both of the few extremely good and valuable, and I am afraid the more

House of Commons, April 16.

numerous class that will fall below that—the normal rate would be twenty years on the basis of the rental which I have described. I must add some important particulars of explanation. An addition may be made to the sum on which the charge will be founded in the case of arrears coming due after November 1885, when it is shown to the satisfaction of the Land Commission that every attempt has been made to collect them, and that it has not been found practicable. An addition may be made to the twenty years in the case of exceptionally good estates, limited, however, by a *maximum* of twenty-two years. It is still more necessary that there should be a power to effect a decrease from the twenty years, and it is not possible to attach a fixed limit to that decrease, because if we were to give a fixed limit we must found it on the farthest case to which it ought to go, and that would imply so considerable a deduction that I think it would shake the confidence and tend to pervert the general impression as to the main aim of the Bill, which is a normal standard of twenty years.

I will illustrate my meaning. This power of deduction I will thus define. It would have by no means an exclusive reference, but a somewhat special reference to small holdings. As regards estates composed principally of small holdings, in the considerable majority of cases, even after making the deductions, they are less valuable than estates which are not made up of holdings so small. But, again, if you were to attempt to meet that, as we thought at one time, by naming a more limited number of years for holdings under certain rates, we should fall into an error, because there are estates, particularly in Ulster, which are made up in a great degree of small holdings, but which are, nevertheless, of extremely good, sound general repute. For that reason we leave this power of distinction in the hands of the Land Commission. I think, sir, that is the end of the general provisions of the Bill which I ought to mention, with the important exception as to the mode in which we are to find the money.

House of Commons, April 16.

Financial security.

I come then to the third question which I have stated to the House. The House has a right to ask me and to ask the Government, "You confess that you are going to make use of the public credit; do you intend, under this Bill, that the country is to undertake a real pecuniary risk, and that Parliament is to be requested to compromise its duties as guardians of the public treasury and of the public credit?" My answer, sir, is twofold. In the first place, in my opinion, the introduction of a plan, founded on the basis I now propose of building upon the responsibility of an Irish State authority, will not increase but will greatly diminish the public risk—that public risk which is inseparable from the condition of the Treasury when it comes to be the creditor of perhaps hundreds of thousands of tenants in Ireland. Observe that you cannot have an extensive plan in Ireland without being prepared to deal with tenants in hundreds of thousands. Therefore I distinctly plead to the House that this Bill, if passed, will not be an increase but will be a diminution of public responsibility.

I do not hesitate to say that it will be a grief to me that I can never dismiss from my mind if, at the end of a very long life, much of which has been devoted to a guardianship, perhaps very ineffectual, but still with the best intention I could give, of the public treasury and of the public credit, I should submit to Parliament a measure founded upon opposite principles, or a measure to which we had not ourselves applied the most jealous scrutiny with a view to obtaining what I will not hesitate to call an absolute security.

The risk which the public might have to undergo would be twofold. We are proceeding upon a basis of not making loans in the market to meet the Irish demand, but of issuing stocks. There are two things, therefore, to be considered. First of all, the certainty of the repayment of the money; but that is not the only question. The other thing is the effect of our issues upon the general credit and the general

House of Commons, April 16.

condition of the public security. I not only do not deprecate but I invite scrutiny of the Bill when printed in relation to both these subjects.

Amount of stock to be issued.

The proposals we make, sir, are these. Of course, one of our great difficulties in this business is that neither we nor any human authority can determine beforehand whether the offer, the great offer, signal and conspicuous, which is now made, will be accepted, universally, largely, or at all. We are obliged to make the best calculation or conjecture that we can. It is quite necessary to make an attempt on what may fairly be called, in reference to ordinary transactions, a large scale. That proposition we accept. Notices coming in will be, of course, limited to certain times. The State cannot remain subject to a perpetual recurrence of proceedings lying so far out of the ordinary road, and the Act will prescribe strictly the notices which may be given and the transactions, issues of public stocks to meet them, which may take place in pursuance of those notices. In respect of the notices which may be given in the financial year 1887–88, we propose to authorize the issue, as a *maximum*, of £10,000,000 of stock, because we assume that, although the notices of that year may be very numerous, if the Act works largely, yet the transactions to be concluded in it cannot by any means be so abundant, for these transactions evidently cannot be carried through in a day, and you cannot have an innumerable army of official persons to carry them through. Therefore we authorize an issue of £10,000,000 for the notices given in 1887–88, a further issue of £20,000,000 to meet notices in or before the year 1888–89, and a further issue of £20,000,000 for notices in or before 1889–90. That will give a total of stock, issuable at par, under the Act, amounting to £50,000,000 should it be called for. The operative portion of the Act, the House will feel, must be provided for, because no notices will be given under the powers of the Act, after March 31, 1890.

House of Commons, April 16.

Effect on the money market.

But the House will understand, with reference to what I described as the second kind of risk which we have to keep in view, that it would not have done for us to say that the purchase may be effected to the extent of £50,000,000, and leave it a matter of chance when the stock shall be issued. We must consider carefully what amount of stock we can undertake to issue within the twelve months, and, at the same time, maintain a reasonable amount of confidence that we shall not by that issue unfavourably affect the general price and credit of securities. This point I consider of very great importance. It is necessary for us to maintain the very high level of the price of the public securities. I would even say, setting apart the extraordinary casualties and combinations of circumstances which no man can predict, it is necessary that we should maintain them at something not very far from the level where they now are, and where they have been for a considerable time. Therefore I may be justly asked, Do you think that £20,000,000 is the amount which in one year you may venture to fix as the limit, and yet feel confident in maintaining your price?

Now, sir, that is a question which thirty or forty years ago it would have been impossible to answer in the affirmative, because the powers of Parliament for purchasing stock were so limited that, when even a second-rate purchase was necessary, the Chancellor of the Exchequer had no option but to go hat in hand to the Bank of England, or lesser authorities, to see what they could do for him. I am able to say now, however, that on our own account we are in a condition, under the normal and regular action of the Acts relating to the disposal of Exchequer deposits and banking deposits at the command of the Chancellor of the Exchequer, to exercise so large a power of purchase in the stock market as effectually to counteract any abnormal depression which might otherwise be threatened by the fact that many of those who may acquire a considerable proportion of stocks under the Act will be desirous to exchange them for others perhaps

House of Commons, April 16.

not quite so stable, but at the same time more lucrative. I think I can give that assurance to the House with considerable confidence after having made it a subject of careful inquiry among those who have the largest experience and the greatest faculty of determining what is the point to which we may safely go.

An improvement in the Bill.

I am evidently open to an important observation. I have said that our policy embraces in its final scope, if they desire to avail themselves of the opportunity, embraces in its final scope all Irish landlords. I am bound to express my hope that a good many Irish landlords, not on pecuniary and fiscal grounds only, but upon moral, social, and political grounds, are in such a position that they will not dream of availing themselves of it in its final scope. I am prepared to say that what we contemplate is that every man who desires to avail himself of it shall have a fair opportunity of doing so. It is evident from what is known of the value of Irish landed property, if we go to its total, falling within the definition of the Bill, it would certainly exceed to a very considerable extent, not 50 millions, but 100 millions; I will not say how much, but very considerably. We do not know what fraction we might safely cut off as the proportion of those who under no circumstances would be likely to exercise the option; but it is obvious that a transaction of that kind, if acted upon to that extent, would not be covered by the final issue. When we commenced first drawing the rudimentary sketch, the dominant idea in our minds naturally was to redeem fully the constructive promise we made to the Irish landlords. Therefore, I certainly thought at the first moment to put in the Bill a larger figure as the sum upon which I founded the computation of what might be provided. That figure was not fifty, but so much as 113 millions. That was the computation on which I founded the figures which I first brought before my colleagues. Two of those colleagues, the right hon. gentleman the member for the Border Burghs, and the right hon. gentleman the member for

House of Commons, April 16.

West Birmingham, in particular, felt jealous of charging the public for Irish land or charging it to that great extent. To their objections I certainly feel indebted for what I think a great improvement in the Bill. Because, although there is no change whatever in the policy of the Government, I certainly have to thank them for having set me to consider more carefully what is the relation between an Executive Government asking an advance of that description from Parliament and Parliament charged with the responsibility of maintaining the public credit.

Why the estimated cost was reduced.

I am not ashamed of saying that this plan is not a plan which sprang up in the brain fully armed at a moment's notice. I have told the House of the extraordinary and unprecedented difficulties under which it has been framed, amid the pressure of Parliamentary business from day to day, and I am very glad to own any assistance which has been given to me. It is very pleasant to me to make it known to my colleagues, as regarding this question, that I had the means of bridging over very considerably such difficulties as might exist between us. The matter never came, strictly speaking, to an issue between us. Now hon. gentlemen may think that I have no real or substantial reason for making this reduction except what might be called meeting a popular outcry. Quite the reverse. Unquestionably it was our duty to consider the probability of the acceptance of the measure. But we had many other considerations, and I must say that, upon considerations quite apart from difficulties in procuring the acceptance of the measure, I arrived at the deliberate conviction that it would have been a great error on our part to ask at this moment, now, at once, for a sum founded upon anything like an outside estimate of the possibilities of the case. I felt we ought to ask from Parliament what would secure an efficient progress of the measure, if it became really an operative measure, but that we ought to reserve to Parliament, after we had reached that limit, an opportunity of exercising its discretion afresh.

House of Commons, April 16.

A safe experiment to be repeated.

Hon. gentlemen must have seen that, so far as we are concerned, there are some things which I have said which may be considered to be in the nature of pledges of good faith as between us and the landlords. To make this offer, to make it in an efficient shape, and with the intention so far as we are concerned of following it up if necessary, I conceive to be a matter of honour and good faith; but there are a multitude of other conditions and considerations affecting the future Irish authority, conditions affecting the Irish tenant, conditions affecting the money market, and the nature of those issues, which are not matters of good faith even for us, but are more or less, though by no means generally or universally, matters of good faith, matters of good policy and expediency. From my point of view, I conceive that it is quite right in an arrangement of this kind that we should secure to Parliament an opportunity of exercising its judgment afresh on the subject we now submit to it. So far as good faith is concerned, I am quite certain of this, that if Parliament accedes to and accepts this particular Bill, if it finds that the promises under which we commend the Bill are fulfilled, if it finds that public credit is duly maintained, if it finds that repayments are duly made, if it finds that the whole complex machinery is so well oiled that it works like a locomotive, and if the public credit is safe, as we are sure it will be, in my opinion Parliament will never under-estimate the moral obligations that may be comprehended in the subject. Therefore, sir, this proposal, subject to the declarations which I have not scrupled to make, is in a manner so far experimental that the discretion of Parliament upon its particulars will be reserved.

How the repayments are to be secured.

But then I shall be asked, perhaps, how these repayments are to be secured. They are to be secured in a manner which I commend to Parliament as simple, as effective, and as warranted by the circumstances of the case. It is proposed that there shall be appointed a Receiver-General under British authority, who shall not levy rents or other revenues in Ireland, but through whose hands all rents and all Irish revenues whatsoever must pass before a shilling of them can be applied to any Irish purpose whatever. It is necessary for the Irish authority, if it is to govern Ireland, to have funds for the purpose. Under the plans we propose, and with the economies which I have not the least doubt they will make, I believe their funds will be ample and abundant; but what we propose is this, that these funds shall be subject to the discharge of prior obligations, and that the right of the Irish authority to the money shall begin at the point where the prior obligations end. For that purpose, except under the limited arrangement as to the Customs and certain Excise duties, we are not going to take the levying of the rents and revenues out of Irish hands. That is the very last thing I should desire to do; that of all others is the thing which would be most opposed to the purpose and the policy of the whole Bill. But we are going to require that the money which has been levied for the service of Ireland shall all converge and run into a certain channel. We shall have the money, as it is sometimes said, between the body and the head, the head being the Irish Government. The money must all pass through the channel of the neck, and the neck is the Receiver-General.

House of Commons, April 16.

Receiver-General.

The Receiver-General will find it necessary to appoint two deputies, but he will have nothing to do with the tax-payer—nothing to do except with the tax receivers; they will receive and collect the revenue for him. He will be subject to audit. He will be liable to prosecution by the State authorities, and he will have full authority over the sub-receivers. He will, however, never annoy the taxpayer, nor come near him, nor, I hope, ever be heard of by him. He will not be the appointer of the collectors of taxes—that is a function we do not wish to see in his hands. The power of bringing actions against the sub-receivers in the Court of Exchequer will rest with the Receiver-General, and that

House of Commons, April 16.

explains the provision which I have already mentioned to the House on a former occasion as to the judgments of the Court being supported by the public forces. This security will extend to everything in Ireland for the central purposes of government, to Customs and Excise, and all public revenues whatever. Perhaps I may be told the old story of calling into existence a new Irish legislative body, and at the same time showing a mistrust of it. With great respect, I show nothing of the kind. These provisions have nothing whatever to do with my notions; they are not intended to satisfy me nor the British public; but these are large operations, and the provisions are intended to satisfy a somewhat peculiar and fastidious class, the class of public creditors.

Maintenance of the public credit.

I say boldly that the maintenance of public credit is a common interest: it is the interest of gentlemen opposite; it is the interest of gentlemen here; above all, it is the interest of the Irish Nationalists, because Ireland will undoubtedly want to organize a credit of her own for public purposes. She will require it—I hope not to excess. She will want to organize her own credit by degrees, and she cannot organize a credit to be worked economically and safely unless the ground is absolutely solid under her feet, and the ground cannot be solid under her feet unless the securities for the fulfilment of all her prior engagements are absolutely unimpeachable. I submit that the Exchequer will be as safe in respect of these advances, under the provisions which I propose, as it is in respect of the collection of the taxes in England for the ordinary purposes of government.

An example worked out.

Now, I will endeavour to exhibit with some exactitude to the House the position of the four parties interested in a pecuniary sense in this plan, namely, the Irish landlord, the Irish tenant, the Irish State authority, and the British Exchequer. The case which I take of the Irish landlord for the sake of simplicity is the case of the landlord who has no public burdens and no encumbrances. I should greatly con-

House of Commons, April 16.

fuse the House were I to take the contrary case, and therefore I take the case of an Irish landlord who is so happy that he has nothing but his rates to pay. I take as an instance a gross rental of £1200 a year and ask, "What will be the deduction?" I can only calculate from general information as to rents. The circumstances of particular estates vary so enormously with regard to outgoings, other than encumbrances, that, while the figure I am going to name would be much too high in some cases, it would be much too low in others. I am obliged to strike an average, and the deduction I take as the average figure is 20 per cent. Therefore my gross rental of £1200 will be reduced by the deduction of £240 to £960, and the normal rate of compensation at twenty years, and here again I put aside exceptional cases, will be £19,200.

Now, what will be the condition of the tenant? The *maximum* that he will have to pay will be £960—that is to say, 4 per cent. upon twenty years' purchase, not of the sum the landlord receives, but of the gross rental which he has hitherto paid. That is the *maximum* payment, because, as I shall show you presently, there is a fund out of which, if it should seem right to the State authority, some further favourable arrangement may be made. On receiving that deduction, he will become subject to half-rates, because he becomes an owner. The 4 per cent. charge will continue for forty-nine years, and the legal ownership will become, at the end of that time, perfectly free ownership, without any annual payment unless taxes should be laid upon the land by the State authority.

Now for the position of the State authority. That authority will receive £960 from the tenant. What will it have to pay to the Imperial Exchequer? It will have to pay 4 per cent. also, not, however, upon the gross rental, but upon the net rental. That will be £768. The cost of the collection of the net rental, we can confidently state, will be very low. It will only be 2 per cent.—that is, £19, 4s.

House of Commons, April 16.

The State authority will therefore receive £960, and the total charge upon it will be £787, 4s. That leaves the State authority £172, 16s., or nearly 18 per cent. Then what is the State authority to do with this £172, 16s.? On the one hand, it may be enlarged, because it will be larger in those cases where the compensation will be below twenty years, and therefore it will be larger if the average is below twenty years. On the other hand, it may be subject to certain deductions on account of the cost of conveyance, because we have thought it fair not to leave the landlord liable to unrestricted charges in respect of proof of title; and we shall accordingly fix very low the *maximum* of the costs which can be charged upon the landlord with respect to conveyance. The State authority may also be liable to a somewhat heavier charge, in respect of the redemption of quit-rents, head-rents, tithe commutations, and jointures, which cannot always be kept within the limit of twenty years. Upon the whole, there is no reason to believe that those considerations will cause any great invasion of the balance which I have shown to be free for the State authority, about 18 per cent. upon the sum payable to the landlord.

Ireland's balance after the debt is paid.

We have proceeded upon the principle that the State authority may in certain cases find it necessary or think it expedient to grant some further remission to the tenant. But we are not acting simply for the interests of the Irish tenant; we are acting also for the interests of the Irish labourer and the Irish community, and it is our duty, if Great Britain is to make an effort by the use of her credit to bring about an improved state of things—it is our duty to leave some fair portion of the resulting profit to be for the advantage of Ireland at large, subject to the distribution and according to the direction of the Irish authority. I may say, that, in case the whole of these transactions should go forward, the sum becoming subject to the discretion of the Irish State authority would be not much less than £400,000 a year.

Now a few words with respect to the position of the

House of Commons, April 16.

Security to Imperial Exchequer.

Imperial Exchequer. The Imperial Exchequer assumes a *maximum* expenditure of £50,000,000. It may, or may not, be that, but I take the *maximum*. The interest at 4 per cent., including sinking fund, will be £2,000,000. That will be the cash which the Imperial Exchequer will receive every year from the Irish authority through the Receiver-General, that admirable personage to whom I have already referred. How will this £2,000,000 be secured? If these transactions take place, the land rents which the State authority will levy will amount to a net rental of £2,500,000, and we have the highest possible security for its vigilance in levying those rents,—first of all, in its sense of right; secondly, in its sense of prudence; and thirdly, in its sense of necessity, inasmuch as until the prior charge is paid it can touch nothing. The sum will in the first place be secured upon this amount of £2,500,000; but it will be secured also upon the balance of all Irish revenue; and thirdly, it will be a first charge on the taxes levied under the Irish State authority, which I have assumed will amount to £5,778,000. You may say there is also the Imperial contribution to be taken into view. Yes, there is; but there is also a large further fund which may be taken into account, namely, Customs and Excise. If I add to the Imperial contribution and to the charge for the constabulary the £2,000,000 which I have now spoken of in respect to land, the sum comes out thus. We want to get £6,242,000, and that is secured upon £10,850,000, no portion of which can be applied for any other purpose until our claim in respect of the £6,242,000 is satisfied. That I conceive to be securing British credit, and that is the only possible foundation for Irish credit also.

England's account with Ireland.

There is one other matter to which I wish to refer; it is the last with which I shall trouble the House. Some people have an idea that, under the present arrangement, we receive from Ireland, if not all that we desire, yet enough to replenish very materially our Imperial resources. That is a woeful delusion. We do nothing of the kind, and I will prove it. I

House of Commons, April 16.

do not say that Ireland does not pay enough, but I do say that we receive very little; and I am bound to add that, with the views I hold with respect to the unwisdom of our policy, I do not think that we deserve to receive more. The present contribution of the Irish taxpayer to the revenues of this country is £6,980,000, and out of that we pay back for Irish civil charges £4,840,000. The residue of £2,000,000, in round numbers, is apparently an Imperial contribution from Ireland for the Army, the Navy, the National Debt, and other Imperial Civil Service charges. But having got that, what do we do with it? We send an army to Ireland of 26,000 men, whom we have not dared to release, and which costs us £3,000,000 a-year, nearly £1,000,000 more than the apparent surplus of £2,000,000 to which I have just referred, without any provision whatever for debt, the Navy, or Imperial Civil charges. That, sir, is the economy of the system which we have to root up from out the land.

Conclusion.

I have detained the House a long time, but this is a complex question. I will detain the House no longer. I commend this measure with the utmost earnestness as a complement to our policy, adopted under serious convictions both of honour and of duty. I commend it to your strict, your jealous, your careful, and your unbiassed examination; convinced as I am that, when that examination has been given to it, both in regard to policy, and honour, and duty, it will be recognized as a fitting part of our proceedings upon this certainly great and, as I believe, auspicious occasion; fitting, I do not say to adorn, but to accredit and sustain the plans of the British Legislature for the welfare of what is, and what has long been, and what I hope will ever be, under happier circumstances than heretofore, an integral portion of Her Majesty's dominions.

IV.

FOURTH HOUSE OF COMMONS SPEECH.

MONDAY, MAY 10, 1886.

THE GOVERNMENT OF IRELAND BILL.

On the order of the day for the second reading of the Government of Ireland Bill, Mr. Gladstone said:—

Introduction.

I was the latest of the members of this House who had an opportunity of addressing the House in the debate on the introduction of this Bill; yet I think no one will be surprised at my desiring to submit some observations in moving the second reading. And this, on the double ground—first of all, because, unquestionably, the discussion has been carried on, since the introduction of the Bill, throughout the country with remarkable liveliness and activity; and, secondly, because so many criticisms have turned on an important particular of the Bill, with respect to which the Government feel it to be an absolute duty on their part that they should, without any delay whatever, render to the House the advantage of such explanations as, consistently with their public duty, it may be in their power to make.

My personal position.

I am very sorry to say that I am obliged to introduce into this speech—but only, I hope, to the extent of a very few sentences—a statement of my own personal position in regard to this question, which I refrained from mentioning to the House at the time when I asked for leave to bring in the Bill. But I read speeches which some gentlemen opposite

House of Commons, May 10.

apparently think it important to make to their constituencies, and which contain statements so entirely erroneous and baseless that, although I do not myself think it to be a subject of great importance and relevancy to the question, yet, as they do think it to be so, I am bound to set them right, and to provide them with the means of avoiding similar errors on future occasions. Although it is not a very safe thing for a man who has been for a long time in public life, and sometimes not very safe even for those who have been for a short time in public life, to assert a negative, still I will venture to assert that I have never in any period of my life declared what is now familiarly known as Home Rule in Ireland to be incompatible with Imperial unity. ("Oh, oh!" from the Opposition.) Yes; exactly so. My sight is bad, and I am not going to make personal references; but I daresay the interruption comes from some member who has been down to his constituents, and has made one of those speeches stuffed full of totally untrue and worthless matter.

I will go on to say what is true in this matter. In 1871 the question of Home Rule was an extremely young question. In fact, Irish history on these matters, in my time, has divided itself into three great periods. The first was the Repeal period under Mr. O'Connell, which began about the time of the Reform Act, and lasted until the death of that distinguished man. On that period I am not aware of ever having given an opinion; but that is not the question which I consider is now before us. The second period was that between the death of Mr. O'Connell and the emergence, so to say, of the subject of Home Rule. That was the period in which physical force and organizations with that object were conceived and matured, taking effect under the name generally of what is known as Fenianism. In 1870 or 1871 came up the question of Home Rule. In a speech which I made in Aberdeen at that period, I stated the great satisfaction with which I heard and with which I accepted the statements of the proposers of Home Rule, that under that name they

House of Commons, May 10.

contemplated nothing that was at variance with the unity of the Empire.

A national desire.

But, while I say this, do not let it be supposed that I have ever regarded the introduction of Home Rule as a small matter, or as entailing a slight responsibility. I admit, on the contrary, that I have regarded it as a subject of the gravest responsibility, and so I still regard it. I have cherished, as long as I was able to cherish, the hope that Parliament might, by the passing, the steady and the continuous passing, of good measures for Ireland, be able to encounter and dispose of the demand for Home Rule in that manner, which obviously can alone be satisfactory. In that hope undoubtedly I was disappointed. I found that we could not reach that desired point. But two conditions have been always absolute and indispensable with me in regard to Home Rule. In the first place, it was absolutely necessary that it should be shown, by marks at once unequivocal and perfectly constitutional, to be the desire of the great mass of the population of Ireland; and I do not hesitate to say that that condition has never been absolutely and unequivocally fulfilled, in a manner to make its fulfilment undeniable, until the occasion of the recent election. It was open for any one to discuss whether the hon. member for Cork — acting as he acted in the last Parliament, with some forty-five members—it was open to any one to question how far he spoke the sentiments of the mass of the Irish population. At any rate, it is quite evident that any responsible man in this country, taking up the question of Home Rule at that time, and urging the belief that it was the desire of the mass of the Irish population, would have been encountered in every quarter of the House with an incredulity that it would have been totally impossible for him to have overcome. Well, I own that to me that question is a settled question. I live in a country of representative institutions; I have faith in representative institutions; and I will follow them out to their legitimate consequences; and I believe it to be dangerous in the highest

House of Commons, May 10.

degree, dangerous to the Constitution of this country and to the unity of the Empire, to show the smallest hesitation about the adoption of that principle. Therefore, that principle for me is settled.

Home Rule and Imperial Unity.

The second question, and it is equally an indispensable condition with the first, is this: Is Home Rule a thing compatible or incompatible with the unity of the Empire? Again and again, as may be in the recollection of Irish members, I have challenged, in this House and elsewhere, explanations upon the subject, in order that we might have clear knowledge of what it was they so veiled under a phrase, not exceptionable in itself, but still open to a multitude of interpretations. Well, that question was settled in my mind on the first night of the present session, when the hon. gentleman the leader of what is termed the Nationalist party from Ireland declared unequivocally that what he sought under the name of Home Rule was autonomy for Ireland. Autonomy is a name well known to European law and practice, as importing, under an historical signification sufficiently definite for every practical purpose, the management and control of the affairs of the territory to which the word is applied, and as being perfectly compatible with the full maintenance of Imperial unity. If any part of what I have said is open to challenge it can be challenged by those who read my speeches, and I find that there are many readers of my speeches when there is anything to be got out of them and turned to account. I am quite willing to stand that test, and I believe that what I have said now is the exact and literal and absolute truth as to the state of the case.

Experiments in politics.

I shall not dwell at any great length on the general argument in favour of the Bill; but I will notice one or two points that have been taken, and which, if they do not express any very definite argument, yet give expression to feelings which are entitled on my part to deference and respect. A great objection which is felt by some hon. gentlemen is much to this effect:—"Do not, in these great matters, experiment

House of Commons, May 10.

in politics; do not let us have this kind of legislation, uncertain as to its effect, involving great issues, and therefore liable to be marked, I may say stigmatized, by the name of experiment." Because, although in one sense every law is an experiment, yet I perfectly understand, and I am the first to admit, that experimenting in politics is a bad and a dangerous practice. Now, what is experimenting in politics? If I understand it, it is the practice of proposing grave changes without grave causes. Is this a case in which there is no grave cause with which we have to deal? Why, sir, we have to deal with the gravest of all causes that can solicit the attention of a Legislature—namely, the fact that we have to treat the case of a country where the radical sentiment of the people is not in sympathy with the law. (Murmurs.) I defy any man, be he an opponent or not, to deny that we have to deal with the case of a country where the radical sentiment of the people is not in sympathy with the law. Of course, I am making general assertions. I do not say that an action on a bill of exchange between debtor and creditor in Ireland could not be settled without reference to any international prejudice. I speak of the most important parts of the law, of those parts which touch agricultural relations, the one great standing, pervading employment and occupation of the country; I speak above all of the criminal law, of the very first exigencies of political society; and I will not argue the question whether the criminal law of Ireland, especially when it concerns agricultural relations, has or has not the sympathy of the people until I find some one who is ready to say, after all he knows about evictions, about the operations of the Land League, and about the verdicts of juries, that the criminal law in Ireland has the sympathy of the people. Not only is this a matter of fact, but it is a matter of fact with which we are constantly dealing, which has run through three generations of men, and that almost without intermission.

Past legislation.

We have tried expedients. What has been our great expedient? Our great expedient has been that to which I

House of Commons, May 10.

admit *primâ facie* a Government will first and justifiably resort. Our first expedient has been that which is known as repression or coercion. Has that class of experiment, has that class of expedient, been successful? I argued this point at full length in introducing the Bill, and I will not argue it now at any detail whatsoever. I will only make this one assertion, which I believe to be absolutely undeniable—namely, that this medicine of coercion, if it be a medicine, is a medicine which we have been continually applying in increasing doses with diminishing results. When a physician has before him such a phenomenon as that, he should direct his attention and his efforts to some other quarter and to some other method. We have, and I am glad to admit it, tried remedies. I see it stated sometimes that nothing has been so miserable a failure as the course of remedial legislation with respect to Ireland, with which the members of the present Government, and I myself, for a long time have been associated. I refer now to the removal of religious disabilities, to the disestablishment of the Church, to the reform of the Land Laws, and to the removal—or, if not the absolute removal, to the enormous mitigation—of the intolerable grievances, perhaps the worst of all after the land grievance, under which Ireland used to labour with respect to education.

Remedial legislation incomplete.

If I am asked what I think of all these measures, I deny that they have failed. We have not failed, but we have not finished. They have had this effect, that the disease of Ireland has taken a different and a milder form. (Cheers and laughter.) I am sorry to arouse scepticism whichever way I go. When I said just now that social order in Ireland was disturbed, there were signs of dissent from hon. members opposite; and now when I say that the disease of Ireland has taken a milder form there are also signs of dissent, and it seems to me impossible that anything said by me can be true. My meaning is this—the disease of Ireland is in a milder form; but, in my opinion, it is in a form still extremely serious, and yet a milder form than it took in 1832, when murders, excesses, and outrages were manifold to what they are now, so as to indicate a different state of things at the present time from what existed then, and an undoubted growth of what are known as law-abiding habits; or I might go further back to the dreadful rebellion of 1798, which demanded a great effort on the part of this country to put down. No, sir, that legislation has not failed. I admit that it is incomplete, that it has not reached, that it has not touched the goal, the terminating point of the race we had to run, and something yet remains to be done.

House of Commons, May 10.

Coercion and concession.

But there is another notion which has gone abroad. I have spoken of former expedients and remedies, but there is now a notion that something might be done by judicious mixtures of coercion and concession. These judicious mixtures are precisely the very thing that we have tried. Go back to the Roman Catholic emancipation. The Duke of Wellington made a judicious mixture upon that occasion. He proposed that we should open the doors of Parliament, and I am thankful he did so, to the Roman Catholics of Ireland, but he at the same time disfranchised the 40s. freeholder on the principle of judicious mixture. When Sir R. Peel in 1843–44 put Mr. O'Connell on his trial, and succeeded in obtaining in Ireland a conviction which was afterwards quashed on a point of form, that was a strong step in the direction of coercion; but he followed it up immediately by the important Act for enlarging the endowment of Maynooth, by an Act for facilitating the granting of charitable bequests to the Roman Catholic Church, and I must also say, although it may shock some hon. gentlemen opposite, by a third Act, which was then viewed as a great boon to the Roman Catholic interest—namely, the Act for the foundation of undenominational colleges. There was another case of judicious mixture. It happened when we were disestablishing the Church there was great disorder in Westmeath, and in the middle, I think, of the Land Bill, we arrested the progress of that measure and introduced a very strong measure of coercion for Westmeath,

House of Commons, May 10.

all on the principle of judicious mixture. The Government which came into office in 1880, and which was put out of office in 1885—the whole course of that Government was nothing but one of rigid and incessant effort in a policy of judicious mixture. Therefore do not let us suppose that the merit of novelty attaches to that recommendation.

Party spirit.

But I have seen another recommendation made, and made, I think, by a person of very great authority, I believe in my hearing, to the effect that if we could only cast away party spirit in dealing with Ireland we should do well. Then, I think, a good many hon. members opposite cheered, indicating that they were ready to cast away party spirit. What is meant by this? Is it meant that party spirit is to be expelled generally from the circuit of English politics? Is that so? Is there a dreamer who, in the wildness of his dreams, has imagined that you can really work the free institutions of this country upon any other principles than those in the main which your fathers have handed down to you and which have made the country what it is? (Cheers and counter cheers.) Those cheers may be meant in sarcasm. I accept them in good faith. I believe that in uttering the words that I have just used I have quite as strong a meaning, and I am ready to act upon the principle which I have laid down quite as much, and perhaps a little more, than a great many hon. members opposite who cheered. It may be said, "We do not think you can get on altogether without party spirit, but do at any rate cast out party spirit from Irish affairs." Is that a more hopeful recommendation?

Visionary suggestions.

It will be convenient to take the case of the two sides of the House separately, and first I ask, is it desirable that the Tory party should cast out party spirit? I should say undoubtedly. But if I should press it upon the right hon. gentleman opposite, he would be entitled to make an answer to me which I should feel to be a crushing answer, because he would say, "Before you talk of casting away party spirit from the handling of Irish affairs, you must show that it has

House of Commons, May 10.

been applied to those affairs in some sense different from its application to other affairs, and in a more guilty and more mischievous manner." I will not speak of the last year or two, during which there may have been strong prejudices. I will go back half a century, to the time when great resistance was offered, and I as a humble and as a silent follower had my share of responsibility for that resistance. I mean the resistance to the extension of the franchise in Ireland, especially of the municipal franchise. I deeply lament that opposition was ever offered; I may say, *quorum pars exigua fui.* The conduct of the Tory party of that day under Sir Robert Peel and the Duke of Wellington, Lord Stanley and Sir James Graham, although very mistaken, was perfectly honest. I am not prepared to say that Irish affairs have been handled in this House, speaking generally, by either party with a larger admixture of party feeling or with a smaller flavour of true patriotic tone than other affairs of the country. It is idle to set up as remedies, as alternatives, and as policies to adopt in great crises these suggestions which are totally visionary and unreal, and which never could become the basis of human action in a Legislative Assembly.

Opinions of statesmen.

So much for experiment. Here I stand upon the ground that a great necessity is before us, that a growing and urgent evil requires to be dealt with, that some strong and adequate application to the case is requisite, and that the whole and the only question is whether the application we propose is the right one. Let me say this upon this particular question of a Legislature for Ireland, that it appears to be a very popular topic with our opponents to say, "Why do you depart from the course taken by all the statesmen of the nineteenth century?" Now let us see what has been done and said by all "the statesmen of the nineteenth century." The great case produced is the famous Repeal debate in 1834, in which I myself was one of the majority who voted against the repeal of the Union. A very remarkable passage from a very re-

Sir Robert Peel.

markable speech of Sir Robert Peel, well deserving to be kept

House of Commons, May 10.

fresh in the memory of posterity, from its terseness and power, has again become familiar to the people of this day, as I myself heard it with my own ears that day with admiration. What was Sir Robert Peel then doing? In the first place, he was opposing the repeal of the Union. You call this repeal of the Union. (Opposition cheers.) You must at least allow us to have an opinion on that subject. For my part, I am not prepared at this moment to say that the question of the repeal of the Union should be reopened. I may be right or wrong in that matter, but my opinion is that Ireland has done much, by wisdom and moderation, by bringing her essential demands within certain limits, to facilitate the task set before us. But even if this were repeal of the Union, I admit, without the least question, that up to a certain point the Union is upon its trial. I admit, without the least question, that in my opinion this Bill constitutes a most important modification of that Act. But was Sir Robert Peel in the same circumstances in 1834 as we found ourselves in 1884? He had had one generation of experience; we have had nearly three. In the days when he spoke, the Statute Book of England was loaded with a mass of Acts inflicting the most cruel grievances upon Ireland, and it was a perfectly rational opinion for a man like Lord Macaulay, who was deeply interested in Ireland, and other politicians of like character, to think that by the removal of those grievances you might save the Union. What was then a matter of reasoning and speculation has now become a matter of knowledge.

Lord Macaulay.

So Lord Macaulay is one who is quoted like Sir Robert Peel. I remember well a passage of splendid eloquence delivered by Lord Macaulay against the repeal of the Union, a Union of which I will not say anything more now than that I do not desire to rake up the history of that movement, a horrible and shameful history, for no epithets weaker than these can in the slightest degree describe or indicate ever so faintly the means by which, in defiance of the national sentiment of

House of Commons, May 10.

Ireland, consent to the Union was attained. I think in 1834,[1] or not very distant from that date, Lord Macaulay, in words of burning eloquence, denounced the repeal of the Union. Lord Macaulay, I think in 1859, or certainly many years later in his life, if not so late as that, in his *Life of Pitt*, declared that the Union without the measures which Mr. Pitt finally hoped to procure from it, and to which it became in fact the greatest impediment—without those measures the Union was union only in name, and, being a union only in name, it was in rank opposition to all the national and patriotic sentiment of Ireland. How was it possible that its authority could commend itself to the people of that country? I do not admit that the question of the Union, so far as it is now on its trial, has been decided, or has been touched, by statesmen of the nineteenth century. Those of whom I spoke never had before them what we have before us, the bitter fact, the rich though painful story of the experience which the rolling years of the last half century have afforded us.

Old Whig traditions.

Well, then, sir, we are told again with extraordinary boldness, "Why do you depart from the old Whig traditions?" If there is one thing more than another which my hon. friend the member for Bedford was doing in his admirable speech which he delivered on this subject, it was in showing that he was acting in strict consonance and conformity with the old Whig traditions. What were the old Whig traditions? The organs of those traditions were Mr. Sheridan and Lord Grey —the Lord Grey of that day, or rather the Mr. Grey of that day, afterwards still more famous as Lord Grey. Then there were Lord Fitzwilliam, and, above all, Mr. Fox, and even above Mr. Fox himself there was Mr. Burke. Upon this great subject of the relations with Ireland Mr. Burke never modified by one hair's-breadth the generous and wise declaration of his youth and of his maturer manhood. Mr. Burke did not live to the date of the Union, but he placed on record in the first place his political adhesion to the opinions of Mr.

Mr. Burke.

[1] The date was February 6, 1833.

House of Commons, May 10.

Grattan, and in the second place he placed upon record his full satisfaction with the state of things that prevailed in Ireland, the political state of things, especially the Acts of 1782 and 1783; and in a letter written not long before his lamented death, he said that he trusted that Ireland had seen the last of her revolutions. By that he meant that the Act of 1782 did amount to a revolution, a blessed and peaceful revolution, but still a revolution, a revolution effected by those peaceful means, by that bold and wise British statesmanship, such as in 1844, and again at a later period, was commended by Lord Beaconsfield.

It may be said with perfect truth that Lord Grey declined at a later date to be a party to the repeal of the Union. In that respect, in my opinion, he was perfectly consistent. For my own part, if I may refer to myself, I do not at all regret the vote which I gave fifty-two years ago against the repeal of the Union, considering what that repeal involved, and considering the amount of information we had with regard to its working. The Union, whatever may be our opinion with regard to the means by which it was obtained, was a statute of vast importance, for it modified and in many respects transformed the relations between Great Britain and Ireland. Such a statute as that cuts deep tracks in history; those tracks cannot be effaced in later times. But we are acting in most complete conformity with Whig traditions and the principles upon which Whig statesmen founded their action. They did not say that the principle of the Union between Great Britain and Ireland was bad in the abstract; they did not say, "We in our minds are opposed to it, and therefore Ireland and Great Britain shall not have it;" but they said it was opposed to the sentiment of the Irish people. They said it was in opposition to all that was most honourable and upright, most respected, and most disinterested in Ireland, and nothing but mischief, nothing but disorder, nothing but dishonour, could come from a policy founded upon the overriding of all those noble qualities, and by means which would not bear the face of day imposing the arbitrary will of the Legislature upon the nation, in spite of its almost unanimous opposition. House of Commons, May 10.

Now, sir, it should be borne in mind that there was at that time in existence the greatest difference of sentiment from what we now witness in Ireland. The north was more opposed to the Union probably than the south. I remember that the town of Cork used to be quoted as a spot on which love of the Union might be detected by the careful observer. Unquestionably the promises held out by Mr. Pitt did induce a division of sentiment among the Roman Catholic clergy of that time. I believe that the Irish national patriotic sentiment which I have mentioned with sympathy was more vivid in the north of Ireland than in any other quarter.

Well, sir, hon. gentlemen say, "Do not talk to us about *Canada.* foreign countries; do not talk to us about British colonies; do not mention Canada, it has nothing whatever to do with the case. Canada is loyal and content; Ireland is disloyal and disaffected." But Sir Charles Gavan Duffy in an able paper admits the charge. He says:—"When it was determined to confer Home Rule on Canada, Canada was in the precise temper attributed to Ireland. She did not get Home Rule because she was loyal and friendly, but she is loyal and friendly because she got Home Rule." Now, sir, I am, on this subject, able to speak as a witness. I sat in Parliament during the whole of the Canadian controversy, and I even took, what was for me, as a young member, an active part in the discussions upon the subject. And what was that Canadian controversy? The case of Canada is not parallel to the case of Ireland. It does not agree in every particular, and the Bill which we offer to Ireland is different in many important particulars from the Acts which have disposed of the case of Canada. But although it is not parallel, it is analogous. It is strictly and substantially analogous. What, sir, was the issue in the case of Canada? Government from Downing Street. These few words embrace the whole con-

House of Commons, May 10.

troversy; Government from Downing Street being, of course, under the Government of St. Stephen's.

The unity of the Empire.

What was the cry of those who resisted the concession of autonomy to Canada? It was the cry which has slept for a long time, and which has acquired vigour from sleeping; it was the cry with which we are now becoming familiar, the cry of the unity of the Empire. Well, sir, in my opinion the relation with Canada was one of very great danger to the unity of the Empire at that time, but it was the remedy for the mischief, and not the mischief itself, which was regarded as dangerous to the unity of the Empire. Here I contend that the cases are precisely parallel, and that there is danger to the unity of the Empire in your relations with Ireland; but unfortunately, while you are perfectly right in raising the cry, you are applying the cry and the denunciation to the remedy, whereas you ought to apply it to the mischief.

Victors vanquished.

In those days what happened? In those days, habitually in this House, the mass of the people of Canada were denounced as rebels. Some of them were Protestants and of English and Scotch birth. The majority of them were Roman Catholic and of French extraction. The French rebelled. Was that because they were of French extraction and because they were Roman Catholics? ("Yes" from an hon. member on the Opposition side.) No, sir; for the English of Upper Canada did exactly the same thing. They both of them rebelled, and perhaps I may mention, if I may enliven the strain of the discussion for a moment, that I remember Mr. O'Connell, who often mingled wit and humour with his eloquence in those days when the discussion was going on with regard to Canada, and when Canada was the one dangerous question, the one question which absorbed interest in this country as the great question of the hour—when we were engaged in that debate, Mr. O'Connell intervened, and referred to the well-known fact that a French orator and statesman named Papineau had been the promoter and the leader of the agitation in Canada. And what said Mr.

O'Connell? He said:—"The case is exactly the case of Ireland, with this difference, that in Canada the agitator had got the 'O' at the end of his name instead of at the beginning." Well, these subjects of Her Majesty rebelled—were driven to rebellion and were put down. We were perfectly victorious over them, and what then happened? Directly the military victory was assured, as Mr. Burke told the men of the day of the American war, the moment the military victory was assured the political difficulty began. Did they feel it? They felt it; they gave way to it. The victors were the vanquished, for, if we were victors in the field, we were vanquished in the arena of reason. We acknowledged that we were vanquished, and within two years we gave complete autonomy to Canada. And now gentlemen have forgotten this great lesson of history. As to saying that the case of Canada has no relation to the case of Ireland, I refer to that little sentence written by Sir Charles Duffy, who himself exhibits in his own person as vividly as anybody the transition from a discontented to a loyal subject—"Canada did not get Home Rule because she was loyal and friendly, but she has become loyal and friendly because she has got Home Rule."

House of Commons, May 10.

The issue.

Now I come to another topic, and I wish to remind you as well as I can of the definition of the precise issue which is at the present moment placed before us. In the introduction of this Bill I ventured to say that its object was to establish, by the authority of Parliament, a legislative body to sit in Dublin for the conduct of both legislation and administration under the conditions which may be prescribed by the Act defining Irish as distinct from Imperial affairs. I laid down five, and only five, essential conditions which we deemed it necessary to observe. The first was the maintenance of the unity of the Empire. The second was political equality. The third was the equitable distribution of Imperial burdens. The fourth was the protection of minorities. And the fifth was that the measure which we proposed to Parliament—I

House of Commons, May 10.

admit that we must stand or fall by this definition quite as much as by any of the others—that the measure should present the essential character and characteristics of a settlement of the question.

Well, sir, that has been more briefly defined in a resolution of the Dominion Parliament of Canada, with which, although the definition was simpler than my own, I am perfectly satisfied. In their view there are three vital points which they hope will be obtained, and which they believe to be paramount, and theirs is one of the most remarkable and significant utterances which have passed across the Atlantic to us on this grave political question. (Cries of "Oh, oh" from the Opposition.) I just venture to put to the test the question of the equity of those gentlemen. You seem to consider that these manifestations are worthless. Had these manifestations taken place in condemnation of the Bills and policy of the Government, would they have been so worthless?

A question so defined for the establishment of a legislative body to have effective control of legislation and administration in Ireland for Irish affairs, and subject to those conditions about which, after all, there does not appear in principle to be much difference of opinion among us—that is the question on which the House is called upon to give a vote, as solemn and as important as almost, perhaps, any in the long and illustrious records of its history.

The exclusion of Irish Members.

Sir, in the interval which has taken place since the introduction of the Bill much discussion has arisen upon a variety of its particulars which I am very far from grumbling or complaining at. One of them, however, is exciting so much feeling that it is quite necessary that it should receive the notice of my colleagues and of myself in the present debate. I mean that which relates to the exclusion or disappearance, for it really can hardly be called an exclusion when it is rather desired and sought for by the parties themselves, of the Irish members from the benches of this House.

Now, sir, in this explanation which I am about to give, I

do not address myself to those who are hostile to the principle of this Bill. I wish with all my heart I could say something, without vitally prejudicing the public interests involved in this measure, that would tend to reconcile or to abridge the differences between Her Majesty's Government and a body of gentlemen with whom hitherto they have had the happiness of acting in as perfect concord—allowing for the necessary freedom of human opinion and the occasional differences that may arise—as ever consolidated together the different sections of the Liberal party. Unhappily, sir, while I have the most cordial respect for those gentlemen, I am not able to promise myself that they will listen with much interest to what I have got to say. There are others who, as I believe, accept not less cordially than Her Majesty's Government themselves what I have declared to be the principle of this Bill, and who at the same time see greater difficulties than we do, though we have seen great difficulties all along, and I never represented this measure as one in which all the points were clearly indisputable. The case bristles with difficulties of detail throughout which only require goodwill and patient intelligence to deal with, and different men feel them in different modes and different degrees.

House of Commons, May 10.

What has happened, sir, is this. I do not deny the fact that many friends of this measure, whom we should be loth indeed to alienate, have taken strong objection to the provisions with respect to the future absence of Irish members from this House under two heads. In the first place, they recall a proposition which I myself stated very strongly in introducing the Bill, namely, the great political principle that there ought not to be taxation without representation. In that I stated what was an obvious truth. It is quite evident that we never would enforce upon Ireland taxation without representation, and nothing but the consent of Ireland could have induced Her Majesty's Government to contemplate such a thing for a single moment. But many gentlemen, and I do not find fault with them, are not satisfied even with the

Objections to this provision.

House of Commons, May 10.

consent of Ireland. Gentlemen will recollect that, though we now hear sometimes of persons being more Popish than the Pope, and many phrases of that kind, the original phrase was *Hibernicis ipsis Hiberniores.* The meaning of that phrase was this,—that those English families, those portions of the English race, who went and planted themselves amongst the Irishry, after a moderate time became more Irish than the Irish themselves. We have had that illustrated wholesale on the present occasion. I must own that this is a difficulty which I regard with respect and with sympathy, and I trust that in any attempt to meet it I shall have the sympathy of the House in general, at all events of those who can on any terms tolerate the principle of this Bill. Besides that objection, which is an objection strictly upon argumentative and constitutional grounds as respects taxation, there is undoubtedly another sentiment more vague, less definite, in a different region of the human mind; there is a sentiment of regret that there should cease to be a symbolical manifestation of the common concern of Ireland with ourselves in the unity of the Empire, and in the transaction of Imperial affairs.

Ireland and foreign affairs.

Well, now, sir, how do we stand with regard to this case? First of all, let me say, however much it may appear to be a paradox to English members, yet history undoubtedly teaches us that, to whatever cause it may be due, foreign affairs, what I may call over-sea affairs, do not stand in exactly the same relations to Ireland as they do to England and Scotland. This is what I mean—I am not raising any disputable proposition—I speak of the feeling of the people; and it appears to me perfectly natural that the inhabitants of a country like Ireland, whose difficulties have been so great, whose woes have been innumerable, whose hopes have been intermittent and continually disappointed—the history of a country like that must throw back the mind of the people upon itself and its own concerns, and in that way it is that I can understand why it is that Irish gentlemen do now, what we all do if we are men of common sense in the common affairs of life, that is, look to the principle, and do not think so much about objects which in their view are secondary as about that which is central and essential,—that which is central and essential being the management of Irish affairs. What I am now going to say has not had so much notice as it deserves. Ireland is not so entirely excluded by the Bill as it stands from Imperial affairs as gentlemen may be disposed to think. I refer, and I by no means refer alone, to the principle which is contained in the 39th clause of the Bill—the clause which provides for the recall of Irish representatives of both Houses before this House can proceed to any alteration of the statute upon which the two Legislatures are not in accord. I hope that is a provision which there will be little, if any, occasion for putting into action. But the principle involved is an important principle.

Besides that, there is another clause which provides that in certain circumstances the Irish Assembly may vote sums of money in relation to subjects which are excluded from its ordinary cognizance. This provision has been misunderstood to mean that the Irish legislative body might in certain circumstances vote money for the establishment of a Church.

Well, sir, I have really not examined whether the words of the statute will bear such a construction as has been put upon them. But if they bear such a construction, undoubtedly an effectual remedy ought to be applied. The meaning of the words is simply this—our belief in drawing the Act was this—that it might be felt right in the event, as I trust the improbable event, of a great war, wherein this country and Ireland were engaged with a common feeling and common interest, for the Crown to send a message to the Irish legislative body to ask them freely to testify their participation in our interests and privileges by voting money and supplies. (Opposition laughter.) Some gentlemen differ from me as to the measure by which they estimate the ludicrous and the serious. My own estimates are sometimes in an inverse relation to theirs. What they think ludicrous seems to me to be

House of Commons, May 10.

serious, and possibly *vice versâ*. It is supposed to be ridiculous that a practically independent body in Ireland—(Opposition cheers)—yes, practically independent in the regular exercise of its statutory functions, should entertain such a proposal. But it was not ridiculous when Ireland had an independent Parliament.

Ireland and foreign affairs.

I said just now that it was a wonderful thing to see how little in other days Ireland had interposed in foreign affairs. I have had the debates looked up during the whole period of Grattan's Parliament, and, if I except certain discussions relating to foreign treaties of commerce—I will speak of that matter by and by—there are only two occasions upon which that Parliament debated foreign affairs, so far as I can discover. Both of those occasions are occasions on which by message from the Crown they were invited to vote sums of money for purposes of war. One of them was in 1790, when there was a seizure of British vessels by Spanish men-of-war. A vote of money was then asked and was given. The second was in 1795, when a contribution was asked towards the expenses of the French war. On the first occasion the Irish Parliament granted the money without question. I do not believe myself that pecuniary illiberality has ever been a vice of Ireland. On the second occasion they granted it, but moved an amendment, full, I think, of good sense, hoping for a speedy conclusion of hostilities. For my part, I heartily wish that prayer of the Irish Parliament had been complied with. I take blame to myself for not having explained to the House the provision to which I have just referred, namely, the provision for the voting of money by the Irish legislative body in answer to the message from the Crown. But my right hon. friend the Chief Secretary will bear me out when I say that after I had spoken I remarked to him that I regretted the omission of which I had been guilty.

Moreover, sir, although the statute will limit the legislative powers of the Irish legislative body, there are other moral powers of influence which it will possess, and which we do not and cannot limit. The privilege of free speech is not going to be taken away from Ireland; that privilege of free speech will attach to the members of this legislative body and to the legislative body collectively, and a considerable influence may be exercised upon proceedings at Westminster through resolution and by address from the legislative body.

House of Commons, May 10.

However, sir, while I wish these provisions to be understood, I do not mean to limit what I have to say by reference to them. I wish to say what Her Majesty's Government have thought to be their duty with regard to the feeling which has been copiously expressed in many portions of the country by gentlemen friendly to the principle of the Bill. Undoubtedly, it is our plain duty to consider how far we can go, without prejudice to the main purpose of the Bill, to meet that desire. We shall do that upon grounds of policy, and upon grounds of principle. We shall make willing steps in that direction as far as duty will permit us to go. There are three things which I had better at once say we cannot do, and are unwilling to entertain in any shape. We are not willing to break up the Parliamentary traditions of this House, or to introduce a principle of confusion into the working of the House. That is the first. The second is, we are not willing to fetter against its will the action of the Irish legislative body in any case except where cardinal and Imperial interests require it. We will do nothing that shall have the effect of placing our measure in such a condition that Ireland, through her representatives, can only offer to it a qualified and a grudging, instead of a free, cordial assent and acceptance. And, third, we can do nothing that will have the effect of placing the Committee of the Bill before the second reading. That may be a phrase mysterious to some, but the meaning of it is this, that to determine in detail, even if upon points of importance, everything which is of great interest touching this Bill before you obtain assent to the principle of the Bill is not practicable, and if it be practicable the rules of this House are based upon folly, for undoubtedly it would be much more

Indispensable conditions.

House of Commons, May 10.

convenient in many respects before you are called upon to assent to the principle of a Bill to have it in the exact form in which it is to be finally adopted.

There is another thing to be considered, and it is this. It has very often happened to me in the course of a great experience in Parliamentary legislation, that you hold communications with one class of gentlemen, you happen to be good-tempered or bad-tempered as the case may be, you feel a great desire to meet the views of that class of gentlemen, and you unwarily pledge yourself to propose the thing they desire. It is settled within the four walls of a private room. Then you come into this House, which happily—I thank God for it—is the place of the most thorough publicity in the whole world, and you find other sets of persons, quite as much entitled to be heard, who are at daggers drawn with the first. But the Government has unwarily committed itself; and a quarrel ensues. All the while it is perfectly possible that if they had been allowed to reserve their discretion, and freely to consider the particulars in the Committee, they might have been able to find means to conciliate those of opposite views, so as to bring about general satisfaction. What I mean is this, and I think the House will agree with me, I admit that when a thing is right, and when you see it to be practicable, you may promise before the second reading of a Bill that if agreeable to the House you will do it. But we cannot do more than promise a fair consideration hereafter to a fair proposal, unless it is such a proposal as we can see our way to embodying in a workable shape. I do not think that is an unfair proposal. In violation of these three conditions we can do nothing. But we are ready and willing to do everything that they will allow.

Taxation and representation.

Then I take the first objection that has been made to the proposed exclusion of the Irish representatives from this Parliament. It is that the principle that representation should accompany taxation would thereby be violated. Now, what I am about to say involves a considerable responsibility;

but the question whether and how far the difficulty may be met has been considered, and I am prepared to say that we can give full satisfaction to those who advance this objection. If agreeable to the House, we will meet it in Committee, by providing that when a proposal is made to alter the taxation in respect of Customs and Excise, Irish members shall have an opportunity of appearing in this House to take a share in the transaction of that business. It will then be impossible to urge against the Bill that it is proposed by the Government that representation should not accompany taxation.

House of Commons, May 10.

In regard to such matters of common interest between Great Britain and Ireland as those which form the subject of foreign treaties, no doubt the objections urged from some quarters may be met in some considerable degree by the adoption of a system of executive communications, which is the system adopted in certain foreign countries. There are cases in which two countries are disunited in their Legislatures, but united in national action and feeling. They find themselves able, by executive communications, to provide for the common handling of common subjects. But we do not feel that the plan of executive communications need of necessity be the only one. There are various plans which have been proposed in order to indicate and maintain common action on Imperial subjects, and which are well worthy of consideration. For example, it has been proposed that a joint Commission should be appointed, representing the House of Parliament on this side of the water, and representing the Irish legislative body, in due proportion of members, and that that Commission should meet from time to time as occasion might arise during the Session of Parliament, to consider common questions, and report their opinions to both legislative bodies upon many, at any rate, of the Imperial matters that are reserved by the Bill as it stands. I hesitate to say upon "any" of those questions, for I incline to the belief, for example, that the question relating to the succession of the Crown, in all the different branches of the subject, ought

Plans for the joint discussion of matters of common interest.

House of Commons, May 10.

not to go to any secondary authority. But I can conceive that many subjects, such, for example, as treaties of commerce, might well be considered by a Commission of this kind. I do not say of this plan as absolutely as I do of the plan as to taxation, that we are quite ready to propose it if it be the wish of Parliament, for it has been little canvassed, and objections may be raised to it which we have failed to anticipate; but I can say that we look at the proposal as one which might satisfy jealousies, might have other advantages, and is not open, so far as we know, to serious objection.

Further proposals.

Another proposal is that a joint Committee of the kind which I have described could be appointed to consider how far and upon what conditions, other than those provided in the statute, Irish members should come here. There is yet another suggestion, that Irish members might be entitled to come to Parliament—I assume generally that corresponding opportunity would be given to Irish peers—upon occasions when the legislative body should, by an address to the Crown, have expressed a desire that they should do so. I do not say that that is open to objection on principle. At the same time, I see considerable difficulties as to the particular way of making it a practicable plan. I will, however, state broadly that it is our duty to give an unprejudiced ear to proposals which others may make for the purpose of insuring the continued manifestation of common interest between Great Britain and Ireland in Imperial concerns. That end, we say distinctly, is a good end; means for attaining it we regard with favour, subject to the condition that they shall not be so handled as to introduce into this House the principle of confusion, nor so handled as to impose on the Irish legislative body limitations of its liberty in any matters except such as affect high Imperial policy. (LORD R. CHURCHILL asked whether the Irish members would reappear in their full numbers.) I am much obliged to the noble lord. The clause now in the Bill contemplating the recall of the Irish representatives in a certain contingency makes no difference

House of Commons, May 10.

from the present arrangements as to the numbers in which they would come. We do not feel that the subject involves a vital principle, nor have we arrived at any binding decision; but my own personal opinion is that if we were to bring back the Irish members in any other numbers than the present, we should first have to devise a new system of election, and I am not sure that it would be wise to complicate the matter in that way. I should be inclined to hope that, so far as it is desirable that Irish members should reappear in Parliament, the Irish people would be liberally and amply, rather than scantily and jealously, represented.

Social order imperative.

There is only one other subject to which I must advert. We propose a change of which, if viewed as an abstract and speculative change, the postponement for a year or even longer would not have been a matter of vital consequence. But this concession, if you like to call it so—in my view it is something much higher than a concession, it is a great reformation and improvement—this change is not proposed upon grounds of general expediency alone, or in the view of abstract improvement alone; it is proposed in order to meet the first necessity of civilized society. Social order is not only broken up in Ireland, it is undermined, it is sapped, and by general and universal confession it imperatively requires to be dealt with. It is because this measure is one for the restoration of social order by the removal not merely of the symptoms but of the cause of the mischief that we recommend it to the consideration of Parliament. We are all agreed up to a certain point—(An Hon. Member: "No")—all except a solitary gentleman opposite. We all agree upon this, that social order in Ireland imperatively requires to be dealt with; but when we come to the method, then, unfortunately, our differences come into view. Were I to take all the individual opinions that have been expressed as to the mode of dealing with Irish questions, I should simply bewilder the House. I will only look at the main and leading divisions of power and influence in this assembly.

House of Commons, May 10.

Tory policy.

There are in the House two great parties, independently of the Irish party, and there is a third body whom I will not call a party, because I am happy to think that as a party we are not yet divided from them, and I trust may never be. But we are vitally divided on this great and significant question from those whom I will not call a party, but whom I must call a body, but who are so important that they may possibly hold the balance and decide the question between the two great British parties in this House. The mass of the Irish representatives have committed in the eyes of many gentlemen opposite a new, a mortal offence, an offence more deadly than any former offence. They have committed the offence of agreeing with us in this matter. As long as their favours were bestowed in another quarter, great toleration was to be expected, and was happily experienced, by them from those who are now very much shocked in their highest moral qualities at our alliance with the Irish party, which alliance amounts simply to a coincidence of views on a great vital and determining public question.

Of the two political parties in the House, both have spoken, and spoken plainly. I do, indeed I must admire the tact, the caution, I will not say the astuteness, with which most of the leaders of the Tory party have abstained from overmuch troubling themselves with forecasts of the future, or pledges as to the mode of meeting it, with regard to the Irish question. Finding that they had on this side of the House allies—I do not use the word in an invidious sense, it is the same kind of alliance that there is with gentlemen from Ireland, that is to say, it is an honourable and conscientious coincidence of opinion—finding that they had allies of that kind ready to do their work, with equal politeness and wisdom they have left the doing of that work to them. But, notwithstanding that, they have spoken and spoken plainly for themselves. When the noble lord the member for Paddington was brought to the point, and when it was said he had not declared a policy, he pointed, and he was justified in pointing, not even to a phrase, but to a date, and he said, "Our policy is the 26th of January." I accept that reply from the noble lord. It is true and it is just, and that was, and that is, the declaration of policy for Ireland from the Tory party.

House of Commons, May 10.

The suppression of the National League.

I remember, and many others may recollect, the fervid and almost endless cheering with which the gentlemen then sitting on this side of the House accepted the announcement of the 26th of January. That is a plain, manly, and straightforward announcement. What was it? The notice did not convey, and we could not expect that it should convey, a full description of the proposals that were to be made; but it so far described them that it indicated one point with perfect clearness, and that was the suppression of the National League. I may say, in parenthesis, that I trust that we shall be suppressors of the National League. That, if it comes about, will certainly be by a different process. The suppression of the National League—what does it mean and what does it come to?

"To drive discontent under ground."

A noble friend of mine, to whom I refer with the greatest respect, when he held office in Ireland, said:—"We want to drive discontent under the ground." I own I thought at the time that that expression was what is called a slip of the tongue, and I suppose there is no man among us who does not occasionally slip into that form of error. But if instead of its being a slip of the tongue it is exalted into a policy, then what is the meaning of the suppression of the National League? It is the conversion of the proceedings of that body, which I am not now called upon to discuss or characterize—it is the conversion of the proceedings of that body, taken daringly but openly in the face of day, into the proceedings of secret societies, the last resort in this and other countries of the extreme and hopeless difficulties of political problems; and, in my opinion, nothing is to be gained by procuring and bringing about the substitution of secret communities for the open action of a body like the National League.

House of Commons, May 10.

To abolish discontent.

It is sought apparently to take away discontent from the surface. We are not contented with so limited an ambition. We desire to take away discontent neck and crop. We desire to abolish it root and branch, or, if I may once more put into requisition a phrase which had its day, we desire to abolish Irish discontent "bag and baggage." I do not believe that Parliament would pass a proposal for the abolition, in the present circumstances, of the National League. If it did pass such a proposal, in my opinion it is doubtful whether it would have made any contribution whatever to a real solution of the Irish difficulty,—whether, on the contrary, it would not have administered a new aggravation to it. However that may be, I own that that party has spoken plainly, and their policy is summed up in the words "repression" or "coercion."

When this Government was formed, it was formed on the principle of looking for some method of dealing with Ireland other than by the method of coercion; and that policy has now taken definite form and shape in the proposal of autonomy for Ireland. You have spoken plainly, and we have spoken plainly. Has the third power in the House spoken plainly? Has that power which is to hold the scales, and which may decide the issue, told the country in what manner, when it is forced to face this tremendous problem, it intends to deal with it?

Lord Hartington's policy.

There are few men in this House, I am sure there is no man outside of it, who does not admire the temper and the courage with which my noble friend the member for Rossendale has behaved on this question. In obedience to his conscience, and to his conscience alone, he has rent asunder with pain, and perhaps with agony, party ties to which he has been among the most faithful of all adherents. And, speaking generally of those who act with him, I believe that in their several spheres the same may be said of them. Nor do I feel, although I may lament that they have come under what I think are narrow and blind influences, that their titles to my respect are one whit diminished by what they have said or done. I make these admissions freely and without stint. My noble friend has assumed an immense responsibility. It is not for me to find fault with those who assume immense responsibility. My responsibility in this matter is perhaps even greater than his. Next to mine, and you will never find me here to extenuate it, I know no subject of Her Majesty that has a greater load of responsibility upon him than my noble friend. I do not blame, I have no title to blame him. All honour and praise to him for his undertaking the task which I know to be of enormous difficulty! But it may be a task of leading the determining and superior forces of Parliamentary opinion towards a conclusion on the Irish question. If that is so, I ask what does he mean to do? Has not the time arrived when we ought to know what his policy is to be?

House of Commons, May 10.

I have endeavoured to search it out by such means as I could. Is it to be the policy announced to the Loyalist minority at Belfast in November last? (A HOME RULE MEMBER: "So-called 'Loyalist minority.'") I assume the phrase. In politics I like to give to every class of men the name by which they like to be called. Well, sir, in Belfast my noble friend made very considerable promises on the 5th of last November, and he said an extremely bold thing. "I should not shrink," he said, "from a great and bold reconstruction of the Irish Government." Well, all I can say is this, that we who are now the Government are exceedingly daring; but our daring is nothing like yours. The man who will undertake to reconstruct the Irish Government without touching the legislative principle from which administrative government derives its life, if he is not a traitor or a fool—these are words not ours, but are reserved for gentlemen quite different from us—he is either a magician or a man not much accustomed to the practical transaction of public affairs.

His offer to reconstruct the Irish Government made in 1885.

That is not all, sir. My noble friend did not stop by promising in the exuberance of his zeal that which I am

A contradiction between then and now.

House of Commons, May 10.

convinced is absolutely impossible—namely, to reconstruct the Irish Government for any practical purpose without providing a new spring of action, which can only be provided on the principle of the policy we propose. But my noble friend did not promise absolutely the principle of the policy we propose, because he said that nothing could be done in the direction of giving Ireland anything like complete control over her own affairs, either in a day or a session or perhaps a Parliament. But he pointed to the means by which it was to be done, namely, by the work of time, by the growth of small beginnings, the superstructure was to be raised on a wise and sound foundation. Yes, but what is the principle really at issue between us? It is this, not whether we are right in proposing at one step to give to Ireland complete control of her own affairs, but whether it is a thing right to be done at all. At Belfast in November my noble friend in this passage implied that it might be a thing right to be done. To-night he is to move that it is a thing wrong to be done. What, then, is his policy? I am sorry to think that since November the movement of my noble friend has not been forwards, but rather, as it appears to me, backwards. We have heard nothing since November of this complete reconstruction of the Irish Government, and the gradual progress on a sound foundation of a well-built structure. But I rejoice in that declaration on one ground, namely, that it implies that the complete control by Ireland of her own affairs is a thing which may be contemplated, and that in the view of my noble friend it is a thing compatible with the unity of the Empire. Therefore, I am convinced that it is not a thing to be renounced *ab initio*, to be renounced and proscribed as a something tending to disintegrate and break up the unity of the Empire.

The bold path is the safe path.

I confess that I do not believe in this gradual superstructure. I believe the meaning of it would be, were it practicable, that a series of boons would be offered to Ireland, every one of which would, with an enormous loss of Parliamentary time and temper, and with an immense obstruction of public business, be either entirely repudiated by Ireland, or be received in a grudging temper and with the fullest notification that whatever power of that kind you gave her would be used simply as an instrument for acquiring more power. I am very disinterested upon that subject. I should have disappeared from the scene while my noble friend's process was in a very early stage indeed. But I own I do not believe that that is the wisest method of dealing with the great Irish question. I believe we have reached one of those crises in the history of nations where the path of boldness is the path, and the only path, of safety. At least we have come to a time when there is one thing we ought to know, and that is our own minds. We ought to know and we ought to tell our minds. There is another thing which I hold to be essential: we ought not to take this great Irish question, and cast the fate of Ireland into the lottery of politics. I think it is obvious that I am not open to the reproach of casting the fate of Ireland into the lottery of politics, because what you tell me is that I am steering Ireland to utter destruction and certain ruin. If we are proposing to drive Ireland down the cataract, point out to us the way of escape. Is it really to be supposed that the last declaration of my noble friend, which was the keeping alive of two or three clauses of the Crimes Act, which we intended to have kept in existence had we remained in office last year—is that really the policy for Ireland? To that no assent, no approval has been given from the important party opposite.

House of Commons, May 10.

The alternatives.

Sir, Parliament is entitled to know at this time of day the alternatives that are open to its choice. You say that we offer the alternative of ruin. At any rate, in our view, it is of a very different character. But even in your view, it is a definite proposal, which is our justification on its behalf, and is the only contribution which we can make to the solution of the question. Parliament is entitled to have before it the

House of Commons, May 10.

alternatives proposed, the alternatives of policy, not of plan, proposed by those who are taking steps which may in certain contingencies with high probability bring into their hands the supreme direction of affairs. The Tory party have announced their policy. Repression—the 26th of January. There is a policy I understand. Here I know with whom, and with what, I have to deal. But as regards my noble friend, I must say that I am totally ignorant with whom, and with what, I am dealing, so far as policy is concerned. I hope that the notice he has given for to-night has been given with the intention of tracing out for us a palpable and visible road into the darkness, and that he will tell us on what principle it is that he proposes to make provision for the government of Ireland. Let us know these alternatives. The more they are examined, the better I believe it will be for us all. It will become reasonably clear, I won't say to demonstration, that we have before us a great opportunity of putting an end to the controversy of seven hundred years, ay, and of knitting together, by bonds firmer and higher in their character than those which heretofore we have mainly used, the hearts and affections of this people and the noble fabric of the British Empire.

V.

FIFTH HOUSE OF COMMONS SPEECH.

MONDAY, JUNE 7, 1886.

GOVERNMENT OF IRELAND BILL.

MR. GLADSTONE, on rising to reply, at the close of the debate on the motion for the second reading of the Government of Ireland Bill, said :—

Mr. Speaker,—I shall venture to make, sir, a few remarks *Introduction.* on the speech of the right hon. gentleman (Sir Michael Hicks-Beach) ; but I will first allow myself the satisfaction of expressing what I believe to be a very widespread sentiment, and saying with what pleasure I listened to two speeches this evening,—the singularly eloquent speech of the senior member for Newcastle (Mr. Cowen), and the masterly exposition, for I cannot call it less, of the hon. member for Cork (Mr. Parnell). Sir, I feel a strong conviction that speeches couched in that tone, marked alike by sound statesmanship and far-seeing moderation, will never fail to produce a lasting effect upon the minds and convictions of the people of England and Scotland. Sir, with respect to the personal question which has arisen between the hon. member for Cork and the right hon. gentleman opposite (Sir M. Hicks-Beach), I think it no part of my duty to interfere. I have avoided, and I shall avoid, in the discussion of this question, so far as I can, all matters which are of a purely polemical character between party and party. I presume that this subject will be carried

House of Commons, June 7.

further. I understand a distinct allegation to be made by the hon. member for Cork with regard to some person, whose name he does not give, but who is one of a limited body. In that limited body it will not be difficult, I conclude, to procure it, if it can be given. Upon that I pass no judgment. I simply make this comment upon a subject which is of considerable public interest. The right hon. gentleman opposite will do me the justice to say that I have not sought, before taking office or since taking it, to make the conduct which right hon. gentlemen opposite pursued on their accession to power matter of reproach against them. ("Oh.") If they do not like to do me that justice, I shall not ask it.

Sir M. Hicks-Beach's "simple facts."

On the speech of the right hon. gentleman I need not dwell at great length. He began by stating a series of what he succinctly described as simple facts. I will not say his simple facts are pure fictions, because that would hardly perhaps be courteous. But they are as devoid of foundation as if they had been pure fiction.

"The Bill of one man."

The right hon. gentleman declared, though I do not see that it has much to do with the matter, that this is the Bill of one man. Well, I am amazed that the noble lord and the right hon. gentleman speak as if they had been at my elbow all day, and every day, through the autumn and winter of last year. How can any man know that this is the Bill of one man? (A laugh.) How can the hon. member who laughs know that this is the Bill of one man? Reference is made to the allegations of my right hon. friend the member for West Birmingham. My right hon. friend could only speak within the compass of his knowledge, and, if he said that it was the Bill of one man, he would know no more about it than the hon. member opposite. What my right hon. friend said, and said truly, was to state the time at which the Bill came before the Cabinet. But, sir, long before that time the subject of the Bill and its leading details had been matter of anxious consideration between me and my nearest political friends. ("Name.") I never heard a more extraordinary demand in my life, not to say gross impropriety. I refer to those of my colleagues who were most likely to give the most valuable aid, and with whom from the first I was in communication.

House of Commons, June 7.

"In office by Parnellite support."

Then, sir, the right hon. gentleman says we were installed in office by the help of the hon. member for Cork. The right hon. gentleman appears to have forgotten the elementary lessons of arithmetic. It is perfectly true that the energetic assistance of the hon. member for Cork might have kept the right hon. gentleman in office. The right hon. gentleman speaks of the party behind him and the Liberal party, as it then was, on this side of the House, as if they had been two equal parties, and only required the hon. member for Cork and his friends to turn the scale. (LORD R. CHURCHILL: "They were.") They were, says the noble lord? The noble lord's arithmetic is still more defective;—335 is by 85 votes a larger party than 250. Then the right hon. gentleman says that with the exception of the Customs and Excise duties no change was made in the Bill after it was first submitted to the Cabinet. He has no means of knowing that, even if it were true; but it happens to be entirely untrue. Provisions of great importance had never been seen by my right hon. friend the member for West Birmingham. My right hon. friend took exception to certain provisions of the Bill without being acquainted with the whole *corpus* of the Bill. That is the fact; so that the right hon. gentleman is entirely wrong also upon this as well as upon his other "simple facts."

A promise to reconstruct the Bill.

Then the right hon. gentleman says that I had announced that this Bill was not to be reconstructed. I announced nothing of the kind. I announced that I did not promise that it should be reconstructed. There are actually gentlemen opposite, members of Parliament chosen to represent the country, who think this a matter of laughter, and can see no distinction between promises that a Bill shall not be reconstructed, and not having promised that it shall be. I conceive that a person who has promised that a Bill shall be reconstructed is bound to reconstruct it. Is that true? A person

House of Commons, June 7.

who has not promised that a Bill shall be reconstructed is free to reconstruct it, but is not bound to do so. I hope I have made a clear distinction; and I am glad to see that the laughter opposite has ceased, as light has flowed in upon the minds of those hon. gentlemen.

I was struck with another observation of the right hon. gentleman. He says that this Bill, whatever else may happen, will at any rate be rejected by the votes of a majority of English and Scotch members, and he is cheered by those who teach us that they are above all things anxious for the maintenance of an absolutely United Kingdom, and an absolutely united Parliament, in which Irish members are in all respects to be assimilated to, and identical with, those representing English and Scotch constituencies. The right hon. gentleman talked about a dissolution, and I am very glad to find that upon that point he and we are much more nearly associated in views and expectations than upon almost any other point.

The principle of the Bill.

After what the right hon. gentleman has said, and the want of acquaintance which he has shown with the history of this Bill on which he dwelt so long, and after what was said by my right hon. friend behind me, I must again remind the House, at any rate, in the clearest terms I can use, of the exact position in which we stand with reference to the Bill. In the first place, I take it to be absolutely beyond dispute, on broad and high parliamentary grounds, that that which is voted upon to-night is the principle of the Bill as distinguished from the particulars of the Bill. (A laugh.) What may be the principle of the Bill, I grant you freely, I have no authority to determine. (Renewed laughter.) The hon. member laughs; I am much obliged for his running commentary, which is not usual, on my observations, but it is our duty to give our own sense of the construction of the principle of the Bill, and I think I drew a confirmation of that construction from the speech of the right hon. gentleman, because he himself said this was a Bill for the purpose of establishing a legislative body in Ireland for the management of Irish affairs.

House of Commons, June 7.

Entire freedom as to details.

Well, sir, that, if we have any power or any title to give our view on the subject, is the principle of the Bill. As respects the particulars of the Bill, I apprehend it to be beyond all question that members voting for the principle of the Bill are in this sense entirely and absolutely free, that if they consider that there is another set of provisions by means of which better and fuller effect may be given to the principle of the Bill, they are at liberty to displace all the particulars they find in it which hinder that better and fuller effect being given to the principle. (A laugh.) That does not admit of doubt. I am quite certain the hon. member who laughs will not rise in his place at any time and say that a member is not at liberty to remove each and all, if he think fit, of the particulars of the Bill, if in good faith he believes that the principle of the Bill can be better and more adequately promoted by a different set of provisions.

Amendments invited subject to conditions.

But the Government have taken certain engagements. They have taken an engagement as to taxation for the intervention of Irish members, to the terms of which I need not refer. They have also taken an engagement on the claim of Ireland to a continued concern through her members in the treatment of Imperial subjects generally. And that has entailed a positive pledge to reconstruct the 24th clause, and to adopt certain consequential amendments connected with it. One more question has been raised, and has excited a deep interest, and that is with respect to other amendments to the Bill. Of course, as to the freedom of members to suggest other amendments, I have spoken in terms which, I think, are abundantly large. As respects our duty, there can be no question at all that our duty, if an interval is granted to us, and the circumstances of the present session require the withdrawal of the Bill, and it is to be reintroduced with amendments at an early date in the autumn—of course it is our duty to amend our Bill with every real amendment and improvement, and with whatever is calculated to make it more effective and more acceptable for the attainment of its end. It is, as a matter

House of Commons, June 7.

of course, and without any specific assurance, our duty to consider all such amendments. We are perfectly free to deal with them; but it would be the meanest and the basest act on the part of the Government to pretend that they have a plan of reconstruction ready beforehand, cut and dry, in their minds at a time when, from the very nature of the case, it must be obvious that they can have no such thing.

The five specified conditions.

So much, then, for the situation, for the freedom of members to propose amendments, for the duty of the Government to consider amendments and improve their Bill if they can, with the view of a fuller and better application of the principle,—but subject, let me add, to conditions, five in number, which have been clearly enumerated on a former occasion, and from which there is no intention on our part to recede. The right hon. gentleman speaks of Ulster as a question of principle. The question of Ulster, or whatever the common name of the question may be, may be one of great importance, but I must say that, while I in no respect recede from the statement made in regard to it at the opening of these debates, yet I cannot see that any certain plan for Ulster has made any serious or effective progress. The hon. and gallant member for North Armagh emphatically disclaims the severance of Ulster from the rest of Ireland, and the member for Cork has laid before us a reasoned and elaborate argument on that subject to-day, which, as it appears to me, requires the careful attention of those who propose such a plan for our acceptance. We retain, however, perfect freedom to judge the case upon its merits.

Irish "Loyalism."

Now, sir, I want to say a word upon the subject of Irish loyalism, because we are obliged to use phrases in debates of this kind which cannot be explained from time to time when using them, and it is well that there should be a little understanding beforehand. When I hear the speeches of the member for Belfast (Mr. Johnston), and of some other gentlemen, it always appears to me that he is under the pious conviction that loyalty is innate in the Irish Protestants, and disloyalty innate in some other persons. I do believe that he is under the impression that at all times, in all the long generations of Irish history, that has been the distinction to be drawn between Protestants and persons who are not Protestants. Is Protestant loyalism a thing that has a date and origin, or is it not? Has the hon. member, or the hon. and gallant member, inquired what was the state of Ireland in the eighteenth century with respect to loyalty? As far as regarded the great mass of the population, the Roman Catholic population, they were hardly born into political life until the close of the century, and for a long period, in the time of Dean Swift, who describes their incapacity for political action as something beyond belief, it would have been absurd to speak of them as loyal or disloyal. But at the close of the century the Protestants and Roman Catholics of Ireland were described in a short passage by Mr. Burke which I shall now read to the House. The date of it is 1796, and it is taken from a letter to Mr. Windham. He speaks of the subject of disaffection.

House of Commons, June 7.

"It"—that is to say disaffection—"has cast deep roots in the principles and habits of the majority among the lower and middle classes of the whole Protestant part of Ireland. The Catholics who are intermingled with them are more or less tainted. In the other parts of Ireland (some in Dublin only excepted) the Catholics, who are in a manner the whole people, are as yet sound; but they may be provoked, as all men easily may be, out of their principles."

What does that mean? That the Protestants, not having grievances to complain of, have become loyal, but in many cases the Roman Catholics, as Mr. Burke says, have been provoked, as all men easily may be, out of their principles of loyalty. And these are words, and these are ideas, which show us what is the way in which to promote loyalty, and what is the way in which we can destroy it.

Federation.

Another subject on which I shall dwell only for a moment is that of federation. Many gentlemen in this House are

House of Commons, June 7.

greatly enamoured of this idea, and the object they have in view is a noble object. I will not admit the justice of the disparagement cast by the right hon. gentleman on the British Empire. I do not consider that this is a "loosely-connected Empire." But I admit that, if means can be devised of establishing a more active connection with our distant colonies, the idea is well worthy the attention of every loyal man. The idea of federation is a popular one. I will give no opinion upon it now, but I suspect that it is beset with more difficulties than have as yet been examined or brought to light. But this Bill, whatever be its rights or wrongs in any other respect, is unquestionably a step, an important step, in that direction. Federation rests essentially upon two things, and upon two things alone as preconditioned. One is the division of Legislatures, and the other is the division of subjects, and both those divisions are among the vital objects of this Bill.

Supremacy of the Imperial Parliament.

The right hon. gentleman has referred to the question of supremacy. My own opinion is that this debate has, in a considerable degree, cleared the ground upon that subject. It is most satisfactory to me to hear the statements of the hon. member for Cork. I own I have heard some astounding doctrines, astounding to an ignorant layman, from learned lawyers; but still, upon the whole, the balance of authority seems to me to have established, as a clear and elementary proposition that cannot be denied, that this Parliament, be it the Imperial Parliament or not, as long as it continues in its legal identity, is possessed now, as it was possessed before the Union and before the time of Grattan's Parliament, of a supremacy which is absolutely and in the nature of things inalienable, which it could not part with if it would, and which it would not part with if it could. There is no doubt a practical question, because it is quite true that in constituting a Legislature in Ireland we do what we did when we constituted a Legislature for Canada and for Australia. We devolve an important portion of power—we did it in Canada,

House of Commons, June 7

and I hope we shall do it in Ireland; and we devolve it with a view to not a partial, not a nominal, but a real and practical independent management of their own affairs. That is what the right hon. gentleman objects to doing. That is the thing which we desire and hope and mean to do. It is obvious that the question may be raised, How are you to deal with the possible cases where the Imperial Government, notwithstanding this general division of affairs, may be compelled by obligations of Imperial interest and honour to interfere? My answer is, that this question has received a far better solution from practical politics, and from the experience of the last forty or fifty years, than could ever have been given to it by the definition of lawyers, however eminent they may be.

Canada.

When the Legislature of Canada was founded, this difficulty arose. We had the case of the Canadian rebellion, where I myself for one was of opinion, and Lord Brougham was also of opinion, I know not now whether rightly or wrongly, that the honour of the Crown had been invaded by the proposition to grant compensation for losses in the rebellion to those who had been rebels and who had incurred those losses as rebels. I say nothing now about our being right or wrong, but in 1849 Lord Brougham brought forward a motion on the subject in the House of Lords, and I myself did the same in the House of Commons. The important part was the declaration which was drawn from Ministers of the Crown. Lord Russell then, in answer to me, laid down what I conceive to be a true and sound doctrine in terms which, I think, may be described as classical and authoritative in their manner of dealing with this question. Lord Russell, speaking on the 14th of June 1849, said:—

"I entirely concur with the right hon. gentleman—and it is, indeed, in conformity with the sentiments which I expressed in a despatch written, I think, some ten years ago—that there are cases which must be left to the decision of the responsible Ministers of the Crown. There are cases where the honour

House of Commons, June 7.

of the Crown and safety of this country are concerned, and in such cases it requires the utmost temper in the Colonies, and the utmost temper and firmness in this country, in order to prevent differences from being pushed to a collision, which might be fatal to the connection between the mother country and the Colonies. I fully admit that there are such cases. But when the right hon. gentleman goes on to say that Lord Elgin has received from the Government of this country instructions by which he is debarred from asking the advice and direction of the Crown upon a question affecting Imperial policy and the national honour, he is totally mistaken in that most unwarrantable assumption."

That passage, as I believe, contains, very justly and clearly set forth, the practical mode by which this question, difficult in the abstract, will be settled now as it has been settled before, and we shall find that, as it has been perfectly easy to reconcile the rights of Canada with the supremacy of the Imperial Parliament, it will be not less easy in practice to reconcile the rights and the autonomy of Ireland with the same supremacy.

Unionists and Separatists.

I wish now to refer to another matter. I hear constantly used the terms Unionists and Separatists. But what I want to know is, Who are the Unionists? I want to know who are the Separatists. I see this Bill described in newspapers of great circulation, and elsewhere, as a Separation Bill. Several gentlemen opposite adopt and make that style of description their own. Speaking of that description, I say that it is the merest slang of vulgar controversy. Do you think this Bill will tend to separation? Well, your arguments, and even your prejudices, are worthy of all consideration and respect; but is it a fair and rational mode of conducting a controversy to attach these hard names to measures on which you wish to argue, and on which I suppose you desire to convince by argument? Let me illustrate. I go back to the Reform Act of Lord Grey. When that Reform Bill was introduced, it was conscientiously and honestly believed by great masses of men, and intelligent men too, that the Bill absolutely involved the destruction of the Monarchy. The Duke of Wellington propounded a doctrine very much to this effect, but I do not think that any of those gentlemen, or the newspapers that supported them, ever descended so low in their choice of weapons as to call the measure "the Monarchy Destruction Bill." Such language is a mere begging of the question.

House of Commons, June 7.

Now I must make a large demand on your patience and your indulgence. We conscientiously believe that there are Unionists and Disunionists, but that it is our policy that tends to union, and yours to separation. This involves a very large and deep historical question. Let us try for a few moments to look at it historically. The arguments used on the other side of the House appear to me to rest in principle and in the main upon one of two suppositions. One of them, which I will not now discuss, is the profound incompetency of the Irish people; but there is another, and it is this. It is, I believe, the conscientious conviction of hon. gentlemen opposite that when two or more countries, associated but not incorporated together, are in disturbed relations with each other, the remedy is to create an absolute legislative incorporation. On the other hand, they believe that the dissolution of such an incorporation is clearly the mode to bring about the dissolution of the political relations of those countries. I do not deny that there may be cases in which legislative incorporation may have been the means of constituting a great country, as in the case of France. But we believe, as proved by history, that where there are those disturbed relations between countries associated but not incorporated, the true principle is to make ample provision for local independence subject to Imperial unity. These are propositions of the greatest interest and importance.

Our policy leads to union, yours to separation.

Gentlemen speak of tightening the ties between England and Ireland, as if tightening the tie were always the means to be adopted. Tightening the tie is frequently the means of making it burst, whilst relaxing the tie is very frequently

Local independence never followed by severance.

House of Commons, June 7.

the way to provide for its durability, and to enable it to stand a stronger strain; so that it is true, as was said by the hon. member for Newcastle, that the separation of Legislatures is often the union of countries, and the union of Legislatures is often the severance of countries. Can you give me a single instance from all your historical inquiries where the acknowledgment of local independence has been followed by the severance of countries? (Cheers, and a voice, "Turkey, Servia.")

Exceptions to this rule.

I was just going to refer to those countries, and to make this admission, that what I have said does not apply where a third Power has intervened, and has given liberty in defiance of the Sovereign power to the subject State. But do you propose to wait until some third Power shall intervene in the case of Ireland as it intervened in the case of America? (An Hon. Member: "We are not afraid," and cries of "Order.") I never asked the hon. gentleman whether he was afraid. It does not matter much whether he is afraid or not, but I would inculcate in him that early and provident fear which, in the language of Mr. Burke, is the mother of safety. I admit that where some third Power interferes, as France interfered in the case of America, you can expect nothing to result but severance with hostile feeling on both sides. But I am not speaking of such cases. That is not the case before us. I ask you to give me a single instance where, apart from the intervention of a third Power, the independence of the Legislatures was followed by the severance of the nations?

Instances of opposite policy.

I can give several instances where total severance of countries has been the consequence of an attempt to tighten the bond—in the case of England and America, in the case of Belgium and Holland. The attempt to make Belgians conform to the ways and ideas and institutions of Holland led to the severance of the two countries. In the case of Denmark and the Duchies, they long attempted to do what, perhaps, gentlemen would wish much to do in Ireland—namely, to force Danish institutions and ideas on the Duchies.

Those long attempts ended, as we all know, together with the insufficient acknowledgment of the ancient institutions of those Duchies, in the total loss of those Duchies to Denmark, and their incorporation in another political connection. But let us not look simply to the negative side. Where local independence has been acknowledged and legislative severance has been given, there, in a number of cases, it has been made practicable to hold countries together that otherwise could not have been held together, and the difficulties which existed either have been lessened or altogether removed. The world is full of such cases. (An HON. MEMBER: "Turkey.")

House of Commons, June 7.

An hon. gentleman imprudently interrupts me by calling out "Turkey." I am going to tell him that in Turkey, with its imperfect organization, in cases where there has not been violent interference, where the matter has not been driven to a point to provoke armed interference by a foreign Power, local autonomy has been tried and tried with the best effect.

Cases of local autonomy—Turkey.

In the Island of Crete, which twenty years ago appeared to be almost lost to Turkey, loosening the ties to Constantinople has immensely improved the relations between the Sultan and that island. (LORD R. CHURCHILL: "Chronic revolution.") Chronic revolution! What are the tests of chronic revolution? Has it paid its tribute? Has it called for the armed force of Turkey to put down revolt?

Crete.

Then I will take another case, the case of the Lebanon. That was the subject of international arrangement twenty-three or twenty-four years ago. The Lebanon was in chronic revolution, and was under the absolute sway of Constantinople. The Lebanon was placed under a system of practical local independence, and from that day to this it has never been a trouble to Turkey.

The Lebanon.

In a case more remarkable, the case of the Island of Samos, which has enjoyed for a length of time, I believe, a complete autonomy, and in which, singular as it may seem, it has never been possible to create disorder, a real attachment to the Turkish Empire, or at any rate a contentment with the

Samos.

House of Commons, June 7.

political tie, subsists and holds that country in tranquillity. So that even Turkey bears testimony to the principle of which I speak. There are numbers of other cases.

Norway and Sweden.

The case of Norway and Sweden is most remarkable, because of these two countries the stronger and more populous can hardly hope to have power to coerce the weaker—two countries completely separate, having absolutely no connection of Legislative or Executive Government, and united together recently, only sixty years ago. That union has been found practicable, and practicable only by means of granting a just autonomy and independence.

Denmark and Iceland.

Take the case of Denmark and Iceland. (Opposition laughter.) Laughter is, with hon. gentlemen opposite, a very common weapon now, and it is very difficult for me to contend with it at this period of my life. Perhaps twenty, thirty, forty years ago I could have defended myself against it with more ease. It has been said that the Parliament of Iceland has been dissolved, and that there have been difficulties. Well, there have been difficulties between the Parliament of Iceland and the Crown of Denmark. The Crown of Denmark is unhappily in difficulties with the legislative body of Denmark, but between the legislative body of Denmark and the legislative body of Iceland there have been, I believe, no difficulties. When the Under-Secretary of State for Foreign Affairs, in his admirable speech, quoted the case of Iceland, gentlemen opposite, with their usual method of rebuke, laughed, and some one, endeavouring to dignify, adorn, and decorate that laughter with an idea, called out "Distance; Iceland is so distant." Well, if it is so distant, I apprehend that that makes it a great deal more difficult for Denmark to hold her down by force, and therefore more necessary for her to choose the methods which are most likely to secure contentment and tranquillity.

Russia and Finland.

But if you object to the case of Iceland on account of distance, what do you say to the case of Finland? Is that country distant from Russia? Are you aware that the social

House of Commons, June 7.

and political difficulties, which have so often threatened the peace of Russia, and which were fatal not many years ago to the life of one of the best and worthiest of her Sovereigns, have no place in Finland? Why? Because Finland has perfect legislative autonomy, the management of her own affairs, the preservation of her own institutions. That state of things has given contentment to Finland, and might be envied by many better known and more famous parts of the world.

Austria and her States.

But the case of Austria is perhaps the most remarkable of all. I won't refer now to Austria and Hungary, further than to say that I believe my right hon. friend the member for East Edinburgh is entirely wrong, for all practical purposes, in what he said as to the mixture of Executive Governments. I may lay down this proposition without fear of contradiction. There is no mixture whatever of Executive Governments so far as local affairs are concerned. As far as joint affairs are concerned it is a different matter, but there is a perfect independence between Austria and Hungary so far as local affairs are concerned. The case there, I should state, was surrounded with difficulties infinitely transcending any before us. But it is not Austria and Hungary alone. It is not too much to say of Austria that that great Empire, with the multitude of States of which it is composed, is held together by local autonomy and nothing else, and that the man who should attempt to banish local autonomy from Austria and to gather together the representatives of her States in Vienna to deal with the local affairs of the provinces would seal the death-warrant of the Empire. Long may she flourish as having based herself upon so just and so enlightened a principle. The most striking instance in the wide circuit of her Empire is Galicia. Galicia is inhabited by Poles. Austria has one of the fragments of that unhappy and dissevered country under her charge. Well, I need not speak of Russia and Poland, while even in Prussia the relations of Prussian Poland are, at this moment, the subject of most serious difficulty. There are no difficulties between Galicia and Austria. Why?

House of Commons, June 7.

Because Austria has treated Galicia upon the principle of placing trust and confidence in her, and has invested her with full practical power over the management of her own affairs.

No instances on the other hand.

Now I do not think that I have thrown out any unfair challenges. I have asked for instances from the other side in which the granting of Home Rule has been attended with evil consequences, but none have been given, whereas I have given a multitude of instances in support of my proposition, which is that the severance which we propose to make for local purposes between the Irish legislative body and Parliament meeting in these walls is not a mode of disunion, but is a mode of closer union, and is not a mode of separation, but is a mode of preventing separation.

Canada.

Before I leave this point I must refer to the case of Canada, because it is so remarkable, and because, notwithstanding the multitude of circumstantial differences between Canada and Great Britain, yet still the resemblances in principle are so profound and so significant. My right hon. friend the member for West Birmingham said, as I understood him, the other day, that he had been investigating the case of Canada. I own I thought I knew something about it, because in the early years of my Parliamentary life I took great interest in it, and some part in the great discussions on the disposal of Canada some fifty years ago. My reading of the history of Canada sustains my original propositions. My right hon. friend announced to the House that he had found that the Legislative Councils in Canada had been established for the purpose of protecting the minority. Where did he find that? I read not long ago the very lengthened and detailed debates in Parliament on the subject of the establishment of those Legislative Councils, and from the beginning to the end of these debates, while the character of the Legislative Councils was abundantly discussed, there is not a word about their being appointed for the protection of minorities.

But I will not rest the case of Canada upon that ground. What does the case of Canada show? It shows two things:

first, that between 1830 and 1840 there were most formidable differences between Great Britain and Canada, and that those differences were completely cured and healed by the establishment of a responsible Government with a free Executive; that is to say, that those differences were absolutely cured by the very remedy which we now propose to apply in the case of Ireland. But, as I have shown, supremacy was not relinquished; it remained, as was stated in the citation from Lord Russell. But after that, what happened? The two provinces changed most fundamentally in their relative importance, and the stereotyped arrangements of the Union of 1840 were found to be totally inadequate to deal with the altered conditions of the provinces among themselves. Recollect that these provinces were united provinces with one Legislature. Discord arose between them. What was the mode adopted of curing that discord? The mode which we now propose of the severance of the Legislatures; the establishment of an extended union, under which at this moment, with the multiplied Legislatures of those provinces, a substantial and perfect political harmony exists. I can understand, then, the disinclination which hon. gentlemen opposite have to go into history as to these cases; but it will be unfolded more and more as these debates proceed, if the controversy be prolonged; it will more and more appear how strong is the foundation upon which we stand now, and upon which Mr. Grattan stood over eighty-six years ago, when he contended that a union of the Legislatures was the way to a moral and a real separation between the two countries.

House of Commons, June 7.

Reasons for dealing with the Question.

It has been asked in this debate, Why have we put aside all the other business of Parliament, and why have we thrown the country into all this agitation, for the sake of the Irish question? (Hear, hear.) That cheer is the echo that I wanted. Well, sir, the first reason is this; because in Ireland the primary purposes of government are not attained. What said the hon. member for Newcastle (Mr. Cowen) in his eloquent speech? That in a considerable part of Ireland

(1) Social order.

House of Commons, June 7.

distress was chronic, disaffection was perpetual, and insurrection was smouldering. What is implied by those who speak of the dreadful murder that lately took place in Kerry? And I must quote the Belfast outrage along with it, not as being precisely of the same character, but as a significant proof of the weakness of the tie which binds the people to the law. Sir, it is that you have not got that respect for the law, that sympathy with the law on the part of the people without which real civilization cannot exist. That is our first reason.

(2) *Reparation for the past.*

I will not go back at this time on the dreadful story of the Union; but that too must be unfolded in all its hideous features if this controversy is to be prolonged—that Union of which I ought to say that, without qualifying in the least any epithet I have used, I do not believe that that Union can or ought to be repealed, for it has made marks upon history that cannot be effaced. But I go on to another pious belief which prevails on the other side of the House, or which is often professed in controversies on the Irish question. It is supposed that all the abuses of English power in Ireland relate to a remote period of history, and that from the year 1800 onwards from the time of the Union there has been a period of steady redress of grievances.

Sir, I am sorry to say that there has been nothing of the kind. There has been a period when grievances have been redressed under compulsion, as in 1829 when Catholic emancipation was granted to avoid civil war. There have been grievances mixed up with the most terrible evidence of the general failure of Government, as was exhibited by the Devon Commission in the year 1843. On a former night I made a quotation from the report which spoke of the labourer. Now I have a corresponding quotation which is more important, and which speaks of the cottier. What was the proportion of the population which more than forty years after the Union was described by the Devon Report as being in a condition worse and more disgraceful than any population in

Europe? Mr. O'Connell has estimated it in this House as 5,000,000 out of 7,000,000, and Sir James Graham, in debate with him, declined to admit that it was 5,000,000, but did admit that it was three and a half millions. Well, sir, in 1815 Parliament passed an Act of Irish legislation. What was the purpose of that Act? The Act declared that, from the state of the law in Ireland, the old intertangled usages and provisions, containing effectual protection for the tenant against the landlord, could not prevail. These intertangled usages, which had replaced in an imperfect manner the tribal usages on which the tenure of land in Ireland was founded, Parliament swept away, and did everything to expose the tenant to the action of the landlord, but nothing to relieve or to deal with, by any amendment of the law, the terrible distress which was finally disclosed by the Devon Commission.

House of Commons June 7.

Again, what was the state of Ireland in regard to freedom? In the year 1820 the sheriff of Dublin and the gentry of the county and capital determined to have a county meeting to make compliments to George IV., the trial of Queen Caroline being just over. They held their county meeting; the people went to the county meeting, and a counter-address was moved, warm in professions of loyalty, but setting out the grievances of the country, and condemning the trial and proceedings against the Queen. The sheriff refused to hear it. He put his own motion, but refused to put the other motion; he left the meeting, which continued the debate, and he sent in the military to the meeting, which was broken up by force. That was the state of Ireland as to freedom of petition and remonstrance twenty years after the Union. Do you suppose that would have been the case if Ireland had retained her own Parliament? No, sir.

Irish freedom in 1820.

Other cases I will not dwell upon at this late hour, simply on account of the lateness of the hour. From 1857, when we passed an Act which enabled the landlords of Ireland to sell improvements on their tenants' holdings over their heads,

House of Commons June 7.

down to 1880, when a most limited and carefully framed Bill, the product of Mr. Forster's benevolence, was passed by this House and rejected by an enormous majority in the House of Lords, thereby precipitating the Land Act of 1881, it is impossible to stand by the legislation of this House, as a whole, since the Union. I have sometimes heard it said, You have had all kinds of remedial legislation. The two chief items are the disestablishment of the Church and the reform of the land laws. But what did you say of these? Why, you said the change in the land laws was confiscation, and the disestablishment of the Church was sacrilege. You cannot at one and the same time condemn these measures as confiscation and sacrilege, and at the same time quote them as proofs of the justice with which you have acted to Ireland.

(3) *Ireland demands to make her own laws.*

I must further say that we have proposed this measure because Ireland wants to make her own laws. It is not enough to say that you are prepared to make good laws. You were prepared to make good laws for the Colonies. You did make good laws for the Colonies, according to the best of your light. The Colonists were totally dissatisfied with them. You accepted their claim to make their own laws. Ireland, in our opinion, has a claim not less urgent.

Alternatives.

Now, sir, what is before us? What is before us in the event of the rejection of this Bill? What alternatives have been proposed? Here I must for a moment comment on the fertile imagination of my right hon. friend the member for West Birmingham. He has proposed alternatives, and plenty of them.

Mr. Chamberlain's plans.

My right hon. friend says that a dissolution has no terrors for him. I do not wonder at it. I do not see how a dissolution can have any terrors for him. He has trimmed his vessel, and he has touched his rudder in such a masterly way, that in whichever direction the winds of heaven may blow they must fill his sails. Let me illustrate my meaning. I will suppose different cases. Supposing at the Election—I mean that an Election is a thing like Christmas, it is always coming—supposing that at an Election public opinion should be very strong in favour of the Bill. My right hon. friend would then be perfectly prepared to meet that public opinion, and tell it "I declared strongly that I adopted the principle of the Bill." On the other hand, if public opinion was very adverse to the Bill, my right hon. friend again is in complete armour, because he says, "Yes, I voted against the Bill." Supposing, again, public opinion is in favour of a very large plan for Ireland. My right hon. friend is perfectly provided for that case also. The Government plan was not large enough for him, and he proposed in his speech on the introduction of the Bill that we should have a measure on the basis of federation which goes beyond this Bill. Lastly—and now I have very nearly boxed the compass—supposing that public opinion should take quite a different turn, and, instead of wanting very large measures for Ireland, should demand very small measures for Ireland, still the resources of my right hon. friend are not exhausted, because then he is able to point out that the last of his plans was four provincial councils controlled from London. Under other circumstances I should perhaps have been tempted to ask the secret of my right hon. friend's recipe; as it is, I am afraid I am too old to learn it. I do not wonder that dissolution has no terrors for him, because he is prepared in such a way and with such a series of expedients to meet all the possible contingencies of the case. Well, sir, when I come to look at these practical alternatives and provisions, I find that they are visibly creations of the vivid imagination, born of the hour and perishing with the hour, totally and absolutely unavailable for the solution of a great and difficult problem, the weight of which, and the urgency of which, my right hon. friend himself in other days has seemed to feel.

House of Commons, June 7.

Lord Salisbury's plan.

But I should not say now that our plan has possession of the field without a rival. Lord Salisbury has given us a rival plan. My first remark is that Lord Salisbury's policy has not been disavowed. It is therefore adopted. What is

House of Commons, June 7.

it? (A laugh.) Another laugh! It has not been disavowed. What is it? Great complaints are made because it has been called a policy of coercion, and Lord Salisbury is stated to have explained in another place that he is not favourable to coercion, but only to legislative provisions for preventing interference by one man with the liberty of another, and for ensuring the regular execution of the law. And that you say is not coercion. Was that your view six months ago? What did the Liberal Government propose when they went out of office? They proposed to enact clauses against the . . . (Cries of "No, no" and "They never made any proposal.") Perhaps not, but it was publicly stated—it was stated by me in a letter to the right hon. gentleman. (SIR M. HICKS-BEACH: "In October.") Certainly, but it was stated in order to correct a rather gross error of the right hon. gentleman. It was stated as what we had intended when we were going out of office; unless I am greatly mistaken, it was publicly stated in this House long before. However, it is not very important. What were the proposals that we were about to make, or that we were supposed to be about to make? Well, a proposal about boycotting, to prevent one man interfering with the liberty of another; and a proposal about a change of venue to ensure the execution of the ordinary law. And how were these proposals viewed? Did not the Tories go to the elections putting upon their placards "Vote for the Tories and no Coercion"? ("No, no" from Sir W. Barttelot.) I do not say that every Tory did it. The hon. and gallant baronet cries "No." No doubt he did not do it; but he had no Irish voters. (COL. BARTTELOT: "If I had I would not have done it.") Then it means this, that these proposals which we were about to make, were defined as coercion by the Tories at the election; and Lord Salisbury now denies them to be coercion; and it is resented with the loudest manifestations of displeasure when any one on this side of the House states that Lord Salisbury has recommended twenty years of coercion.

Lord Salisbury recommended, as he says himself, twenty years of those measures which last year were denounced by the Tories.

House of Commons, June 7.

His advocacy of coercion.

But what did Lord Salisbury call them himself? What were his own words? His words were: "My alternative policy is that Parliament should enable the Government of England to govern Ireland." What is the meaning of those words? Their meaning, in the first instance, is this—the Government does not want the aid of Parliament to exercise their Executive power; it wants the aid of Parliament for fresh legislation. The demand that the Parliament should enable the Government of England to govern Ireland is a demand for fresh legislative power. This fresh legislative power how are they to use? "Apply that recipe honestly, consistently, and resolutely for twenty years, and at the end of that time you will find Ireland will be fit to accept any gift in the way of local government or repeal of coercion laws that you may wish to give." And yet objections and complaints of misrepresentation teem from that side of the House when any one on this side says that Lord Salisbury recommended coercion, when he himself applies that same term in his own words.

Why the Government introduced this measure at this time.

A question was put to me by my hon. friend the member for Bermondsey (Mr. Rogers) in the course of his most instructive speech. My hon. friend had a serious misgiving as to the point of time. Were we right in introducing this measure now? He did not object to the principle; he intimated a doubt as to the moment. I may ask my hon. friend to consider what would have happened had we hesitated as to the duty before us, had we used the constant efforts that would have been necessary to keep the late Government in office and allowed them to persevere in their intentions. On the 26th of January they proposed what we termed a measure of coercion, and I think we were justified in so terming it, because anything attempting to put down a political association can hardly have another name.

House of Commons, June 7.

Can it be denied that that legislation must have been accompanied by legislation against the Press, legislation against public meetings, and other legislation without which it would have been totally ineffective? Would it have been better, if a great controversy cannot be avoided—and I am sensible of the evil of this great controversy—I say it is better that parties should be matched in conflict upon a question of giving a great boon to Ireland, rather than (as we should have been if the policy of January 26th had proceeded) that we should have been matched and brought into conflict, and the whole country torn with dispute and discussion, upon the policy of a great measure of coercion.

The voice of Ireland now first clearly expressed.

That is my first reason. My second reason is this. Let my hon. friend recollect that this is the earliest moment in our Parliamentary history when we have the voice of Ireland authentically expressed in our hearing. Majorities of Home Rulers there may have been upon other occasions; a practical majority of Irish members never has been brought together for such a purpose. Now first we can understand her; now first we are able to deal with her; we are able to learn authentically what she wants and wishes, what she offers and will do; and as we ourselves enter into the strongest moral and honourable obligations by the steps we take in this House, so we have before us practically an Ireland under the representative system able to give us equally authentic information, able morally to convey to us an assurance the breach and rupture of which would cover Ireland with disgrace. There is another reason, but not a very important one. It is this. I feel that any attempt to palter with the demands of Ireland so conveyed in forms known to the Constitution, and any rejection of the conciliatory policy, might have an effect that none of us could wish in strengthening that party of disorder which is behind the back of the Irish representatives, which skulks in America, which skulks in Ireland, which I trust is losing ground and is losing force, and will lose ground and will lose force in proportion as our

House of Commons, June 7.

policy is carried out, and which I cannot altogether dismiss from consideration when I take into view the consequences that might follow upon its rejection.

A question only of time and circumstance.

What is the case of Ireland at this moment? Have gentlemen considered that they are coming into conflict with a nation? Can anything stop a nation's demand except its being proved to be immoderate and unsafe? But here are multitudes and I believe millions upon millions out of doors who feel this demand to be neither immoderate nor unsafe. In our opinion, there is but one question before us about this demand. It is as to the time and circumstance of granting it. There is no question in our minds that it will be granted. We wish it to be granted in the mode prescribed by Mr. Burke. Mr. Burke said in his first speech at Bristol:—

"I was true to my old-standing invariable principle that all things which came from Great Britain should issue as a gift of her bounty and beneficence rather than as claims recovered against a struggling litigant; or at least that if your beneficence obtained no credit in your concessions, yet that they should appear the salutary provisions of your wisdom and foresight; not as things wrung from you with your blood by the cruel gripe of a rigid necessity."

The difference between giving with freedom and dignity on the one side, with acknowledgment and gratitude on the other, and giving under compulsion, giving with disgrace, giving with resentment dogging you at every step of your path—this difference is, in our eyes, fundamental, and this is the main reason, not only why we have acted, but why we have acted now.

A golden moment in our history.

This, if I understand it, is one of the golden moments of our history; one of those opportunities which may come and may go, but which rarely return, or, if they return, return at long intervals, and under circumstances which no man can forecast. There have been such golden moments even in the tragic history of Ireland, as her poet says:—

"One time the harp of Innisfail
Was tuned to notes of gladness."

House of Commons, June 7.

And then he goes on to say—

> "But yet did oftener tell a tale
> Of more prevailing sadness."

But there was such a golden moment; it was in 1795; it was on the mission of Lord Fitzwilliam. At that moment it is historically clear that the Parliament of Grattan was on the point of solving the Irish problem. The two great knots of that problem were, in the first place, Roman Catholic emancipation, and, in the second place, the reform of Parliament. The cup was at her lips, and she was ready to drink it, when the hand of England rudely and ruthlessly dashed it to the ground in obedience to the wild and dangerous intimations of an Irish faction.

> "*Ex illo fluere ac retro sublapsa referri*
> *Spes Danaûm.*"

There has been no great day of hope for Ireland, no day when you might hope completely and definitely to end the controversy till now—more than ninety years. The long periodic time has at last run out, and the star has again mounted into the heavens. What Ireland was doing for herself in 1795 we at length have done. The Roman Catholics have been emancipated; emancipated after a woeful disregard of solemn promises through twenty-nine years, emancipated slowly, sullenly, not from goodwill, but from abject terror, with all the fruits and consequences which will always follow that method of legislation. The second problem has been also solved, and the representation of Ireland has been thoroughly reformed, and I am thankful to say that the franchise was given to Ireland on the readjustment of last year with a free heart, with an open hand; and the gift of that franchise was the last act required to make the success of Ireland in her final effort absolutely sure.

Ireland must be heard.

We have given Ireland a voice; we must all listen for a moment to what she says. We must all listen: both sides, both parties, I mean, divided as they are on this question, divided, I am afraid, by an almost immeasurable gap. We do

House of Commons, June 7.

not undervalue or despise the forces opposed to us. I have described them as the forces of class and its dependants, and that, as a general description, as a slight and rude outline of a description, is, I believe, perfectly true. I do not deny that many are against us whom we should have expected to be for us. I do not deny that some whom we see against us have caused us by their conscientious action the bitterest disappointment.

The people's heart and the promise of the future.

You have power, you have wealth, you have rank, you have station, you have organization. What have we? We think that we have the people's heart; we believe and we know we have the promise of the harvest of the future. As to the people's heart, you may dispute it, and dispute it with perfect sincerity. Let that matter make its own proof. As to the harvest of the future, I doubt if you have so much confidence, and I believe that there is in the breast of many a man who means to vote against us to-night a profound misgiving, approaching even to a deep conviction, that the end will be as we foresee and not as you do, that the ebbing tide is with you and the flowing tide is with us.

The prayer of Ireland.

Ireland stands at your bar expectant, hopeful, almost suppliant. Her words are the words of truth and soberness. She asks a blessed oblivion of the past, and in that oblivion our interest is deeper than even hers. My right hon. friend the member for East Edinburgh asks us to-night to abide by the traditions of which we are the heirs. What traditions? By the Irish tradition? Go into the length and breadth of the world, ransack the literature of all countries, find, if you can, a single voice, a single book, find, I would almost say, as much as a single newspaper article, unless the product of the day, in which the conduct of England towards Ireland is anywhere treated except with profound and bitter condemnation. Are these the traditions by which we are exhorted to stand? No, they are a sad exception to the glory of our country. They are a broad and black blot upon the pages of its history, and what we want to do

House of Commons, June 7.

is to stand by the traditions of which we are the heirs in all matters except our relations with Ireland, and to make our relations with Ireland to conform to the other traditions of our country. So we treat our traditions, so we hail the demand of Ireland for what I call a blessed oblivion of the past. She asks also a boon for the future; and that boon for the future, unless we are much mistaken, will be a boon to us in respect of honour, no less than a boon to her in respect of happiness, prosperity, and peace. Such, sir, is her prayer. Think, I beseech you; think well, think wisely, think, not for the moment, but for the years that are to come, before you reject this Bill.

ADDRESSES

TO THE

ELECTORS OF MIDLOTHIAN

IN MAY AND JUNE 1886.

VI.

ADDRESS TO THE ELECTORS OF MIDLOTHIAN *IN MAY* 1886.

ON May 1, 1886, Mr. GLADSTONE issued the following address to his constituents, the electors of Midlothian, on the question of Home Rule for Ireland:—

GENTLEMEN,—I could have wished to take a part in the active operations of the Easter recess, particularly as they have been pushed within the limits of your county. You have given me from your local meetings good reason to believe that I should have found the echoes of those walls, within which I have so often had the honour to address you, much the same as they have been on former occasions. But age grows upon me, and I am obliged to reserve my limited power of voice for any effort which may be required in the House of Commons. I therefore use my pen to revert to the subject which I opened in my address to you of last September. I then said that any concession of local self-government to Ireland which was duly adjusted to the paramount conditions of Imperial unity would, in my view, be a source not of danger but of increased security and strength to the Empire. Since that time a Bill has been introduced by the existing Cabinet on some important provisions of which, as was to be expected, differences of opinion prevail among its friends, but which could not have met, as I conceive that it has met, with such wide and warm

Address of May 1.

approval in the country unless it had been felt, first, that the principle of local autonomy, or Home Rule for Ireland, is reasonable; and, secondly, that the demands of Imperial unity have at least been carefully studied in the provisions of the Bill. I have never known an occasion when a Parliamentary event so rung throughout the world as the introduction of this Bill under the auspices of a British Government. In extending our view beyond our shores we sometimes obtain valuable aid towards the conduct of our affairs from the opinions formed in other countries upon great internal questions of our own, which they often view with a frank goodwill lifted entirely above the level of any sectional or local prejudice. Naturally we look with the greatest interest to the sentiments of that vast British and Irish public which has already passed beyond one hundred millions, and which spreads with a rapidity unabated from year to year over some of the widest spaces of the globe. From public meetings and from the highest authorities in the Colonies and America, from capitals such as Washington, Boston, and Quebec, and from remote districts lying beyond the reach of all ordinary political excitement, I receive conclusive assurances that the kindred people regard with warm and fraternal sympathy our present effort to settle on an adequate scale and once for all the long vexed and troubled relations between Great Britain and Ireland, which exhibits to us the one and only conspicuous failure of the political genius of our race to confront and master difficulty, and to obtain in a remarkable degree the main ends of civilized life. We must not be discouraged if at home, and particularly in the upper ranks of society, we hear a variety of discordant notes—notes alike discordant from our policy and from one another. Gentlemen, you have before you a Cabinet determined in its purpose, and an intelligible plan. I own I see very little else in the political arena that is determined or that is intelligible.

I will now proceed to speak to you on the state of things

in Parliament and beyond its walls, and also upon the nature and import of the next great step to be taken in the progress of the measure. I speak at present of the Irish Government Bill, and I leave the Land Purchase Bill to stand on the declarations we have already made, adding only an expression of the regret with which I find that, while the sands are running in the hour-glass, the Irish landlords have as yet given no indication of a desire to accept a proposal framed in a spirit of the utmost allowable regard to their apprehensions and their interests. I heartily concur with Lord Hartington — whose absolute integrity and manly courage in this controversy, like Mr. Bright, I find it a pleasure to acknowledge—in holding that, on a question of supreme rank like that of the Irish policy, party, if need be, must give way, and sound argument, at all hazards and all costs, must rule. I do not under-estimate the grave importance of the differences of opinion on this great subject which have been exhibited within the circle of the Liberal party. Some are inclined to rule the whole question against us by authority, and to say: "Surely such a number of persons—all of them declared, many of them able and consistent, some of them even extreme, Liberals—would not have parted from their friends except in obedience to the imperative dictates of truth and reason?" I will say nothing of the motives which have determined us to confront the risk of such a parting. But I earnestly recommend on all the parts and at all the stages of this controversy a reference to the lessons which history supplies. It is not the first time in the history of Liberalism when sections, under chiefs of high distinction, character, and ability, have dissented from the general view of the party, to the great joy, and no doubt at the moment to the great advantage of the Tories. In 1793 a great, indeed an illustrious, secession of this kind brought on the tremendous war finally closed in 1815. It left the party thinned and impoverished; but the party lived while the secession died, and, what is more, we know now that the party was right and the

Address of May 1.

secession wrong. We have a second instance in 1835. Lord Derby and Sir James Graham seceded from their party to maintain the Irish Church Establishment. The judgment of the country has again shown that in principle the party were right and the secession wrong. In comparing the present secession with the examples I have cited (and I am aware of no examples the other way), it is impossible not to be struck by one great, nay, vital, difference. Each of the two former secessions was agreed within itself upon an active and substantial policy. It was war in the first case; it was the sacredness of Church property and of the principles of a Church Establishment in the second. It is not so with the present secession. Some are for coercion without limit, others for the moderated doses of it which we have tried without effect (but with a tendency to increase) during eighty years; a few are against it altogether. On the other side, some are for giving no local government, some will give it to counties, some to provinces, some would give an administrative centre to Ireland but not a legislative—some a legislative organ but not an executive; some go beyond the Government and actually recommend federation; some agree with themselves no more than with one another, and their proposals alter in every speech they make—a proof not of weakness in the men, but of hopelessness in their cause. We, gentlemen, have at least the advantage as to aim and principle of speaking with one voice. The secession, however respectable and estimable in other ways, is as to positive policy for Ireland a perfect Babel. It is admitted on all hands that social order is the first of all political aims, and that its bases are dangerously sapped in Ireland. To meet this state of things the secessionists offer us either a hundred conflicting remedies or no remedy at all. I speak of what is notorious, and I content myself with general statement now; the proof in detail is for another place. These remarks, gentlemen, are not less applicable to Tory than to Liberal opponents. In the speeches of both alike I find one remark-

Address of May 1.

able omission. Whether they suggest, or whether they only criticize, one thing they almost uniformly fail to do—they fail to express confidence in the permanent success of their opposition. To live from hand to mouth appears to be the height of their expectation. They seem to suspect what we well know—that the strife which they are stirring can only end one way, can only end in the concession of self-government to Ireland. If this be so, then the real question before us is, not the triumph of Irish autonomy, but the length and the character of the struggle by which it is to be preceded. We say, let it be short; they seek to make it long. We say, let us give freely; they say, by their acts if not in words, let us only give when we can no longer withhold. We say, let us give now, when the position of our country in the affairs of the world is free and strong; they seem to prefer waiting for some period of national difficulty that we may yield to Irish demand in terror, as we did to the fear of foreign war in 1778, to the demands of the volunteers in 1782, to the growing terrors of the conflict with France in 1793, to the alternative of civil war in 1829. We say, let us act now, when moderation of thought and language rules in Irish counsels, and when by willing concurrence on all sides every arrangement for the reservation of the Imperial prerogative can be made complete and absolute; they would postpone the settlement until a day when demands may be larger and means of resistance less; we say, deal with this matter as a matter between brothers—a matter of justice and of reason; they renew the tale—alas! too often told—which has for its prologue denial with exasperation and resentment, and for its epilogue surrender without conditions and without thanks. Now, however, a new terror is brought upon the stage, the terror of Home Rule for Scotland, and some add for Wales; but this suggestion, gentlemen, brings no alarm to me. Give us a little time only, that we may look at each question in its order and on its merits. I am not sorry they are named, for all serious

Address of May 1.

naming of them, all naming of them except in caricature, will serve to help our movement on behalf of Ireland. I can draw no vital distinction of right between the case of Ireland and other cases. There are many distinctions of circumstance. For many years I have hoped that it might be found practicable to apply decentralizing processes, even perhaps to portions of England, with a careful consideration of the different conditions of each case, which will naturally require for it differences of treatment. Subject to primary Imperial obligations, I believe that a standard measure of good government for Scotland and for Wales will be eventually determined by the public opinion of Scotland and of Wales, and this without the painful and disparaging circumstances of controversy with which we are now threatened in the case of Ireland, whose woeful history for centuries emboldens some of us to treat her as if she had but a limited share in the great inheritance of human right, and none at all in the ordinary privilege or immunity from gross and wholesale insult —emboldens, I say, some of us, but only some of us, and not, I rejoice to think, the nations of Scotland or of England.

Watching from day to day the movement of the currents of opinion during the present conflict, more and more I find it vital to observe the point at which the dividing lines are drawn. On the side adverse to the Government are found, as I sorrowfully admit, in profuse abundance, station, title, wealth, social influence, the professions, or the large majority of them—in a word, the spirit and power of Class. These are the main body of the opposing host. Nor is this all. As knights of old had squires, so in the great army of Class each enrolled soldier has, as a rule, dependants. The adverse host, then, consists of Class and the dependants of Class. But this formidable army is in the bulk of its constituent parts the same, though now enriched at our cost with a valuable contingent of recruits, that has fought in every one of the great political battles of the last sixty years and has been defeated. We have had great controversies before this

Address of May 1.

great controversy—on Free Trade, free navigation, public education, religious equality in civil matters, extension of the suffrage to its present basis. On these and on many other great issues the classes have fought uniformly on the wrong side, and have uniformly been beaten by a power more difficult to marshal, but resistless when marshalled—by the upright sense of the nation. Lord Hartington has reminded us—and I cordially agree with him—that this question, which may be turned over in a thousand ways, and placed in a thousand partial lights, can only be settled and set at rest by the nation. From the first I have stated, and I think I may speak for the Government at large, that here is my main and capital reliance. I rely on my colleagues; I rely on an upright and enlightened House of Commons; I rely on the effect of free discussion; but the heart and root, the beginning and ending of my trust, is in the wise and generous justice of the nation.

I have still to say a few words on the issue which is more immediately before us at this moment. I know, gentlemen, from a happy experience during the last seven years, that you, when you have a great aim before you, are not apt to be drawn away from it by the artful raising of side issues. We have a great aim before us now. It is to restore your Parliament to efficiency by dividing and by removing obstacles to its work; to treat the Irish question with a due regard to its specialities, but with the same thoroughness of method by which we have solved Colonial problems that fifty years back were hardly, if at all, less formidable; to give heed to the voice of a people speaking in tones of moderation by the mouth of a vast majority of those whom we ourselves have made its constitutional representatives, and thus to strengthen and consolidate the Empire on the basis of mutual benefit and hearty loyalty. Such is the end. For the means we take the establishment in Dublin of a Legislative body, empowered to make laws for Irish, as contradistinguished from Imperial, affairs. It is with this that we are now busied, and

Address of May 1.

not with details and particulars. Their time will come. They are now employed with art before their season to bewilder unwary souls. So it has been before. You remember well how the campaign against the recent extension of the suffrage was carried on by setting in the front of the battle the pretended difficulties and dangers of the redistribution of seats. We are not now debating the amount of Irish contributions to the Empire, or the composition of the Legislative body, or the maintenance of a representative connection with Westminster. On these questions and many more, we may or may not be at odds; but what we are at this moment debating is the still larger, and far larger question which includes, and, I think, absorbs them all—the question whether you will or will not have regard to the prayer of Ireland for the management by herself of the affairs specifically and exclusively her own. This and no other is the matter which the House of Commons has at once to decide. If on this question it speaks with a clear and intelligible voice, I feel the strongest assurance that the others, difficult as some of them are, will nevertheless, with the aid of full discussion—with the aid of a wise and conciliatory spirit—be found capable of a rational and tolerable settlement.

It is little, gentlemen, which I can do in this most grave matter; it is no more than to devote with cheerfulness to the cause the small available residue of my active life. But let me, in these closing words, extend my view beyond my own honoured constituency, and in one sentence say that you, my countrymen of Scotland and of England, can do much. With you essentially, and not with any person, or class, or section among you, it rests to deliver the great Ay or No, on your choice between which depend all the best hopes of Ireland, and much that touches, in its honour and high interest, Great Britain and all the mighty Empire of our Queen.—I remain, Electors of Midlothian, Your dutiful and grateful servant,

W. E. GLADSTONE.

HAWARDEN, 1st *May* 1886.

VII.

ADDRESS TO THE ELECTORS OF MIDLOTHIAN

IN JUNE 1886.

ON June 12, 1886, Mr. GLADSTONE issued the following address to the electors of Midlothian, in view of the dissolution of the Parliament elected in the end of 1885, the Government having been defeated on the motion for the second reading of the Government of Ireland Bill:—

GENTLEMEN,—In consequence of the defeat of the Bill for the Better Government of Ireland, the Ministers have advised, and Her Majesty has been pleased to sanction, a dissolution of Parliament, for the decision, by the nation, of the gravest, and likewise the simplest, issue which has been submitted to it for half a century.

It is only a sense of the gravity of this issue which induces me, at a period of life when nature cries aloud for repose, to seek, after sitting in thirteen Parliaments, a seat in a fourteenth, and with this view to solicit for the fifth time the honour of your confidence.

At the last election I endeavoured, in my address and speeches, to impress upon you that a great crisis had arrived in the affairs of Ireland.

Weak as the late Government was for ordinary purposes, it had great advantages for dealing with this crisis. A comprehensive measure, proceeding from them, would have received warm and extensive support from within the Liberal party. It would probably have closed the Irish controversy within the present session, and have left the Parliament of 1885 free to prosecute the now stagnant work of ordinary legislation,

Address of June 12.

with the multitude of questions that it includes. My earnest hope was to support the late Cabinet in such a course of policy.

But, on the 26th of last January, the opposite policy of coercion was declared to have been the choice of the Government—Lord Carnarvon alone refusing to share in it.

The Irish question was thus placed in the foreground, to the exclusion of every other. The hour, as all felt, was come, and the only point remaining to determine was the manner in which it should be dealt with.

Coercion or Self-government for Ireland the issue.

In my judgment, the proposal of coercion was not justified by the facts, and was doomed to a certain and disgraceful failure. Some method of governing Ireland other than coercion ought, as I thought, to be sought for, and might be found.

I therefore viewed without regret the fall of the late Cabinet; and, when summoned by Her Majesty to form a new one, I undertook it on the basis of an anti-coercion policy, with the fullest explanation to those whose aid I sought as colleagues, that I proposed to examine whether it might not be possible to grant to Ireland a domestic Legislature, under conditions such as to maintain the honour, and consolidate the unity, of the Empire.

A Cabinet was formed, and the work was at once put in hand.

You will now, gentlemen, clearly understand how and why it is that the affairs of Ireland have, not for the first time, thrust aside every other subject, and adjourned our hopes of useful and progressive legislation. As a question of the first necessities of social order, it forced itself into the van. The late Government, right in giving it that place, were, as we thought, wrong in their manner of treating it. It was our absolute duty, on taking the government, if we did not adopt their method, to propose another. Thus, gentlemen, it is that this great and simple issue has come upon you, and demands your decision: will you govern Ireland by coercion, or will you let her manage her own affairs?

Address of June 12.

To debate, in this address, this or that detail of the lately defeated Bills, would be only to disguise this issue, and would be as futile as to discuss the halting, stumbling, ever-shifting, ever-vanishing projects of the intermediate class which have proceeded from seceding Liberals.

Two clear, positive, intelligible plans are before the world. There is the plan of the Government; and there is the plan of Lord Salisbury. Our plan is, that Ireland should, under well-considered conditions, transact her own affairs. His plan is, to ask Parliament for new repressive laws, and to enforce them resolutely for twenty years: at the end of which time he assures us that Ireland will be fit to accept any gifts, in the way of local government or the repeal of coercion laws, that you may wish to give her.

I leave this daring project to speak for itself in its unadorned simplicity; and I turn to the proposed policy of the Government.

Our opponents, gentlemen, whether Tories or seceders, have assumed the name of Unionists. I deny their title to it. In intention, indeed, we are all Unionists alike, but the Union, which they refuse to modify, is in its present shape a paper Union, obtained by force and fraud, and never sanctioned or accepted by the Irish nation. They are not Unionists, but paper-Unionists. True union is to be tested by the sentiments of the human beings united. Tried by this criterion, we have less union between Great Britain and Ireland now than we had under the settlement of 1782.

Enfranchised Ireland, gentlemen, asks, through her lawful representatives, for a revival of her domestic Legislature: not on the face of it an innovating, but a restorative, proposal.

She urges, with truth, that the centralization of the Parliaments has been the division of the peoples. But she recognizes the fact that the Union, lawlessly as it was obtained, cannot and ought not to be repealed. She is content to receive her Legislature in a form divested of prerogatives which might have impaired Imperial interests, and better

Address of June 12.

adapted than the settlement of 1782 to secure to her the regular control of her own affairs.

She has not repelled, but has welcomed, stipulations for the protection of the minority. To such provisions we have given, and shall give, careful heed. But I trust that Scotland will condemn the attempt so singularly made to import into this controversy the venomous element of religious bigotry. Let us take warning from the deplorable riots at Belfast and some other places in the North.

Among the benefits, gentlemen, which I anticipate from your acceptance of our policy are these:—

The consolidation of the unity of the Empire, and a great addition to its strength;

The stoppage of a heavy, constant, and demoralizing waste of the public treasure;

The abatement and gradual extinction of ignoble feuds in Ireland, and that development of her resources which experience shows to be the natural consequence of free and orderly government;

The redemption of the honour of Great Britain from a stigma fastened upon her, almost from time immemorial, in respect to Ireland, by the judgment of the whole civilized world;

And lastly, the restoration of Parliament to its dignity and efficiency, and the regular progress of the business of the country.

While, gentlemen, the first question now put to you is, How shall Ireland be governed? there is another question behind it, and involved in it, How are England and Scotland to be governed? You know how, for the last six years especially, the affairs of England and Scotland have been impeded, and your Imperial Parliament discredited and disabled. All this happened while Nationalists were but a small minority of Irish members, without support from so much as a handful of members not Irish. Now they approach ninety, and are entitled to say, "We speak the voice of the Irish nation." It is impossible to deal with this subject by half measures. They are strong in their numbers, strong in the British support which has brought 313 members to vote for their country, and strongest of all in the sense of being right.

Address of June 12.

But, gentlemen, we have done our part. The rest remains with you, the electors of the country. May you be enabled to see through and to cast away all delusions, to refuse the evil and to choose the good.

I have the honour to be,

GENTLEMEN,

Your most faithful and grateful servant,

W. E. GLADSTONE.

10 DOWNING STREET,
June 12, 1886.

SPEECHES

DELIVERED DURING THE

PARLIAMENTARY ELECTION

OF 1886.

VIII.

FIRST MIDLOTHIAN SPEECH.

FRIDAY, JUNE 18, 1886.

DELIVERED to an audience of over 2200 Midlothian Electors in the Music Hall, Edinburgh.

ON Mr. Gladstone entering the Hall, the whole audience rose and accorded him a most enthusiastic welcome. The platform was reserved for members of the Midlothian Executive, and besides Mr. and Mrs. Gladstone, and Mr. W. H. Gladstone, there were present the Countess of Aberdeen; Earl of Elgin; Hon. R. Preston Bruce, M.P.; Hon. Walter James, M.P.; Right Hon. H. C. E. Childers, M.P.; Sir Charles Tennant, Bart., M.P.; Sir George Campbell, M.P.; Mr. C. S. Parker, M.P.; Mr. P. M'Lagan, M.P.; Mr. P. W. Campbell, W.S., Mr. Gladstone's election agent; Mr. Holmes Ivory, W.S., and others.

Sheriff BRAND moved that Mr. John Cowan of Beeslack take the chair, and after a few introductory remarks by that gentleman, Mr. GLADSTONE said—

Mr. Cowan and Electors of Midlothian,— *Introduction.*

It was said after the battle of Inkermann by Mr. Sidney Herbert during the Crimean war that the battle of Inkermann was the soldiers' battle. It was not won by the tactics and ability of the generals, but by the valour and determination of the soldiers. You may anticipate that I mean to say to you that the present dissolution is the people's

Edinburgh, June 18.

dissolution, and the present election is the people's election. We have to lament, here and elsewhere, the absence of some who might perhaps have been on this platform, who might have been with us as in former battles, instead of being against us, as they were on Monday the 7th of this month. The question is, whether the determination of the country, with its strong sense of justice, and its sympathy with their fellow-subjects in Ireland, will make up for these defections. For my part, I have perceived signs, ever since this question came to the front, which inspire me with a strong conviction that the determination of the people will carry it through in spite of the defection of the chiefs. I have lived through many periods of political interest and excitement, I have seen many manifestations of fervour and enthusiasm, but never did I know interest so profound, never did I know enthusiasm so abundantly poured forth, as it has been since the great question of our relations with Ireland has come forward to be determined; and the signs of yesterday, when, departing from the great Metropolis of the South, I reached the Metropolis of the North, would have been enough to convince the most incredulous. I had heard, and I had read in London, that Scotland was doubtful or adverse upon this question. My answer was, I did not believe it. My hope was that I might have an opportunity in some degree of putting it to the proof; and I saw enough in the course of my progress yesterday to show me that the heart of Scotland never was more deeply and profoundly touched, and the will of Scotland was never more earnestly bent upon a work of policy and justice than it is upon the accomplishment of the great enterprise which we have now in hand.

The seceding Liberals.

Gentlemen, I have referred to the sad and painful subject of the absence of some among our friends, who are acting under the dictates of their own consciences, with the same claim to credit for honourable intentions that we might ask for ourselves, and that claim we have freely accorded them. Yet, notwithstanding, we cannot overlook this fact, that the vote was carried against us by a portion of the officers of our own army, and the Conservatives and the Tory party have been well content to leave the work in their hands, and in the performance of that work they have shown a portentous and superhuman zeal. These I venture to call the Liberal seceders; but I will not now discuss the particularities of their position. Unfortunately we cannot agree at all about even the terms which we are to use in this controversy. They call themselves Unionists, they call us disintegrators. But that union upon paper, which they wish to preserve without alteration—that union on paper, which it has mainly been, has destroyed the real union, the union of heart and mind; and while we feel that union upon paper ought to be respected in so far as it is innocent, and especially to be conserved in so far as it is valuable, it is the union of heart and mind which we seek, and which we are struggling to restore.

Real unity and a paper union.

I have said that this is the people's election. Let me in one point express my concurrence with my noble friend Lord Hartington. He hopes that by a great majority the electors may pronounce against the claims of Ireland. My concurrence is not upon the point of opposition to the claims of Ireland. It is upon the point of the great majority. Rely upon it, it is desirable that this great controversy should be brought speedily to a close. I will give, as opportunity offers, the reasons, the convincing reasons, which make that so highly requisite for every interest of this country; but nothing, in my opinion, can be more clear than that the position of all parties will be deplorable, that public business will be interrupted, public confidence will be shaken, social order in Ireland will not be restored, unless the people to whom the appeal is now made, and whose right to decide it is on all hands recognized, shall speak out with a clearness, with a manfulness, and with a decisiveness such as the question requires. Do not let it be said of this great nation that it is unequal to deal with it. Some have flinched from the difficulty, some have turned their backs in the day of trial,

Importance of a decisive verdict.

Edinburgh, June 18.

but let not that be the case of the nation. Let the nation speak clearly and decisively; and, rely upon it, if that voice be given, as we hope it may be given, in defence of the cause we are now advocating, then when that cause shall have been settled, and the excitement attending the contest shall have passed by, it will be just like the old questions of religious disability, of Parliamentary reform, of freedom of trade; people will wonder how it was that this opposition could have arisen. As before, they forgot that they had opposed the reform of the Corn Laws and the removal of religious disabilities, so they will forget that they ever were the opponents of the change which we are now striving to bring about.

The General Election of 1885.

It is a little curious to look back—if I may carry you back to last November—it is a little curious to look back upon the circumstance that has placed us in our present position. Strangely enough, it has happened that the Irish claims have been defeated entirely through Irish agency. What happened at the last election? You returned the Liberal party to Parliament with a majority of 85 over the Conservatives; but the Conservative party, which possessed 250 seats, owed 40 of those seats to the direct action of Mr. Parnell and his friends. I am not going to treat that as a matter of praise or blame at the present moment; I am only referring to it as a matter of fact. Suppose that 40 had been deducted from the number of our opponents in the division of the 7th June, that would have made the number 301 instead of 341; and suppose 40 had been added to our 311, that would have made us 351 instead of 311. As far as England and Scotland were concerned, but for that singular agency of the Irish party and the Irish vote, it seems absolutely beyond dispute that the action of English votes and of Scottish votes at the General Election in November would have returned us in force amply sufficient to carry the Bill through Parliament, and to have saved you the trouble of the present election. I must own that the exertions made by Scotland at the last election were great exertions. I rejoice

Edinburgh, June 18.

to look back upon them. I cannot say that I am not in some degree disappointed at the result, inasmuch as the Scottish members have yielded a larger proportional contingent to the ranks of the seceding Liberals than the English, and far larger than the Welsh members. But I look to Scotland to set all that right. She understands her own affairs, and if she is convinced, as I believe she is, and I am confident she will be convinced, that we are advocating the cause of justice and of policy, then most certainly she will know how to provide that her voice shall not be misrepresented in Parliament.

As I have come down to you for the purpose of a general election, it is natural that I should endeavour, in the manner most convenient, to go through the various topics that are connected with the issue now submitted to you. As regards the general policy, the time has been so short since I had the honour of addressing you on a number of questions of public interest, that I may well refer to the declarations of last winter as setting forth the present creed. Perhaps there are one or two points which it may be requisite to mention. One I may mention now, and I only name it in passing. There was an understanding at the last election, as I believed, that the question of the Church in Scotland was to be maintained in a description of neutrality, not binding individual liberty undoubtedly, but at the same time there was to be no great and systematic movement upon the subject. I may say I do not know how to reconcile with that understanding the introduction of the Bill of Mr. Finlay. That Bill of Mr. Finlay was an attempt essentially and fundamentally to alter the relations between the great Presbyterian bodies in Scotland; and I cannot express any regret, but on the contrary I incline to feel decided satisfaction, that that Bill did not receive the approval of the House of Commons. I only mention that, because it may be considered as an exceptional circumstance, which has a little varied the features of the session in regard to general politics since I had the honour of last addressing you. But I will venture to express also my satisfaction on

The Scotch Church question and Mr. Finlay's Bill.

Edinburgh, June 18.

The Crofter question.

another point deeply interesting to Scotland. It is gratifying to me to think that even within the short period, and amidst the great pressure of the Irish question, it has been found practicable to attempt the legislative settlement of that difficult subject relating to the crofters of the Highlands, a settlement which may not perhaps satisfy every extreme desire, but commands, I believe, the decided approval of the moderate and right-thinking mass of the people of Scotland.

The Irish question is the issue.

But I must devote my speech to Ireland. It is upon Ireland that Parliament has been dissolved; and with regard to the Irish question itself there is far more to be said than I can possibly lay before you this evening. The Irish question has a special aspect as well as a general aspect. It has a special aspect intimately concerning the feelings of Scotland, and the history of Scotland, and the circumstances of Scotland; but addressing, as I do, not you only, but the electors of the country in general—for, through the machinery of the press, such is the character now given to every local address—I think it my duty not to enter to-night, especially as I may have an opportunity two or three days hence of entering into the consideration of the specifically Scottish aspect of this subject, but to touch on its general aspect. For there is a question to be answered which it is of vital importance that the electors should have clearly and beyond all dispute before them. What is the real issue which they are called upon to decide? I know that is a matter which is much disputed, and I wish to put two questions. Is it, in the first place, a choice between opposite policies in respect to Ireland, between opposite principles of action; or is it a choice to be made upon the particulars of a large and complicated Bill? I should not have thought of discussing such a question, if it had not been the fact that very important organs of opinion have been addressing themselves to the purpose of showing that the electors of Scotland are not to consider the policy that is to be pursued, but are to entangle themselves in the particulars of this or that particular method of establishing that policy. Now, I hold that the electors and that the nation are excellent judges of the policy. In a question of this kind, which appeals to the broad principles of justice before and above all things, in my opinion there are no judges so competent as the electors of this country. But if we are to enter into the details of this clause and that clause, to ask how many Irish members ought to sit at Westminster, and on what occasions, and of how many members the Irish legislative body is to be composed, and whether they are to be of one order or two orders, why, gentlemen, you will all tell me that those are the very matters for the settlement and discussion of which you send us to Parliament. It is laid down to you on broad principles; it is for us, under your commission, to deal with particulars and details. I am going to quote from a source that I have not often occasion to quote from, a newspaper which opposes us ten times, and censures us ten times for once that it supports us; but that makes it tolerably impartial in this matter. I am referring to the *Pall Mall Gazette*, which used these words yesterday. It aims at answering the inquiry, What is the question before the electors—Is it a principle or is it the particulars of a plan? and the *Pall Mall Gazette* writes thus: "The Ministerial faith is this, that we are to agree to establish a legislative body in Ireland for the management of exclusively Irish affairs. This is the one article of the true Ministerial faith, which except a man believe faithfully he cannot be saved from rejection at the hands of the local caucuses as a Coercionist, a Hartingtonian, a Chamberlainite, or as an heathen man and a publican." I cannot commend to you for imitation the good taste of that paragraph, because it is a parody of language which has been used for many centuries in connection with the most sacred of all subjects, but I am not looking at the form of it. I am looking at the substance of it; and as to its substance, I affirm that it is strictly accurate. The question you are asked to decide in the affirmative or in the negative is the proposition

Edinburgh, June 18.

Edinburgh, June 18.

that we agree to establish a legislative body in Ireland for the management of exclusively Irish affairs. It is a policy, and it is a principle, upon which you are called to vote. It is not a detail, a particular, or even a Bill.

It is a policy, and not the particulars of our Bills, that is in question.

Now I will try the question yet more closely, and bring it to an issue from which, as I hope, there is no escape; because among the great defections—the great and painful defections, the honour and honesty of which we never question, but the effect of which we deeply lament—is that of our powerful ally, the *Scotsman* newspaper, which has, as I think and perhaps you will allow, rendered great and valuable service to Liberal policy. On this occasion it has at least this merit, that it goes to the root of the matter; it puts the issue in a way in which it can be met, and that is a very great merit, if you are to deal with your antagonists in Parliament. You know that there is a section of them, a small section, yet a section sufficient to turn the scale, who will not vote for the Bill, but who are yet in favour of Home Rule; who are in favour of the principle of the Bill, but yet who will not vote for the Bill, but will vote against it, because they are opposed to the details of the Bill. Now, the *Scotsman* puts this question in a manner that I think is fair and clear. It writes thus: "No general professions on the part of Ministerialists of a desire for self-government in Ireland will serve them. One question can be put which will test the value and the meaning of those professions. Let the candidate be asked if he would in a new Parliament support Mr. Gladstone's Bill, if it were reintroduced with the alterations pointed to at the Foreign Office. If he will, he is for disunion, and he ought to be rejected. No play upon words will help him out of this position." Now mark the coming words—"Safe self-government for Ireland is one thing, and a most desirable thing. Mr. Gladstone's Bill is another, and a most undesirable thing." Well, now, I am ready to make a very handsome offer to the *Scotsman* newspaper, and to all those who think with the *Scotsman*. The *Scotsman* says that safe self-government for Ireland is a most desirable thing. I am sure that when they speak of "safe self-government" they do not mean by the epithet "safe" to emasculate the substantive; they mean that reasonable precautions ought to be taken, and a true, real, effective control of Irish affairs ought to be given to the Irish people. That, says the *Scotsman*, is a most desirable thing. But that is all we want. That is all we ask of you. We never asked Parliament to tie itself to the particulars of our Bill. I stated in the most distinct manner that there was no part of it which Parliament would not be perfectly free to change. I went further, and said that if the change were compatible with the principle, and calculated to forward the application of the principle better than the provisions embodied in the Bill, we would welcome and accept that change. This is no novelty; it is the declaration, as my friend Mr. Childers will tell you, which I made on the part of the Government, and made by the authority of the Government. The case is this: We have before us, in the first place, this principle, the establishment of the local statutory legislative body or Parliament in Ireland for the management of affairs exclusively Irish. We then laid down several conditions which, as we held, were essential to the application of that principle. It must be compatible with and conducive to the union of the Empire. It must be founded on political equality. It must embrace an equitable distribution of Imperial burdens. It must, as we think, provide reasonable safeguards for the minority. And finally it must afford a rational prospect of being accepted as a settlement of the question. Nobody has questioned those conditions. They are admitted to be just and rational. The principle has been stated over and over again, and once again I have stated it to you now, and I tell you this, it is idle to say that the country is to be asked to vote upon the particulars of the Ministerial Bill. The Ministerial Bill is dead. The principle of that Bill survives. I certainly will never be guilty of the dishonesty of promising you, without due consideration, a new plan for

Edinburgh, June 18.

Edinburgh, June 18.

giving effect to that principle. I never will accept a new plan unless it be with the belief that it is better than the old one. But I must tell you, in the first place, that I have been grievously disappointed with the barrenness of mind shown by the critics of our plan; for, when they have taken an objection, the very last thing they have shown themselves competent to do has been to suggest an improvement. Perhaps it is because they would not waste the treasures of their minds upon such an unprofitable audience as the present Government. Perhaps when they come up again to Parliament, or such of them as get there, they will produce one or more excellent plans. Well, if they do, they will find us the first and the most eager to welcome them, and I promise in the name of my colleagues that we will cast our own Bill to the winds the moment it is shown to us that a better plan for giving effect to our views can be produced, and the moment it is shown to us that the new plan is not an evasion of the subject, and is not an artful machinery devised for the purpose of defrauding the Irish people out of their hopes and their just rights. Let it not be said, therefore, that Ministerial candidates are to be tested by the Bill placed by us before the present Parliament, because it was the best that we could frame. No doubt there are better men than we are, who can frame a better Bill, or put us in the way of doing it. If they do, they will not be more happy than we shall be, perhaps not quite so happy as we shall be. I hope that matter is made clear. There are not many propositions in politics that cannot be denied, but the proposition I am now going to put to you is, I think, one which scarcely can be denied. The *Scotsman* says: "Every Ministerialist is taken to be a man pledged to support the late Bill of the Government." He can hardly be pledged to support the late Government Bill as a Ministerialist when the Ministry itself do not ask it or expect it of him. We do not ask or expect it of him. What we ask and expect is that he shall in good faith, knowing the meaning of his words and not using other words as a feint and screen, or a subterfuge, in order to escape from it, give Ireland the real and effective control over her own local affairs. If he is ready to do that, he is a good Ministerial candidate; if he pledges himself to do that, let him speak by the hour, and by the yard if he likes, to the satisfaction of the *Scotsman* and its editor, against the defects, and the weakness, and the follies of the Ministerial Bills. Now I hope I may have in some degree disposed of that portion of the question, and shown you that what is before you for your decision—one of the gravest decisions the country ever was called upon to take—is not a clause, not a particular, not a method, not a Bill, but is a policy and a principle. He who accepts the policy and the principle is our brother-in-arms. He that resists, he that repels it, he that shirks it, he that uses fictitious means to falsify it, he is not our brother-in-arms, but unfortunately, and regarded in all Christian charity, our adversary in the fight, whom we must do our best, without injury to his life, his limb, or his reputation, to discomfit and to defeat.

The alternative policies.

I have shown you that the question before you is the question of policy and of principle. Now, I come to a question still more conclusive, still more weighty. What are the alternative policies that are before the country? It is due to you that you should know them; it is due to you that there should be no mystery and no concealment about them. And here I may say that I endeavoured to turn to account at Carlisle yesterday an interval of a few minutes by calling attention to an incident of the most interesting character, and that is the episode in our political history of the communications between Lord Carnarvon and Mr. Parnell. I hope you will believe me when I say that I have pleasure in referring to this matter, because I do not, in the least degree, feel called upon to blame either the one or the other of those gentlemen. You may remember that at the last election, although I called on you to give the Liberal party the utmost possible strength, and make it independent of the support

Lord Carnarvon and Mr. Parnell.

Edinburgh, June 18.

of Mr. Parnell, which happily you did, yet I never censured Mr. Parnell for his disposition to enlist the late Government on his side, and I never censured the late Government for any disposition they showed to take his side. Not one word of that kind was ever uttered by me to you. But it is extremely important that we should know what did happen between them. Mr. Parnell, as you are aware, stated that a member of the late Government, who afterwards turned out to be Lord Carnarvon, had offered to him that the Conservatives, if successful in the elections, would grant to Ireland a measure of what is known as Home Rule, together with the right to protect Irish manufactures. Lord Carnarvon denied the accuracy of this statement; Mr. Parnell adheres to it; and I make not the smallest question that both this distinguished nobleman and this very remarkable man are both of them speaking with perfect veracity, whatever be the point disputed between them. Lord Carnarvon told us what he did not say to Mr. Parnell, and also told us that he did not make known the conversation to the Cabinet. Now Lord Carnarvon told us one very important thing besides. He told us what were his own views as Lord-Lieutenant of Ireland and as a member of the late Cabinet. He told us that he was in favour of a plan which would meet in full the wants of the Irish in respect of local government, and which would to some extent satisfy her national aspirations. Lord Carnarvon may not like it, gentlemen, but in substance he is our man, and not theirs. If he is ready to meet the wants of Ireland as to local self-government, and also in some degree to satisfy the national aspirations of Ireland, I am persuaded there is no room for dispute between him and us. Lord Hartington has carefully avoided saying that he is ready in some degree to satisfy the national aspirations of Ireland, and so has Mr. Chamberlain. Rely upon it, gentlemen, this, and no other, is the turning-point; and these are the opinions of Lord Carnarvon. But that is not all. I have given you what he

Lord Carnarvon is with us on this subject.

Edinburgh, June 18.

did say, but I wish to call attention, and I wish to call his attention, and I mean to call it repeatedly if necessary, to what he did not say. He did not tell the House of Lords or the public what it was that he did say to Mr. Parnell. He did not tell the House of Lords or the public to whom he told what he did say to Mr. Parnell. I believe, gentlemen, and I shall believe it until it is contradicted, that he told Mr. Parnell at least what he told the House of Lords; that he was for satisfying fully the wants of Ireland with regard to local self-government, and of satisfying to some extent her national aspirations. Let us know whether this is so or not. It is important to know whether Lord Carnarvon was a disunionist or disintegrator or dismemberer of the Empire; because that is the language bestowed upon us, because we wish, in some degree, in a very moderate degree, to satisfy the national aspirations of Ireland. I want to know how it was that these Tories sat in the Cabinet with this disintegrator and this disunionist, and did not put him out, but, on the contrary, were excessively sorry to lose him. But Lord Carnarvon says he never told the Cabinet. I have not a doubt that was true; but I say this, until I am told the contrary, I shall hold that Lord Carnarvon did tell Lord Salisbury. Why do I hold that? Because it was his absolute duty to tell Lord Salisbury. If he did communicate to Mr. Parnell what he says are his real opinions, he had no right to make such a communication to Mr. Parnell, and to withhold that fact from the head of the Government. As he is a man of honour, and I have no doubt knows his duty to the head of the Government, I cannot for one moment doubt that he told that conversation to Lord Salisbury. But I ask the question, Did he? If he kept that secret to himself, let him say so; if he told it to Lord Salisbury, then we shall know that Lord Salisbury, who now denounces us for disintegration and dismemberment, was from the month of August or September last in possession of the fact that his colleague was in communication with the

Edinburgh, June 18.

great disintegrator and dismemberer, and told him that he wished to satisfy in some degree the national aspirations of Ireland. Do not suppose that I am finding fault with Lord Salisbury. If he himself entertained an inclination in the same direction as Lord Carnarvon, I think it was a very wise inclination. The summit of my ambition would have been, to support him in giving effect to that wise inclination, but I say if he paltered and coquetted with the subject till after the election was over, and forty seats were secured, and withheld his opinion respecting the national aspirations of Ireland and disintegration and dismemberment, then I think he has a very serious responsibility, and a very heavy and difficult account to render for the conduct he then pursued, placed in contrast with the conduct he now pursues. As far as depends upon me, I intend to contribute what little I can towards elucidating the whole matter on your behalf, by putting questions to which I now respectfully solicit a reply. What was it that Lord Carnarvon told to Mr. Parnell? To whom did he communicate the purport of the conversation with Mr. Parnell?

The alternative policies.

But I have still to deal with this great subject, What are the alternative policies before the country? There is one that I know you understand, the plan of the Government; a real, effective self-government for Ireland, for the management of Irish affairs,—having this for its principle, and having for its form and method the very best plan that we could devise, or the best that anybody else can devise, to which we are ready to give in our hearty adhesion. But I am obliged to say that there are a great many schemes, notions, ideas put before you as alternatives that are not alternatives at all; and I am sorry to be obliged to connect with the first of them the name of one of the most honourable men I have ever known, that of my late colleague and my present friend, as I trust I may say, Lord Hartington. I am only now testing Lord Hartington as to his alternatives. I am obliged to tell you what, so far as I know, have been

Lord Hartington's alternative.

Edinburgh, June 18.

Lord Hartington's proposals. Three years ago he formally declared that no concession, great or small, should be made to Ireland in the matter of local self-government, until there was a fundamental change of conduct, a real penitential reformation, in the conduct of the whole body of the Nationalist members from Ireland. That was Lord Hartington's starting-point. Nothing was to be given until this great conversion had been accomplished. The conversion is very far from having been accomplished. On the contrary, they persevered, they persisted. They did not entitle themselves to any of the benefits of Lord Hartington's reservation. They went on, and they became worse and worse. They were more and more determined to disturb the course of English politics, and I must say I think in some not inconsiderable degree to weaken the hands of the Executive, and, though I do not say they intended it, even the administration of justice in Ireland. Therefore they have deserved nothing from Lord Hartington since he made that declaration. But since that, while they have only moved in the wrong direction, Lord Hartington has been moving towards them. Last year he appeared to think that, by a certain number of degrees, you might give to Ireland complete control over her own affairs. At Belfast his words, I think, were these, that you cannot give Ireland complete control over her own affairs at one stroke; it must be a gradual process. He appeared to think that a gradual process might be perfectly allowable. Then, on another point, he said he would undertake to make a great and bold reconstruction of the Irish Government. I ventured to tell him in the House of Commons that a declaration more visionary than that never issued from the lips of man. I am not now upon the merits; I am only showing what it is you have to look to in other quarters. I have shown you what you have offered to you by the Government, and I have now shown you what you have offered to you by Lord Hartington. But now again he no longer advocates the gradual process, but in his address

Edinburgh, June 18.

published yesterday he says certain powers not mentioned are to be delegated to certain bodies of number unknown, and this plan he has produced for the first time. Well, now, I want to know what is to be expected from any one who finds it necessary thus to vary his propositions, not to vary them in detail, but to vary them fundamentally and radically; at one time telling you that nothing can or ought to be done; at another time telling you that everything can be done if it is done gradually; and then, again changing his ground, saying with perfect honour and entire honesty and good-will, that some bodies may be appointed with some delegated powers, but not saying what, or how, or where, or when. Gentlemen, these plans are contradictory to one another. They are the plans of an individual, of a very eminent individual, taken up by nobody. Above all, gentlemen, I ask you whether you intend to have a plan with some finality about it, or not. The plan that we proposed is accepted by Ireland, by the mouths of her representatives, and through the length and breadth of the land, and yet, even then, our jealous opponents say, "Oh, it will not be final." Then what are we to say to a plan with respect to which not one of these representatives of Ireland tells you he will for a moment accept it, or acquiesce in it? Gentlemen, it is trifling with the subject.

Mr. Chamberlain's plans.

I turn to Mr. Chamberlain. Last year Mr. Chamberlain is supposed to have proposed a plan of a Central Council for the whole of Ireland, with very large administrative powers. That plan, as I believe, was not Mr. Chamberlain's plan, but Mr. Parnell's plan, and Mr. Parnell was willing to accept it as long as his expectations made him think that was the best that could be got. After the Tory Government came in, after Lord Spencer was censured and condemned for his brave and manly government of Ireland, after the determination to repudiate coercion was expressed, Mr. Parnell then said he must have something of the nature of a Parliament. I cannot blame him. I think it was quite consistent on his part; but

Edinburgh, June 18.

I only mention this as the first plan that Mr. Chamberlain gave his adhesion to, and of which he seemed disposed even to claim the paternity. Then, at the beginning of this year, Mr. Chamberlain went a great deal further. He said—"We must have a large scheme on the lines of federation." I showed in the House of Commons that our Bill is a Bill which advances two material steps towards federation; that it does two great things, which two things are absolutely indispensable to any plan of federation. However, Mr. Chamberlain said he would have a large scheme on the lines of federation. He did not end there. Having propounded that large scheme, he next propounded in the same session an extremely small scheme. He said that he thought that the best plan would be to have four provincial Councils in Ireland by way of satisfying, as Lord Carnarvon says, or rather not by way of satisfying, as Lord Carnarvon says, to some extent the national aspirations of Ireland, but cutting the national aspirations into quarters, as a man was hanged, drawn, and quartered of old. So high flies Mr. Chamberlain like the lark; and so low flies Mr. Chamberlain like the swallow before a shower, according to the suggestions of his teeming brain. If you think I ought not to criticize him in his absence, I assure you I did my best to criticize him quite as freely in his presence, and, if need be, possibly may do it again. You would think that I have shown you proof enough of the fertility of that remarkable mind. But he has not done yet, because yesterday he attended a meeting to found a Radical Unionist Association to frame a plan of local self-government for England, Scotland, and Ireland. Poor Wales is apparently to be left out. Yet the Welsh are a nation, the Welsh have national peculiarities, and I say fairly, if we are to have regard to national peculiarities anywhere, theirs ought to be considered according to degree and circumstances. But I think it is not necessary for me to go further; indeed, I could not now undertake to discuss a plan of local government for these three countries, as a mode,—recollect what it is,—a

Edinburgh, June 18.

mode of dealing with the great and crying subject of social disorder in Ireland. That is this one broad, glaring, and blazing difference between the countries, that whereas these are well governed, well constituted, and on the whole contented communities, you have in Ireland a community with regard to which it is admitted on all hands that the primary purposes of civilized life have not been and are not attained. Now, gentlemen, I think I may say, having on the part of the Government pointed out to you that we have a policy, and that we have done our best in regard to it, and are ready to improve that best as far as we can, or to accept from others what is better—I think I may fairly ask you whether you think that these suggestions of Mr. Chamberlain can be taken as a substitute for the plan of the Government. I did, in an address to you written at Hawarden in the month of May, describe the plans of the seceding Liberals in language which I am afraid Lord Hartington thinks contemptuous. I look back to it to-day. I described them as halting, stumbling, ever-drifting, ever-vanishing projects of seceding Liberals. And it was a true description, it was even a moderate description, it did not do full justice to the incessantly shifting and fluctuating character of those schemes, which are hatched from week to week, essentially different from one another, and put before the country, it cannot be for a substantive purpose, but for the negative purpose of impeding and destroying the projects of the Government.

The policy of coercion.

Now, if you hear me for a few minutes more, I come to the real rival policy. The real rival policy is a policy of coercion. Not to quarrel about the mere word, it is a policy of special repressive criminal legislation for Ireland to be enforced in that country, and not in the other parts of the United Kingdom. That is the other policy. It is between that policy and our policy that you have to choose. It is between the policy of coercion, and what is called the policy of conciliation or of local self-government. Now, I must entreat you to accompany me while I look at the character of the

Edinburgh, June 18.

declarations of Lord Salisbury. Yesterday I read a letter of his in a newspaper, dated 16th June. He had received a letter from a nameless person, by which I mean a person whose name, if it were mentioned, would not make you a bit the wiser. The writer said Mr. Gladstone had alleged that Lord Salisbury's plan was to ask for new repressive laws, and to enforce those laws for twenty years, and Lord Salisbury in answer to the letter says—"You designate this as one of the most deliberate misstatements on record, and I think your language is hardly exaggerated." Well, Lord Salisbury, the late Prime Minister, says of the present Prime Minister of this country, that it is hardly too much to say that I have made one of the most deliberate misstatements on record. Now, Lord Salisbury is a man of many brilliant gifts, for whom in various respects I have a very sincere admiration and regard, but I am bound to tell you this, that his modes of language have never tended to elevate, but always to lower the standard of Parliamentary manners. Having said that, I will endeavour to avoid the use of a single epithet in my reference to him, and will deal simply with the facts. But in regard to that "deliberate misstatement" of mine, that it was deliberate I most fully admit. I hold by it; I mean to repeat it; I mean to impress it upon the country as well as I can, and the country shall fairly have the means of going to an issue upon it, to know whether it is true or false. There is no question about its being deliberate; but the question is about its being a misstatement; and upon that I crave your attention for a few minutes. Lord Salisbury goes on thus: "I have never proposed to enforce new repressive laws for twenty years in Ireland." I affirm that Lord Salisbury has proposed it, and I will give you the proof directly. I pass on; I do not ask you to accept my assertion. I will give you the proof directly. Lord Salisbury then says —"The only occasion on which I have mentioned that period of time is in asking for honest, resolute, and consistent government. If the prevalence and character of crime should be

Edinburgh, June 18.

such as to require repressive laws at any time, of course in the interest of the innocent population they must be made, but whether that necessity will exist, and at what time, is a question on which I have expressed no opinion whatever." Can you believe your own ears? Can you believe that the noble Marquis, who says he has expressed no opinion whatever on the question whether a necessity will arise at any time, and if so, at what time, was the Prime Minister of the Government which on the 26th of January announced in both Houses coercive laws for Ireland? That had been heralded by the Speech from the Throne, in which Her Majesty was advised to inform Parliament that there was a most formidable state of things with regard to social order in Ireland, and that she expected that repressive legislation would probably be necessary. That was the speech of the Queen on the 21st of January. On the 26th of January, in the House of Commons, the announcement was made that immediately, and as a matter of the greatest urgency in point of time, a law would be introduced, of the severest repressive character, to put down a political association, the National League, and that other coercive legislation, of course of the same character, would follow; and that announcement was received with the frantic cheers of the whole of the Tory party, which rang loud and long in the hall in which we sat, as though they had been learning some intelligence dear to their hearts, and causing rejoicing to every one whose ears it should thereafter reach. So much for the first of these assertions of Lord Salisbury. I place in contrast the declaration he makes in his letter on the 16th of June, that he has not expressed any opinion whatever upon the question whether Ireland would require repressive laws at any time,—I put in contrast that assertion on the 16th of June with his own responsible announcement on the 26th of January. I have kept to my word, gentlemen; I have not used one single epithet to heighten the facts: they speak for themselves. And now, did I make a misstatement or did I not? ("No.") Wait a moment, please! I said that the plan of Lord Salisbury was to ask for new repressive laws and to enforce them resolutely for twenty years. Gentlemen, that was a mild statement; I might have said that he had asked for new measures of coercion. I wished to be strictly within the facts, and I said, for new repressive laws. He now says he has not. What are the words of his own speech? "My alternative policy is that Parliament should enable the Government of England to govern Ireland." I say, I put it to your judgments, that that is a demand for new laws. Parliament does not enable the Executive to discharge the executive duties of the Government. They are discharged without the smallest reference to Parliament. If my right hon. friend there, Mr. Childers, advises Her Majesty to remit, or shorten, or abridge a penal sentence, he does a most important and responsible act, but Parliament has no more to do with it than you have. We do not want the aid of Parliament. The law gives us the power. We are in our places by the confidence of Parliament, and, being in our places, we do not ask Parliament to enable the Government to govern the country. Lord Salisbury said what was requisite was that Parliament should enable it. I say that that means that there should be legislation to enable it. And what follows absolutely proves my assertion. Lord Salisbury says, "to govern Ireland resolutely," and, in parenthesis, I want to know whether Lord Salisbury considers that his Viceroys of Ireland—those with whom he had to do, the Duke of Abercorn, the Duke of Marlborough, and Lord Carnarvon—did or did not govern Ireland resolutely? Apparently they did not, because he says that the one thing necessary is that it should be governed resolutely. Well, I know one man who did govern it resolutely. Lord Spencer did govern it resolutely, and the reward he got for governing it resolutely—not from Lord Salisbury, I must do him that justice, but from the colleagues of Lord Salisbury—was censure, disparagement, and condemnation in the House of Commons. That is only in a parenthesis. That is no part of the policy now before us. My point is to

Edinburgh, June 18.

Edinburgh, June 18.

show that the policy now before us as the alternative to the policy of the Government is the policy of coercion. What says Lord Salisbury after the words I have quoted? It is "to govern honestly, consistently, and resolutely for twenty years." Then come the remaining words—"And at the end of that time you will find that Ireland will be fit to accept any gifts"—after this blessed course of education—"in the way of local government or repeal of coercion laws that you may wish to give her." What he wants is government,—government that does not flinch. I am continually, gentlemen, tempted to deviate into parentheses; Lord Salisbury's writing is very suggestive. When he speaks of government that does not flinch, my memory involuntarily goes back for 250 years to the time of Strafford and of Laud, when they said in their correspondence with one another that the policy of the Government ought to be what they called "Thorough." That name "Thorough" was a very favourite and important name at that period, and I think it ought to be reprinted and republished for the benefit of Lord Salisbury. Lord Salisbury's words are these:—"At the end of that time Ireland will be fit to accept any gifts in the way of local government or repeal of coercion laws that you may wish to give her." Repeal of coercion laws! But there exist no coercion laws at this moment. How then are they to be repealed? They have to be passed because Parliament is to enable Government to govern. Then they will be repealed or not, as the case may be, at the end of twenty years, and then, and then alone, you give grammatical and rational meaning to the words of Lord Salisbury, from which he is in vain endeavouring to escape, and in the net of which he is inextricably coiled.

I think, gentlemen, I have made good my point. There are certain unreal alternatives, halting, stumbling, ever-shifting, ever-vanishing, which I defy you to take your stand upon any more than you can take your stand upon a quicksand, with the knowledge that before you have been on it a few moments

Edinburgh, June 18.

you will be as the poor Master of Ravenswood was in the immortal romance of Scott, with nothing but a feather remaining above to indicate the spot where he had sunk. Be not caught on those quicksands, by whatever imposing names they may be recommended to you. There are two policies before the nation—two policies which alone have support. 250 Tories are at the back of Lord Salisbury; 310 or 320 Liberals, at any rate, are at our backs. There are but two real policies. You may convert the 250, if you like, into 350 or 400. You may reduce us from our 310 or 320 to be 250 or 200. It is all, gentlemen, in your power. Reflect, in the name of Almighty God, each one of you, in the sanctuary of his chamber, in the sanctuary of his heart and of his soul—reflect what it is in this year 1886, after nearly a century of almost continual coercion, becoming weaker and weaker, more and more odious, less and less effective as we go along, and repudiated now by a large majority of your representatives—reflect what it is to propose this, and only this, as an alternative to the policy of local government for Ireland. It is with you, gentlemen, if there are Conservatives among you; it is with you, and consider it for yourselves. I rejoice that you are here upon a footing with us all. Consider it for yourselves; consider what you have to do; consider what you have to answer for. Don't allow yourselves to be led away by craven fear. Have some belief that acting justly you will act strongly. Justice is always strong. Join us in the effort to close this painful, this terrible, this awful chapter of the relations of England with Ireland, which for centuries and centuries have been the opprobrium of our country in the eyes and judgment of the world. Join us in that happy, I would almost say that holy effort; and rely upon it that, if we are enabled to attain the object in view, we shall have done perhaps even more for the honour of Great Britain than for the happiness of Ireland.

The right hon. gentleman, after having spoken for an hour and a half, sat down amid loud and continued cheers.

A resolution of continued confidence in Mr. Gladstone, cordially approving of the Irish policy of his Government, and enthusiastically welcoming him to Scotland, proposed by Mr. C. C. Cotterill, Fettes College, and seconded by Mr. W. K. Dickson, was put to the meeting and carried by acclamation.

Mr. Gladstone expressed his thanks for the passing of the resolution, and the meeting concluded with a vote of thanks to Mr. Cowan for presiding.

IX.

SECOND MIDLOTHIAN SPEECH.

MONDAY, JUNE 21, 1886.

Delivered to a meeting of 2500 electors in the Music Hall, Edinburgh.

THIS vast audience gave Mr. Gladstone a most hearty and cordial welcome. The right hon. gentleman was accompanied to the platform by Mrs. Gladstone, the Countess of Aberdeen, Mr. W. H. Gladstone, Mr. Cowan, Mr. Childers, M.P., Mr. R. B. Haldane, M.P., Mr. C. S. Parker, M.P., Mr. Jacks, M.P., Mr. Robert Wallace (now M.P. for East Edinburgh), Mr. W. M'Ewan (now M.P. for Central Edinburgh), and also by a large number of the Midlothian Executive Committee.

On the motion of Dr. Smith, Lennox Lea, Currie, Mr. Cowan took the chair. The Chairman, after referring in loyal and graceful terms to the commencement of the fiftieth year of Her Majesty's reign, called upon Mr. Gladstone, who spoke as follows:—

Introduction.

Mr. Chairman and Gentlemen,—It must be very irksome, I am well aware, to you to hear, as it is irksome to me to speak in your hearing nothing, practically nothing on this occasion except one repeated cry of Ireland, Ireland, Ireland! I had hoped, gentlemen, at any rate to-day, to speak to you upon those aspects of the Irish question which have a special interest for Scotland; such as the position of Ulster; such as the history of the Scottish Union, and the comparison between

Edinburgh, June 21.

that and the Union with Ireland; such as the apprehensions that have been freely expressed by one or more deputations from Ireland, freely expressed among you, of persecution of Protestants by a dominant Roman Catholic power; and, finally, such as the idea that whatever is done in the matter of local government ought to be done upon a rigid cast-iron system for all the three countries and for Wales at once, quite irrespective of all the diversified circumstances of their history. But this task I must put off on account of what seems more urgent; and I will say, before addressing myself to those Irish matters, I admit it is disappointing, it is tantalizing in a high degree, to reflect upon what we are now about to do, and to compare with it what we might have been doing. We might, gentlemen, if we had in other days observed a wiser Irish policy—we might now have been free to retrieve the long arrears of British legislation, and to address ourselves to the consideration of those questions, both civil and ecclesiastical, embracing, in fact, all the varied interests of society, on which the minds of so many among us—I might say with regard to one or other of them, the minds of you all—are set. Well, gentlemen, what I hope is, and what I desire is, that we shall get the hands of Parliament set free at the earliest possible moment to deal with those questions in their order. I know nothing in the Parliament about to die, when I compare it with previous Parliaments, that would derogate from its capacity so to act. And my hopes are hopes dependent, not upon the great ones of the land, but upon the masses of the people. My hopes are that the Parliament about to be elected will even surpass the Parliament you chose in November and December, from which we had hoped, and in many respects had reasonably hoped, so much.

"Ireland blocks the way."

Gentlemen, I think you thoroughly understand why it is that my anxiety to deal with English, Scottish, and Welsh questions induces me to insist at this moment so pertinaciously upon the Irish question. I will endeavour to illustrate what I think the position is. It may be briefly stated in one word

Edinburgh, June 21.

familiar to those who attend parties in London, or perhaps in Edinburgh, and who want to get away from them, but their carriage cannot get to the door—"Ireland blocks the way." Now supposing, gentlemen, you are in a railway train, and part of its diversified and momentary population, all anxious for one reason or another to reach their destination—one to transact an important matter of business, one to visit a sick friend or relative, one to welcome a child returned from distant lands—and with some trial of your patience and some temptation to irritation, you find that the train has come to a standstill. Immediately every window of it is filled by the protrusion of a large portion of the person of a passenger; and if they can get sight of a guard, they ask angrily, "Why do you stop the train?" The guard points along the line. He shows that the rails are occupied by a set of stones, placed there probably by some mischievous person; and I am sorry to say that innumerable persons are responsible, by their neglect or by their misdeeds, for having placed this Irish difficulty in the way of the nation. But you understand the first duty is to get the rails clear; when you have got the rails clear, the train will go on, and you will reach your destination. The whole question in this election, is a question of clearing the rails, and it is to clear the rails that I entreat your aid, and that I rely upon your energies to make that aid thoroughly effective.

Two corrections.

I must refer for a moment, gentlemen, to the speech I made on Friday, because I have been told that it contains an error, which I am anxious at once to set right. It is perfectly immaterial to the argument of the speech. In referring to a variety of plans for dealing with Ireland, which had proceeded from one of my late colleagues, I mentioned the first of these as having been, I believed, the plan of Mr. Parnell. I am told that that plan—what is known as the plan of Central Councils—was not the plan of Mr. Parnell. I wish to withdraw my statement so far as Mr. Parnell is concerned. Whether it be accurate or not, it matters not to the present purpose. I intended to indicate it as the

Edinburgh, June 21.

first of the plans, of the numerous plans, to which Mr. Chamberlain had given his adherence. Well, then, I have again to name Mr. Chamberlain with reference to a speech which he has since made. He states in that speech, as it is reported, apparently with accuracy, that on a certain recent occasion in the House of Commons Mr. Sexton taunted Mr. Chamberlain with having been Mayor of Birmingham, and said that position was exactly up to the level of his ability. Then Mr. Chamberlain says he was surprised to see that Mr. Gladstone cheered that sentiment. There never, gentlemen, proceeded a grosser error from the mouth of man. I cheered no such sentiment. Whatever you may think of Mr. Chamberlain's present action, I am quite sure you will agree with me that nothing can be more honourable to him than his career at Birmingham. It so happens that it is a subject I have been very fond of referring to in conversation with my friends, if not in public; for I do not know a more remarkable example of the operation of a principle vital to our institutions, namely, the great and immeasurable usefulness of local self-government in training men for Imperial functions. Therefore I look with regard and admiration on Mr. Chamberlain's career at Birmingham, and I have never for a moment depreciated, and never shall depreciate, the signal abilities of debate which, reared on that comparatively narrow ground, Mr. Chamberlain has since developed in Parliament.

The Carnarvon conversation.

One other point, gentlemen. I referred on Friday to a subject of interest which we called the Carnarvon conversation. My purpose is to get to the bottom of the relations which have subsisted between the Tory party and Mr. Parnell before the last election, not since the election—about that I am indifferent—in order not to fix censure upon them, but to see what sort of views they then took on the subject of Home Rule, which they now denounce as amounting to the dismemberment of the Empire. Lord Salisbury did me the honour to notice on that very evening some words which, as

Edinburgh, June 21.

he says, I delivered in a spasmodic interval at Carlisle, between the snorting of the engine when it arrived and the snorting of the engine when it departed. Lord Salisbury, in his notice of what I said, has elaborately answered—made a reply to everything that I did not say, and has as elaborately overlooked what I did say. I put two questions to him and to Lord Carnarvon, and I now put them again, for they are of great weight. What communication did Lord Carnarvon make to Mr. Parnell in the conversation which took place, I rather think, last July? That is the first question. And, secondly, did he make known the result of that conversation and its purport to Lord Salisbury as the head of the Government? I wait for full and explicit answers to those two questions; and I conceive that the country is entitled to those answers.

The representation of Edinburgh City.

Now, electors of Midlothian, you will bear in mind that a relation has always been established, on the various occasions when I have come among you for an election, between the election for the county and the election for the city. It has been my desire upon former occasions, if it were at all in my power, consistently with propriety, to lend a helping hand to friends, and a not helping hand to opponents, upon these occasions. You will readily understand that I am tempted under such circumstances to refer to the present state of the representation of Edinburgh. There has been, gentlemen, a Liberal secession, much stronger, undoubtedly, than we could have desired, in the House of Commons, but that secession represented something more than one-fourth of the Liberal party, leaving to us, who call ourselves the Liberal party, nearly three-fourths of the whole. Well, now, I want you to compare that state of things, not the most satisfactory in the world, with the state of things in Edinburgh. In Edinburgh there is a division into three-fourths and one-fourth, but the one-fourth is with the Liberal party, and the three-fourths are with the seceders. It is a matter of interest, gentlemen, to consider; and perhaps you may say,

Edinburgh, June 21.

"You are the county member; you have nothing to do with it,"—but I cannot help it. It is a matter of interest, that I cannot avoid, even to me, to consider whether that state of things is to continue. I hope it is not an impertinence, but I cannot help suspecting that the capital of Scotland will make some stout and sturdy effort in order to set right that state of things. Edinburgh has been accustomed to lead in the van of Liberal politics, and has not been accustomed to find her members among the obstructors of national justice and national welfare. It is not for me, indeed, to enter upon the cases of particular districts and particular contests, but there is one contest in actual progress, and one gentleman whose great distinction requires that I should name him. That is the case of East Edinburgh, and the gentleman whom I name is Mr. Goschen. I can only name Mr. Goschen, gentlemen, in the first instance as a man of very great ability, of remarkable keenness and assiduity, and of unquestioned and unquestionable honour. About that I think there is no doubt. But Mr. Goschen, besides being one of your local representatives, is also a great public character, and has been in a very large degree the soul of the opposition to the Irish Bills. At the last election I am aware that I used words of honourable reference to Mr. Goschen, which were thought by the opponents of Mr. Goschen to constitute a somewhat unfair interference of mine in his behalf. At any rate, I certainly understood that Mr. Goschen at that time was a conforming and an orthodox member of the Liberal party. Your phraseology in ecclesiastical matters is very expressive. I think you have a word by which you indicate the case of men who depart from the established system, and you are accustomed to say that they "deviate." I don't think anybody at that time supposed that Mr. Goschen would "deviate." Well, now, I am very sorry for one of his proceedings in particular. A meeting has been recently held in London of some of the richest men in the country. They have been the seceding Liberals; and you know that we have lost nearly all, certainly a very large portion, of the wealthier men who belong to our party. Mr. Goschen is reported at this meeting to have said that the great object of the meeting was to provide a long purse—I am quoting from the newspapers—to provide a long purse in order to run as many candidates as possible. Against whom were these candidates to be run? I am afraid, gentlemen, the circumstances supply the answer. They were to be run against any candidate supporting the principles and the policy of the Government, and the majority of the party. I am extremely sorry for this. I do not think it consorts with the spirit of Liberalism, to hold a great meeting for the purpose of creating a long purse in order to create Parliamentary contests, Parliamentary contests that would otherwise not exist, and in order to keep poor men out of the field of political contests. Mr. Goschen would be a most admirable candidate, as far as I can judge, with incomparable claims for a Tory constituency. He is an undoubted Liberal in his own belief, in his own most sincere belief; but it is somewhat unfortunate that, being a man of the greatest talent and an undoubted Liberal, his energies for years and years past have been mainly directed towards stopping the purposes of Liberalism. For years together he conscientiously opposed that extension of the franchise, which, gentlemen, as you recollect, was a matter of great difficulty to accomplish, and was very nearly costing the country the anxieties of a dissolution. All this it was hoped at the last election was over. Mr. Goschen in his proceedings sincerely professed the creed of Liberalism. It was most unfortunate that, when his past time had been occupied in resisting an extension of the franchise, his future time was from the very commencement again to be occupied in resisting the purposes of the great bulk of the Liberal party, and this not alone on the question of Home Rule. Recollect that on the very first evening of the session, when a motion was made, which was the immediate cause of the retirement of the Government, with respect to introducing the agricultural labourer to an interest in the

Edinburgh, June 21.

Edinburgh, June 21.

land, Mr. Goschen at once took the opportunity of that motion to deliver a most keen and vehement speech against the policy of the Liberal party in general, and against myself, who had taken some part in the debate, in particular; and it is a very unfortunate thing that while his past was a record of resistance to the greatest object of Liberalism, so his future was to be a record of renewed resistance to that which has, by compulsion, become the main object of Liberal policy. Gentlemen, all that, I hope, will remain well in the hands of the electors of Edinburgh, and I feel convinced that Edinburgh will continue to maintain her place, to assert for herself her place, in the forward ranks of Liberalism, for the advantage of the country at large.

The seceding Liberals.

Gentlemen, I must not lay upon Mr. Goschen more blame than belongs to him, nor do I presume to blame him; I speak simply of the action he has conscientiously pursued, and of his enormous claims to the suffrages of a constituency hostile to the purposes of Liberalism. But I go on to speak of that most important body—for they are a very important body—whom we have termed the seceding Liberals. They call themselves Unionist Liberals. But we contend that they are paper Unionist Liberals,—that the union they recommend is a union which was brought about by fraud and force, and which never has commended itself to the people whom it principally affected. We want a union, gentlemen, of flesh, of the hearts and minds of men. And we will never consent that they are to be called Unionists who set up against it a union upon paper and a union in name. Well, now, why do I call them seceding Liberals? Gentlemen, when a body splits into two, one side much larger and the other much smaller, it is not a very unnatural privilege for the larger part to say that they are the body, and that those who depart from them are the seceders. How does the matter stand here? As I have told you, the seceders amount in the House of Commons to more than a fourth, I believe almost exactly to two-sevenths or nearly two-sevenths. How do they stand in the Liberal Associations throughout the country? Why, there they are about one-fifth or from that to one-tenth. How do they stand among the mass of the Liberal party out of doors? Why, I will venture to say—and my own knowledge and personal experience give me some title to speak upon that subject—that among the masses of the Liberal party out of doors, the masses of those who now possess the franchise, the seceding gentlemen are not one-twentieth, perhaps not one-fiftieth of the whole. Gentlemen, they have acted according to their consciences; they have acted on what they believed to be honour and duty. Let us respect their action. I should be the last to imply the smallest disrespect for it, though I protest against the assumption of titles to which I think they have no claim; but I never, gentlemen, could speak without feelings of regard, as well as regret, concerning a body which contains—though he may be isolated in it, but still he has been associated with it by his vote—I don't think he takes part in its action—which contains that venerable patriot Mr. Bright,—a man whose services to his country have been such that they can never be forgotten; and however much we may differ from anything he may say or anything he may do upon this occasion, it can hardly make the smallest sensible deduction from the debt of gratitude which we owe to him. I might mention many more, men like Lord Hartington, who are the very flower of truth and honour; or, going out of the paths of statesmanship, men like the Duke of Westminster, less known to you than to us in England, but a princely nobleman, who, in every relation of life, sets a most noble example to every rank of the community in the performance of every description of duty. Therefore do not suppose it is disrespect on my part; but I must contend that these are seceding Liberals for two reasons, and not for one alone: first, because they are but a small fraction of the Liberal party; secondly, because they have abandoned the traditions of the Liberal party.

Edinburgh, June 21.

Mr. Bright.

Lord Hartington.

Duke of Westminster.

Edinburgh, June 21.

Traditions of the Liberal party. Mr. Fox.

The Liberal party has the most honourable traditions on the subject of Ireland. I will read to you an extract upon that subject from Mr. Fox. And if Mr. Fox were now alive, and were now to deliver these sentiments, I want to know what sort of reception he and they would receive from the seceding Liberals. Mr. Fox is speaking of those who described the Irish people as traitors, and he goes on—"Such the laws proposed by these hon. gentlemen tell you the Irish are, that is to say, traitors; but such I tell you they are not. A grosser outrage upon truth, a greater libel upon a generous people, never before was uttered or insinuated. They who can find reason for all this in any supposed depravity of the Irish people misunderstand their character. Sir, I love the Irish nation. I know a great deal of that people. I know much of Ireland from having seen it. I know more from private friendship with individuals. The Irish may have their faults, like others; they may have a quick feeling of injury, and not be very patient under it; but I do affirm that, of all their characteristics, there is not one feature more predominant in every class of the country, from the highest to the lowest order, than gratitude for benefits and sensibility to kindness. Change your system towards that country, and you will find them another sort of men. Let impartiality, justice, and clemency take the place of prejudice, oppression, and vengeance, and you will not want the aid of martial law or the terror of military executions." Those sentiments of Mr. Fox were not mere generalities. Mr. Fox, with every genuine Whig, was a strong opponent to the Act of Union, predicted its ruinous consequences, and all the difficulties with which we are now endeavouring to struggle. Not he alone, but I believe every great family, certainly the bulk of the great families of the Whig connection, followed Mr. Fox in that policy; and we are now defending the policy of the Fitzwilliams, and the Cavendishes, and I know not how many more of that day, against their descendants, who resist us in the present. Therefore, gentlemen, I object to the claim to represent the Liberal party by the seceding section, upon the ground not merely that it is a small minority of the Liberal party, but because it has abandoned the generous and wise traditions with which the name of the Liberal party is associated. (A voice, "No.") A gentleman says "No." Has it not abandoned the traditions of the passage I have just now read from Mr. Fox? I know perfectly well it may be said that since that time Lord Grey and others—the Greys of that day were among the most illustrious opponents of the Union, as the Greys of the present day—some of them, I am thankful to say not all—are among our strongest opponents—Lord Grey said, about fifty years ago, that he would not consent to alter the Union. Gentlemen, in my opinion he was perfectly right. So vast a measure as that was a measure which, having been passed, it was absolutely necessary to try, to try patiently, to try for a length of time to see whether it could be made to work, to see whether by abolishing, by removing the frightful grievances of Ireland that then subsisted, you could bring the Irish people to love it. Why, gentlemen, if that could have been brought about, I should never have been here to ask you in the smallest degree to modify or qualify that Union. But Lord Grey never, to my knowledge, nor any one of those distinguished men, so far as I know, ever in the slightest degree retracted or in the slightest degree regretted this stern and strenuous opposition which they had offered, not merely to the Act of Union itself, but to the whole Irish policy upon which that Act was founded.

Edinburgh, June 21.

The Land Purchase Bill.

Now, gentlemen, there is another question which has been so much made the subject of discussion that I don't think I ought to pass it by without a word of notice, although I cannot on this occasion deal with it at any length. I know it has perplexed the minds of some, and I know it was desired to put questions to me on the subject of it. I mean the Land Purchase Bill. Now it will be very hard upon you to ask you to make yourselves acquainted with my views by reading a speech of thirty or forty pages upon the

Edinburgh, June 21.

subject—they are there set forth with tolerable fulness—delivered in the House of Commons; and I don't see any occasion to recede from any of the opinions delivered in that speech, as they were applicable to the time when it was spoken. I think, perhaps, I cannot do better than read to you the substance of part of a letter which I lately wrote to a friend on the subject of the Land Purchase Bill. He felt it to be a stumbling-block in the way of supporting the policy of the Government, and I am bound to make the admission that many others have so felt it. I make another admission. Undoubtedly, as I stated at the time, the great motive with us in making that proposal was the hope that we might mitigate the bitterness and avoid the prolongation of a formidable political controversy. What has happened? Those for whose direct benefit it had a particular application have done nothing to support it. Lord Hartington, who was supposed to desire intensely the passing of such an Act, instead of supporting it, has described it in public as a Bill of which nobody seems to approve. Undoubtedly the people of England and of Scotland have, in a large measure, withheld from the Land Purchase Bill the support, and sympathy, and approval which they have given to the substance of the plan of Irish Government. Gentlemen, I wrote this, which I conceive to be not an unfair statement of the case. What I take to be the case is that both our Bills are for the moment dead. One carries on its tombstone the accorded sanction of a large minority of the House of Commons, so far as its principle is concerned; the other, no sanction beyond that of the Cabinet. If the verdict of the constituencies be not favourable, we shall be dead also together with our Bills. Only one survival is, I think, certain, that is the survival of the principle and policy of self-government for Ireland. For candidates this proposition leaves an absolute freedom as to means for giving effect to the self-government for Ireland, and, of course, as to the question of land purchase. As for us, you will find, if you have patience to read my speech, that the declarations contained in it have reference to the time when it was spoken. Our offer was inseparable in our minds from the principal Act, but it was inseparable at that moment. The Parliament was not bound to join these Acts together, and I stated for myself and for the Government that the acceptance or rejection of our offer evidently must have an important influence on the future course of the question. You will see, therefore, gentlemen, that, with regard to all the other particulars of our plan, we are at perfect freedom to consult for the benefit of the country, and to find the best and safest means to attain our object, namely, the establishment of self-government in Ireland for Irish affairs, with perfect security for the fabric of Imperial unity. That is the principle, and that is the sole principle, which ought to guide us in our future deliberations; and our policy in every point, as to the choice of means, will receive its inspiration from that source, and from that source alone. We shall be as anxious as ever to maintain the obligations of honour and policy; and if we continue in the Government, which it is for you and other constituencies to decide, it will be upon that basis alone that our counsels will be founded.

Edinburgh, June 21.

I am sorry to refer to any personal question. But so much has been said about my own conduct in this business that I must for a very short time detain you in relation to it. I am accused of having concealed from you at the period of the election all idea of what was about to approach,—of having treated the question of Ireland as a very secondary question, and of not having given to any one the means of understanding that, in my opinion, a great crisis was about to arrive. I tell you now, gentlemen, what actually took place. Returning from a short trip to Norway at the beginning of September, I immediately prepared an address to the electors, two months and more before the dissolution of Parliament. You may ask, Why did you go so prematurely into the field? Well, gentlemen, if I am to tell you, I must

A personal explanation. The Address of September 17, 1885.

Edinburgh, June 21.

tell you my special purpose was this, to keep upon tolerable terms together several important gentlemen who are now united in most harmonious resistance to us. That was the reason of my very early address. In that address I treated the question of local government and self-government for Ireland quite apart from the question of local government and self-government for Great Britain, and I said that everything in my opinion ought to be given to Ireland which she was constitutionally shown to desire, and which was compatible with the unity, strength, and honour of the Empire. That is in my address of the 17th September. But I want to call your attention—and, although I have got a volume in my hands, I am not going to read the contents of it—I want to call your attention to what I said to you when the dissolution was really approaching. On the 9th of November I had the honour of first addressing you in connection with the last election, and at page 36 of the speeches I then delivered, you will, if you take the pains to refer to it, find these words:—"We must take into view the likelihood that that party"—namely, the Nationalist party—"will make a demand for the concession of large powers to Ireland in that direction. Well, now, gentlemen, it is quite plain that if that contingency should arise it is a grave and serious contingency. Don't let it fill any of us, gentlemen, with alarm. Depend upon it that, as long as we act liberally, equitably, and at the same time prudently to Ireland, these countries have nothing to fear from any contingency that can arise in the relations of these islands." I only quote that passage as showing that I exhorted my countrymen to be courageous, and to act upon principles of justice and of prudence. Was that a speech confined to a contemplation of grand juries and of county government? On the contrary, it spoke of national relations, and of a serious question in connection with them. I went on at page 38 as follows:—"I have declared that in my opinion it would not only be allowable but beneficial, when once the wishes of Ireland should be constitutionally ascertained—not only allowable, but highly beneficial to the three countries and to the Empire at large, that everything should be given to Ireland in the way of local self-government which is consistent with the maintenance and unity of the Empire, and the authority of Parliament as connected with the unity of the Empire." That is precisely the language we now hold. We are endeavouring to give to Ireland local self-government, consistently with the unity of the Empire and the supremacy of Parliament necessary to its maintenance. One more passage, gentlemen, I have to quote. It is in page 44—"If such a matter comes forward at the outset of the proceedings of the new Parliament as I have described, namely, a demand made constitutionally by the vast majority of the representatives of Ireland, for the concession of large local powers of self-government, accompanied with an admission that the unity of the Empire is not to be impaired"—now I entreat your attention to these words—"the magnitude of that subject, and its character, will sweep into the shade for the moment all those subjects of ordinary legislation on which I or on which others have addressed you, and the satisfactory settlement of that subject, which goes down to the very roots and foundations of our whole civil and political constitution, will become the first duty of the Parliament." I ask you, and I ask every candid man, whether I did conceal from you the ideas which I entertained. I pointed out to you that a great crisis was coming on; and people have the audacity to reproach me with not endeavouring to force upon Parliament—to force upon them by efforts that would be absolutely vain—the consideration of the other subjects of legislation I had referred to, when I told you in the plainest language that if this great majority was returned from Ireland, and if this demand were made, it would sweep into the shade the whole of that legislation, and you would hear no more of it until this business was settled.

Edinburgh, June 21.

The approach of the Irish crisis plainly intimated in November 1885.

Now, gentlemen, consider with me for a moment whether it was possible for me to go beyond that. Ought I to have

Edinburgh, June 21.

That intimation necessarily of a general character.

produced upon that occasion the Irish Government Bill? Should I have told you that we ought to be prepared to give a legislative body or statutory Parliament in Dublin for the consideration of Irish affairs? I am putting now a question to myself, and I will proceed to answer it. I will give you most conclusive reasons, not only why it was not necessary, but why it would have been extremely wrong on my part if I had entered upon the consideration of such a subject.

The result of the elections not then known.

First of all, the election at that period had not taken place. People say it was foreseen. Certainly it was foreseen; but there is a difference, gentlemen, in human things, as we are not inspired prophets, between things that are foreseen by the ordinary use of human intelligence, and things that, being seen, have become part of human experience. It was my duty to prepare you to the best of my power for great events that might come on. I had given you preparation, and that was all that was justifiable.

The exact demands of Ireland not then ascertained.

But, secondly, it was to be foreseen that probably a great demand would arise from Ireland, but how was it to be foreseen that that demand would be so wise and moderate that it could safely be given? These gentlemen now tell us, Oh, they were quite innocent and ignorant in this affair; they foresaw nothing, they had no idea that anything was going to happen in Ireland. And yet these same people find fault with me for not committing myself to making a boon to Ireland before I knew what would be the boon she would ask for. Gentlemen, this question is of vital consequence. It is forgotten; nay, more, it is artfully concealed in many cases, in particular by our Tory opponents, that Ireland is not asking at this moment for what she formerly asked. She formerly asked for the repeal of the Union. It was very much to be apprehended at that time that she would continue to ask for repeal of the Union. I will tell you frankly, I am not prepared to consent to the repeal of the Union. The repeal of the Union means the constitution, that is to say, not

Edinburgh, June 21.

the constitution, but the revival, the permitted revival, by the abolition of an Act of Parliament of the old original national Parliament of Ireland with independent legislative authority,—the Parliament which claimed exclusive title to make laws that were to bind the people of Ireland, and the Parliament which obtained in the years 1782 and 1783 from this proud and powerful country a formal statutory acknowledgment of the validity of that claim. Well, now, gentlemen, it was with regard to a proposition of that kind that Sir Robert Peel delivered in 1834 a very noble passage of Parliamentary eloquence, which I have frequently seen quoted now as if it were applicable to the present proposals. The passage turned upon a fine simile or comparison which he drew between the revival of that old Irish Parliament, and the launching into space of a new planetary body without being able to fix the laws that would govern its motion. That was a cogent argument in 1834. I am not prepared to say that it might not be a cogent argument still. But Ireland had been asking for Repeal at that time. Ireland, gentlemen, has done her utmost to allay your fears, to consider even your prejudices, to overcome your difficulties, and by a careful limitation of her own demand to make it easy for you, if you have justice and policy to guide you, to meet her and to consummate the work of peace. But inasmuch as at the time of the last election the claims of the Nationalist party had usually been to the effect that what they looked for was at least the revival of the old Irish Parliament, I ask you whether it was possible for me with tolerable prudence to commit myself to those claims before I knew the shape that they were likely to assume?

Possibility of a Home Rule measure from late Tory Government.

Well, gentlemen, I had a third reason for not entering further on the matter, which was, if possible, of still greater force, and it was this. I hoped—I was sanguine in the hope—that the ideas we now know possessed the mind of the Tory Lord-Lieutenant of Ireland would also be those of

Edinburgh, June 21.

the Tory Cabinet—"to meet the demand of Ireland for local self-government, and to satisfy to some extent her national aspirations." These are the golden words which proceeded from the mouth of Lord Carnarvon; these are the ideas with which he governed Ireland; these are the ideas which, until I know the contrary, I shall feel morally certain that Lord Salisbury knew him to entertain, and the ideas which Lord Salisbury, with the election and the Parnellite vote in view, did not deem in any respect a disqualification for his being the Viceroy and the representative of the Queen in Ireland. What said at that time Lord Salisbury himself? Why, gentlemen, he spoke in the very terms, substantially in the very terms, that I have quoted to you from my own address. On the 9th of November, at the Lord Mayor's dinner, he said in effect simply this, as I have said—that everything should be given to promote the peace, happiness, and contentment of Ireland, which was consistent with the unity of the Empire and the supremacy of Parliament. Therefore, gentlemen, my hope was that we should have a Tory measure of Home Rule. Was it not my most solemn duty to cherish that hope? What would have happened if you had had a Tory measure of Home Rule? Why, that the greater part of those Tories who are now opposing us as dismemberers of the Empire would, notwithstanding, have been true to the call of their own leaders, and would have trooped into the lobby to support them rather than let them be turned out. And what would have happened on the other side, because these Tories after all were but 250, and no doubt, I fully admit, the 15 or 20 Tories from Ulster would have raved upon the subject just as violently as they have been doing of late, but the bulk of the Tories would have followed their leaders into the lobby? Would they have gone there alone? Of course they would have had the Irish Nationalists, but even that would not have sufficed to carry the measure. No, gentlemen, I tell you what they would have had. They would have had that which we can never hope for on a question such as this; they would have had from their opponents, the mass of the Liberal party, a fair and candid hearing. Numbers of us would have followed them into their lobby, and heartily and loyally supported them in the endeavour to consummate a great and noble work for the benefit of their country. I have seen it ludicrously remarked in a journal—not an Edinburgh journal—that professes to be of the highest intelligence, that if I had the intention to support Lord Salisbury, in the event of his proposing a measure of Home Rule, I ought not to have buried it in my own breast, but ought to have made it known to him. But it so happens, gentlemen, that is the very thing I did do. I made it known in speech and in letter to a near relative of Lord Salisbury's, who communicated it to Lord Salisbury, and I received an acknowledgment of that intelligence, through him, from Lord Salisbury; and not only so, but I stated it in the House of Commons, and it was acknowledged to be true from the Opposition benches. So much for the wisdom and so much for the accuracy of information which is often served up at breakfast for the enlightenment or the bewilderment, as the case may be, of intelligent people of this country. Therefore, gentlemen, I hope you will see that I was shut up between two walls of duty. On the one hand it was my duty to point out to you as well as I could that a serious time was probably about to arrive in Ireland, about to become in all likelihood the engrossing, commanding, absorbing question of the day. On the other hand I was forbidden by equally solemn duty to decide on things on which as yet I was imperfectly informed; and I was, above all, forbidden to abandon the hope of seeing a Home Rule measure from a Tory Government. Why, gentlemen, in what I have been stating to you now do not suppose I am speaking my own dreams without reference to political experience. What happened in the case of the repeal of the Corn Laws? Sir Robert Peel proposed it. Had Sir Robert Peel Tory force enough to carry it? One hundred and nine of the

Edinburgh, June 21.

Edinburgh, June 21.

Tory party supported him. His majority for the repeal of the Corn Laws was made up of from 200 to 300 Liberals, who, knowing the object to be good, were above all considerations of the quarter from whence it proceeded. Just so it had been before in the case of Roman Catholic emancipation, and so, gentlemen, I trust—speaking in this Liberal country—so I trust it will always be; that, while you will value your party as a good and effective instrument for the government of the country, you will always hold the supreme ends of patriotic policy to be above the ends of party, and will support good measures be they proposed by whom they may.

The actual situation—a majority of members of the late Parliament opposed to Home Rule.

Now, gentlemen, one word upon the actual situation. I have spoken in terms of honour of the Parliament now expiring; of course I deeply regret and, as far as I can do it with propriety, I condemn its rejection of the Bill of the Government. But I can well understand many reasons that go to explain that rejection. It is impossible at a moment's notice to get rid of old rooted prejudice, and we cannot deny, if we keep our eyes open, that there are prejudices, and have been prejudices, between this country and Ireland; prejudices on the other side of the water, and prejudices on this side of the water. I must say also much had happened of late years. The conduct of the Irish Nationalist members, whatever apology they have had, yet was certainly of a provocative character, and I further add that it does take a certain time, perhaps, for a great country like this fully to embrace all the bearings of a huge and novel subject. Therefore I am not now complaining of the decision that has been come to, but I wish it to be exactly known what that decision was, because artful attempts are made in some quarters, and I cannot call them less than artful attempts, to contend that the existing Parliament has not declared against the principle of Home Rule for Ireland,—Home Rule meaning the management in Ireland and by Ireland of affairs exclusively Irish, while Ireland remains subject to the Imperial Parliament for all that is Imperial. Now, gentlemen, I can give you the clearest proof that Parliament has rejected, has refused to sanction this principle of the government of Ireland by domestic legislation. There were 93 Liberals who voted in the majority of 341 who rejected the bill—93 Liberals and 248 Tories. Now, will you be so kind as to follow me—the figures are simple enough—in the explanation I have to give. It is known from public declarations and indisputable evidence that out of these 93 Liberals 67 at least voted with Lord Hartington, and under his frank and ingenuous declaration that he was opposed to establishing a domestic legislature in Ireland for the management of Irish affairs. I may just say a word upon the rest. The rest were 26 in all. I believe five of these were immediate adherents of that very distinguished gentleman, whom I need not name again, the member for West Birmingham, and twenty-one were a body of gentlemen who voted, I believe, under various motives, some of them, I know, because they did not consider that they had received sufficient authority from their constituencies to sanction so considerable a change. It is not necessary for me to analyse either the five or the twenty-one, or to enter into the question whether they were really opposed to Home Rule or not. What I insist upon is this—there were 248 Tories, of whom there is not the least doubt that they were opposed. And there were 67 Liberals of whom there is no doubt they were opposed, for they have made it perfectly indisputable. Add 67 to 248 and you have 315, as against 311 who voted in the lobby of the Government; and therefore, without investigating the motives of others, and assuming for a moment that in some shape or other some of them persuaded themselves that they were favourable to Home Rule, and only objected to the particular plan, 315 at the least were opposed to it out and out, and were determined that there should be no statutory Parliament in Dublin for the management of Irish affairs. Therefore, gentlemen, that is the situation, and it is upon that situation and upon that alone that the appeal is made to the country.

Edinburgh, June 21.

Edinburgh, June 21.

Why self-government has not been granted to Ireland before now.

One thing I observe is said, Why did you not do this before? Why is it now in 1886 that you make this proposal? Some I believe say, I have read it I believe to-day, that if I were a man good for anything, I ought to have done it fifty years ago. Well, I think I can give very good reasons why it has not been done until the present time. Will you be good enough to allow me to recall your attention to the great periods in the history of the Irish movement since 1800. The Act of Union left Ireland in a state of burning indignation from one end of the country to the other; but the mass of the population, the Roman Catholic population, at that time were without organs, and had no power, as you have now given them power, to make their sentiments effective. That indignation passed, under the leadership of Mr. O'Connell, into a demand for repeal; and, speaking roughly, I say without doubt that for the first fifty years of this century the demand of Ireland, as far as it was known, was a demand for repeal. Well, gentlemen, I have given you some reasons to-day why, in my opinion, that was a demand that, at that time certainly, it would have been most unwise to accede to, and a demand which for myself I am not prepared to accede to at the present moment. That disposes of the time down to 1850. What came then? There came then a period of about fifteen years—again I speak roughly—during which you had attempts at armed outbreaks in Ireland, coercion laws, armed outbreaks not very successful, but secret conspiracies established under the general name of Fenianism, which took a deep hold upon the people of Ireland. At that time there was no Parliamentary Irish question, but about the year 1865 the Parliamentary question began; and then came the period of attempts at reform. Then it was that we abolished the Irish Church Establishment with your help, gentlemen. I remember well being on the hustings as candidate for South Lancashire in the close of 1868, and hearing on these hustings with joy that in Mid-Lothian, then a fortress of Toryism, the Liberal candidate had been carried.

Edinburgh, June 21.

I had no forecast then of ever having the honour of being your member; but that intelligence warmed my heart. So we abolished the Irish Church Establishment in 1869. We endeavoured to reform the Irish land laws in 1870; and undoubtedly at that period such was the satisfaction given in Ireland at the moment of these changes, and such were the favourable circumstances of the time, with good harvests and good prices, for an agricultural people, that at that time it was not at all unnatural to cherish the expectation that perhaps the Irish people might become reconciled to the Act of Union as it stood. I cherished that expectation for one; that hope, at least, for one. Well, gentlemen, but after that, and shortly after that, a Parliamentary party began to arise which demanded, not the repeal of the Union, but Home Rule; and you, I think, perfectly understand the difference between the two, the difference between an independent Parliament and a statutory Parliament. The first leader of the party was Mr. Butt. Mr. Butt stated his views with moderation, but Mr. Butt was hardly in a condition to speak for the whole people of Ireland, for I don't believe that on any occasion he was able to bring into the lobby an actual majority, certainly nothing like a decided majority, but I doubt even an actual majority of the Irish members. Mr. Butt died. Mr. Shaw was the next leader of the Home Rule party. Mr. Shaw declared his views in the House of Commons, and said he was sure they would be able to convince the British Parliament that Home Rule was a thing perfectly consistent with loyalty, with the Constitution, with the supremacy of the Crown and of Parliament; and, gentlemen, at that moment, at that hour, when Mr. Shaw sat down, I rose in that debate and expressed the delight and satisfaction with which I had heard his declaration. Mr. Shaw's leadership was short. It was under Mr. Parnell that the Nationalist party was fully organized. But, gentlemen, they were organized as a minority of the Irish members. No minority of the Irish members was authorized to speak for Ireland. It was

The rise of the Irish Parliamentary party.

Edinburgh, June 21.

never, until the last dissolution, that on the one hand an immense majority of the Constitutional representatives of Ireland were marshalled in one band to tell you what Ireland wanted, and, secondly, were prepared to reduce and limit the demands of Ireland within bounds, which I think the Liberal party in general acknowledge to be reasonable and safe.

The present opportunity.

Now that is the reason why it would have been premature, certainly on my part, in any way to have directly associated myself with this movement until the proper time arrived. The proper time did arrive, gentlemen, when, living under representative institutions, we heard the voice of the representatives of the sister country. Is that matter nothing? What would you say if upon some subject vitally touching your interests or your feelings, whether it were Establishment or Disestablishment I do not now inquire—I have nothing to do with the particular opinion for the purposes of the present moment—but if you returned sixty out of your seventy-two members to make with one voice upon a Scottish affair a distinct demand on behalf of Scotland, with respect to which it was clear that the interests of the Empire were not threatened, what would you think of the rejection of that demand? I ask you now, gentlemen, and entreat you not to let slip what I have elsewhere described, and describe again, as this golden opportunity. It is not often in the history of countries, in the vicissitudes of politics—it is not often that such opportunities arrive. Rarely, indeed, in the case of Ireland, have they been known. The first of them that I am aware of was the opportunity that the Treaty of Limerick provided for the establishment of an equality of civil rights, independently of religious distinctions, among the whole population of that island. Ah, gentlemen! had that Treaty of Limerick been executed, the last two hundred years would have told a very different tale; and an indelible blot of disgrace which the judgment of the civilized world had fixed upon England for its treatment of Ireland would never have been found to sully her brilliant and illustrious escutcheon.

Gentlemen, I am sorry to say it was Protestant bigotry and it was national perfidy that trampled under foot the articles of the Treaty of Limerick. A hundred years elapsed. Again in 1795 Lord Fitzwilliam went to Ireland, and found an Irish Parliament ready to redress the grievances of Ireland, ready to emancipate the Roman Catholics of that country by admitting them to Parliament, ready to abolish the monopoly of the suffrage; and Lord Fitzwilliam's whole heart was in these purposes; but an Irish faction poisoned the ear of the English Ministry, who recalled Lord Fitzwilliam. The Irish Parliament actually passed addresses lamenting his recall, and expressing confidence in his purposes. But England, and the Parliament of Great Britain—I wish I could say of England alone—the Parliament of Great Britain ruined the fair hopes that that opportunity brought, and again there came another miserable period. The people, provoked to wrath, became disaffected. Protestants were already disaffected and rebellious, and Roman Catholics irritated joined in similar feelings. Then came the rebellion of 1798 and all the subsequent history which we have so much to regret, and which has brought about our present embarrassments.

Edinburgh, June 21.

Probable result of neglecting it.

Well, now, gentlemen, I do not say that you will have another century; though these opportunities, thus far, have come about at intervals of centuries; the end of the seventeenth century, the close of the eighteenth century, and now again the close of the nineteenth century. No, the case is now very different. You have put such weapons into the hands of Ireland as Ireland will naturally know how to use: the weapons of the constitution, the weapons of freedom, the weapons of representative government, which are the strongest of all weapons. You may, on this occasion, reject her prayer, but you will not thereby have settled the question; you will not even obtain an interval of precarious repose. Do you remember what Mr. Burke said during the American war, when the supporters of that ruinous war said they would be able to put down American resistance? He said the moment

Edinburgh, June 21.

of the attainment of your military success will be the commencement of your political difficulties; and if you do put down armed resistance in America, you will never be able to govern America. Gentlemen, I do not hold out to you the terror of civil war in Ireland. I leave that to the loyal Orangemen who are to line the country with rifles from Belfast to the Boyne. No, gentlemen, it is no such terror as that. If it were, you could put it down. You have force enough, and ten times enough, to put down any such resistance as that. But, gentlemen, you will never be able under the present system, above all, you will never be able after what has happened in the last six months, which have stamped upon our history facts ineffaceable in themselves, and certain in their results—you would never be able, if that prayer be rejected, again to govern Ireland. You would find that disappointment would bring about exasperation; you would find social order more and more impaired, society at large more and more disquieted and disturbed by agrarian outrage; you would find the time of Parliament incessantly occupied by odious battles upon coercion demanded, coercion resisted, coercion defeated, coercion, if ever adopted, yet again withdrawn, and the same miserable round of weakness and disappointment, in the face of all the experiences we have had, continuing to dishonour the history of our country.

The prayer of Ireland.

Gentlemen, to avert all these mischiefs we ask the nation to listen to a prayer that has been reduced within the limits of reason and of safety; we ask you to put an end to these miserable and apparently almost interminable sorrows. We call upon the nation: because it was the nation, and not the great ones of the nation, that in 1868 returned a Parliament to disestablish the Irish Church and to reform the Land Laws; it was the nation, and not the great ones of the nation, that in 1880 returned a Parliament to reverse the fatal foreign policy that had for some years prevailed; it was the nation, and not the great ones of the nation, who were, unfortunately, continually falling away even at that time from the Liberal party, that in 1885 vindicated the title of that party, and returned it with a large majority. And now I ask you to achieve another victory, not merely for the Liberal party, but for objects far higher than those of any party—to achieve a victory for the interests of the Empire, a victory for the interests of civilization, a victory for the best and highest interests of mankind. Edinburgh, June 21.

Mr. Gladstone resumed his seat amid the cheers of the audience, having spoken for an hour and a half.

A few questions having been put and answered, Mr. J. J. Wilson, banker, Penicuik, moved the same resolution which had been passed at the meeting of electors on the 18th June. Mr. Rae, West Calder, seconded, and the motion was carried by acclamation.

The meeting concluded with three cheers for Lady Aberdeen.

X.

SPEECH AT GLASGOW.

TUESDAY, JUNE 22, 1886.

Delivered in Hengler's Circus, Glasgow, to an audience of upwards of 6000 people, including Liberal delegates from all parts of the country.

MR. GLADSTONE'S entrance was the signal for a tremendous demonstration—the vast audience rising to their feet and cheering and waving hats and handkerchiefs. In addition to Mrs. Gladstone and Lady Aberdeen, the Premier was accompanied by Sir Charles Tennant, M.P.; Mr. Gilbert Beith, M.P.; Mr. J. G. C. Hamilton, M.P.; Dr. Cameron, M.P.; Mr. R. Cunningham Graham of Gartmore, now M.P. for the North-West Division of Lanarkshire, and others.

On the motion of Sir Charles Tennant, Mr. Beith was called upon to preside.

Mr. Beith, having taken the chair, in a brief speech introduced Mr. Gladstone, who said:—

Introduction.

Mr. Chairman and Gentlemen,—It would be idle for me to attempt to address this vast assemblage, unless I am favoured in that quarter—(pointing to the high gallery on the right)—as well as in all the rest of the body of the building, with the great privilege of the silence of all those here assembled. It is not want of will, but want of physical strength, that would entirely preclude my entering into a contest with even the smallest minority of the crowds that are here before me.

Glasgow, June 22.

Gentlemen, I have not forgotten that during the election of last November, when we were assembled at a meeting in Edinburgh, there came from Glasgow the news that "We are seven." The results of that announcement have been somewhat curtailed and crippled by subsequent events. But I feel the utmost confidence that, in the coming Election, Glasgow, mindful of her great position, will make true and solid work in the Liberal cause.

I propose to address you to-day upon a portion of the great Irish subject which has not yet been touched by me. I mean those aspects of it which peculiarly touch Scotland, or which have a special interest for Scotland. Before I go to my discourse, I wish to select a proper text, and I am going to take my text from a work, a printed work, of a man. whose name is remembered, and will ever be venerated, in Glasgow,—I mean the work and I mean the name of the famous Dr. Chalmers. A correspondent has reminded me of the sentiments delivered by Dr. Chalmers in a sermon preached in the year 1818, on a question deeply touching Ireland. He took occasion to deliver his sentiments on the subject of the Irish nation, and he spoke, gentlemen, as follows:—"I speak of the great mass of the Irish people, and I do think that I perceive a something in the natural character of Ireland which draws me more attractively to the love of its people"—(laughter caused by the chairman lighting a match to allow Mr. Gladstone to see the document from which he was reading. A small candle was brought in, and the right hon. gentleman proceeded)—"than any other picture of national manners has ever inspired." That is the opinion of Dr. Chalmers on the Irish people; and he goes on to say how you must treat them, how you must persuade them that you wish them well, and what

Dr. Chalmers' testimony as to Irish character.

Glasgow, June 22.

will be the consequence when you have thus persuaded them. And then he says :—"You will find a people whom no penalties could turn, whom no terror of military violence could overcome, who kept on a scowling front of hostility that was not to be softened, while war spread its desolating cruelties over that unhappy land. This very people will do homage to the omnipotence of charity, and when the mighty armour of Christian kindness is brought to bear upon them, it will be found to be irresistible." (A number of candles stuck in bottles borrowed apparently from a neighbouring shop were at this stage placed amid great laughter beside the right hon. gentleman. Mr. Gladstone proceeded)—Now, gentlemen, we have got rid of our little impediment. We shall, I hope, proceed smoothly; and I don't doubt you will agree with me that those words which I have read, and which I trust have reached your ears, are the words not only of Christian benevolence, but likewise of high Christian wisdom. And I ask you to approach this great subject in the spirit which those words are calculated to inspire.

Scottish aspects of Irish question.

Now, gentlemen, the points which I believe to be of special interest to Scotland and Scotchmen in connection with the Irish question are the state of the Protestants of Ulster; the fear of religious persecution in Ireland as the result of a scheme of local self-government; the arguments that have been drawn from union between Scotland and England; and, finally, a subject into which much interest has been inspired, especially by the discussion of the Irish question, namely, the subject which goes by the name of Home Rule for Scotland.

Ulster.

And first, as regards the security of Ulster, I may perhaps be allowed to read to you some words that I used on the introduction of the Irish Government Bill; for I think they contained and set forth in a clear manner the views of the Government with regard to that portion of Ireland. I said—"Various schemes short of refusing the demand of Ireland at large have been proposed on behalf of

Glasgow, June 22.

Ulster. One scheme is that Ulster itself, or perhaps, with more appearance of reason, a portion of Ulster, should be excluded from the operation of the Bill we were about to introduce. Another scheme is, that separate autonomy should be provided for Ulster, or for a portion of Ulster. Another scheme is, that certain rights with regard to certain subjects, such, for example, as education and some other subjects, should be reserved, and should be placed to a certain extent under the control of Provincial Councils. These, I think, are the suggestions which have reached me in different shapes. There may be others. It may be that free discussion, which I have no doubt will largely take place after a Bill such as we propose shall have been laid upon the table of the House, may give to some one of those proposals, or to some other proposal, a practicable form, and that some such plan may be found to be recommended by a general or predominating approval. If it should be so, it will at our hands have the most favourable consideration, with every disposition to do what equity may appear to recommend. That is what I have to say upon the subject of Ulster."

Since that time, some persons have spoken about Ulster, and Lord Hartington complains that I made no further advance about Ulster. Why have I made no further advance? In the first place, Lord Hartington has not assisted me to make any further advance. In the second place, Major Saunderson—a gentleman of some ability, and, I think, of perfect onour and integrity,—Major Saunderson has declared that he, and his Orangemen at his back, will not hear of the separation of Ulster from Ireland. What they modestly demand is that a large majority of Irishmen shall adopt and follow the will of the small minority of Orangemen in Ulster. And lastly, Mr. Parnell has made an argument, which every one who heard it felt was a powerful argument, showing what a misfortune it would be, in his judgment, to Ireland were the intelligent and energetic Protestants of the north to be separated from the south, and how much he

Glasgow, June 22.

covets the assistance of every Irishman in the work of governing his country. I can only say, therefore, that we remain open to consider any and every reasonable proposal, if such can be devised, for the purpose of giving separate satisfaction to the portion of Ulster in which Protestantism greatly prevails.

The Roman Catholic majority and the Protestant minority.

But, gentlemen, not being very hopeful upon that subject —I recollect that two and a half months have now elapsed and no progress has been made—I pass to another question in which many of you as a Presbyterian people have felt, I know, a considerable interest. Is there any reason to suppose that the Roman Catholic majority in Ireland, if it had the power, would be disposed to persecute the Protestant minority? Or, if they were so disposed, would they have the power under the Bill which we have introduced? Now on that subject I wish to address to you a few words. You must be aware that when you address a jealous mind, apprehensive of some particular contingency, it is extremely difficult to give satisfaction. Suppose, gentlemen, I were accused of a deliberate plan to turn my wife and children out of doors, and it was confidently predicted that I was about to do it, I have not the least doubt there is a certain, though I believe a small, portion of my countrymen who would say, "He is up to anything, and it is highly probable that he will do something of the kind." To those gentlemen I should have great difficulty in supplying satisfactory reasons to the contrary, and I do not hope to convince any persons who approach this particular subject in the spirit of such gentlemen. But I ask the reasonable Scottish public—and that means the enormous majority—why we should suspect the Irish Roman Catholics of gross intolerance.

Supposed grounds of fear.

I know of but two grounds that can possibly be urged in support of such a suspicion. One of them is that they are favourable to denominational education. But denominational education, duly guarded, is not persecution. It is persecution if you force your denominational education on the conscience

Glasgow, June 22.

of somebody else who objects to it. But that is prohibited by the Bill that we introduced; and I am bound to observe that not only are the whole Tory party in favour of denominational education to a man, but even many persons who are not Tories are decidedly favourable to it. There is one other ground of charge, and that is that the Roman Catholic Nationalists, to my great regret, in the last Parliament refused to accompany the Government and the great bulk of the Liberal party in allowing Mr. Bradlaugh to take his seat. We supported Mr. Bradlaugh in that behalf upon the broad ground that civil disabilities ought not to be imposed on account of religious opinions. The Nationalists of Ireland, to my regret, voted against us; but with whom did they vote against us? With the whole bulk of the Tory party, with the very men that are now accusing them of the disposition to persecute, and the only evidence of that disposition is that they joined in an act in which the Tories were their leaders. Their leaders, gentlemen, so long as they were in Opposition. As long as that was the case, why, as you know, the whole Christianity of the country was at stake, and would be forfeited if Mr. Bradlaugh was let in; but when they were in office the scene rapidly shifted. Nothing more was heard of the dangers attending the admission of Mr. Bradlaugh, and there Mr. Bradlaugh sits among us in peace and tranquillity.

This fear prevalent in the North, not in the South.

I want to point out to you a very remarkable fact, and it is that, so far as I have been able to observe, these apprehensions of persecution in Ireland have all proceeded from the North of Ireland. But in the North of Ireland the Protestants are strong enough to defend themselves. There are a number of Protestants, scattered throughout the South of Ireland, and, so far as I have observed, and so far as I am informed, those Protestants, who are among their Roman Catholic neighbours one in ten, one in twenty, one in fifty, one in a hundred, have, as a rule, no fear of persecution. While I lament that some of the Presbyterian bodies and ministers in the North have raised this cry, unless I am mistaken, their Presbyterian

Glasgow, June 22.

Argument a fortiori *from religious tolerance in other Roman Catholic countries.*

brethren, ministers in the South, disapprove of this cry, and have no sympathy with it whatever.

Well, gentlemen, surely we may look abroad. Ireland is not the only Roman Catholic country. Belgium is a Roman Catholic country. France is a Roman Catholic country. Italy is a Roman Catholic country. And in which of these countries are Protestants persecuted, I should like to know? Why, in none of them. But look at the difference. These are independent countries, where, if they were so disposed, the Roman Catholic majority might persecute the Protestants, with no one to call them to account. Ireland will not be an independent country. Ireland contentedly submits to statutory restrictions. In that very Bill which was before the late Parliament, what was Ireland forbidden to do? She was forbidden in the fourth clause to pass any law respecting the establishment or endowment of religion, or to prohibit the free exercise thereof. And I believe that a good many people are raising this cry of probable persecution who do not at all object to the establishment and the endowment of their own religion. But the establishment and endowment of the Roman Catholic religion is forbidden to the Roman Catholic majority. They are also forbidden to impose any disability or to confer any privilege on account of religious belief. They are also forbidden to abrogate or derogate from the right to establish or to maintain any place of denominational education or any denominational institution or charity. All these provisions are intended to secure perfect freedom; and how were these restraints received by the Irish Nationalist members? They were received, gentlemen, not only with content, but with enthusiasm. They would not part with these restraints. They are as desirous as we can be on their behalf that they should be saved the painful controversies that exist among ourselves about Establishment and Disestablishment. And what has been their history? They have been a Roman Catholic people all along: whom have they chosen for their leaders? Why, their leaders,

Glasgow, June 22.

gentlemen, the men who have enjoyed their confidence, including the remarkable man who at this moment enjoys their confidence—probably in a higher degree than any of his predecessors—the great bulk of these leaders and the most distinguished among them, from the days of Grattan to the days of Parnell, with the distinguished exception of Mr. O'Connell, have not been Roman Catholics, but have been Protestants. Well, then, gentlemen, I say under those circumstances it is hard, it is unjust, it is irrational to impute intolerance to these men, when, with the slight exception of the act into which the Tories seduced them in the last Parliament, they have been in favour of religious freedom, and to charge that nation with entertaining ideas and plans conclusively refuted by the whole of their conduct during the last century of years. But even if that were not enough—and I think I have almost said enough on this point—even if that were not enough, pray recollect that the Royal veto upon the Acts of the Irish Parliament remains, and that it would be the duty of the Government of this country to advise the exercise of that veto against any law infringing the letter or impairing the spirit of the provisions which I have read to you for giving perfect security to religious freedom. I will not detain you any further upon that subject, because I really feel that these alarms are not only needless, but they are frivolous alarms; and I should not have noticed them so particularly had it not been that I am bound to treat with respect the names of some of those who have felt them, and the apprehensions which are due rather, I think, to the unsettlement of mind always accompanying a great political change, than to any real and reasonable suggestion directly connected with the particular case.

The Scottish Union.

Now I come to a subject that you must feel is very germane to the present Irish question: namely, the subject of the Scottish Union. People have said, "The Scotch are content with their Union, why should not the Irish be content with their Union?" Well, now, gentlemen, I

Glasgow, June 22.

will make some remarks upon that subject. This is a question of history, and one of the observations I make about our opponents is that they have made among themselves a kind of threefold self-denying ordinance. The first point of this ordinance is never to have any regard to history at all. The second is never to pay attention to any experience derivable from foreign countries. And the third point is never to derive any lesson from our own experience in our own colonies throughout the British Empire. But on a particular day, gentlemen, a man of great ability in his profession, Mr. Finlay, did depart from this self-denying ordinance, and did make an historical treatment of the question of the Scottish Union; and he actually proved, gentlemen,—no man who heard his speech could deny it,—that he had undertaken the gigantic labour, with the view of illustrating this question, of making himself perfect master of Sir Walter Scott's *Tales of a Grandfather*, and that he was as well qualified to pass an examination in that book as Mr. Hugh Littlejohn himself could have been. Well, gentlemen, some things Mr. Finlay said were perfectly true, some, I think, very questionable, and some totally irrelevant. He said that as the Irish Union was obtained by bribery so the Scottish Union was obtained by bribery, but that the Scotch sold themselves cheaper. It is a known fact that the English Government expended a sum, the very lowest statement of which is a million and a half, in corrupting the Irish Parliament; but because it appears that between £12,000 and £20,000 were paid at that period to certain Scotchmen, we are told that these gentlemen sold Scotland, and that while the value of Ireland was a million and a half or two millions, Scotland in the open market only fetched twelve or twenty thousand pounds. Sir Walter Scott gives countenance to this idea of bribery, and from Sir Walter Scott the notion was derived; but you know the work of your last historian, Mr. Burton, a work of great research and learning, a work of a professed historian, whose business it was to deliver

Glasgow, June 22.

judicial sentences; and Mr. Burton deliberately, and in arguments, holds that that charge of bribery, which the very figures go far to confute,—that charge of bribery, as having been the cause of the passing of the Union, cannot be maintained, and has not been proved.

Scottish and Irish Union contrasted.

But, gentlemen, it is true that the Union was unpopular in Scotland, and it is true that it remained unpopular for a certain time, I think till shortly after the rebellion of 1745. The reason was this. There is no doubt that it was unpopular at the time when it was passed, and it served the purpose of the Jacobites and Episcopalians, who were divided from the rest of the country, to maintain and keep alive that unpopularity. They worked it in favour of their own cause, just as the Tories worked Mr. Bradlaugh in favour of their own cause. But the case of Scotland was totally different in all the most essential respects from the case of Ireland. In the first place, it was the particular conditions of the Union on which the Scotch were dissatisfied, for in 1689, on the invitation of King William III., the Scottish Parliament had passed an Act to appoint a Commission to consider and to settle the terms of the Union with England. After that there arose great exasperation, and the two countries nearly went to war. The English Government was actually arming the English Border. The failure of the Darien Company produced the utmost national estrangement. The Scottish Parliament passed an Act under which the succession to the Crown might have run differently in Scotland from the course which it was to take in England. Well, gentlemen, it was in these circumstances, not on the principle of Union, but on the particulars of the Union, and in connection with the quarrels of the moment, that there was great dissatisfaction in Scotland. But this was the fundamental difference of all: Scotland had always been able, with the rarest exceptions, to hold her own. Scotland met England on a footing of equality. Scotland was governed on the footing of national and political equality; and if she was not so rich and not so

Glasgow, June 22.

populous, that makes it redound the more to her honour that she was on a footing of equality. Scotland had an Executive Government of her own; Ireland was subject to the English Executive Government, and through that Executive Government to England. The foulest and the most monstrous corruption, joined with the grossest intimidation, was exercised to defile the minds and to purchase the votes of a miserably constituted Parliament,—a Parliament of 300, in which there were 116 placemen, and in which a large number of the remaining members were returned by nomination burghs. Gentlemen, the Scottish Parliament and the Scottish anti-Unionists were, according to Mr. Burton, betrayed by their own friends, and especially by the Duke of Hamilton, who was their leader. But all these questions are secondary. The real point to observe is this, that the Union with the lapse of time commended itself, in Scotland, to the mind and heart of the people at large, and the people at large became contented with that Union. Scotland was divided, and always had a strong party of Unionists; but in Ireland the entire nation was against the Union. Protestants and Roman Catholics—it is hardly possible to find the name of a man of high character—they may be counted upon your fingers the men of character and station who were not opponents to the Irish Union; and, as that Union has lasted longer and longer, the mind of the Irish country instead of becoming reconciled to it, as was the case in Scotland, has become more and more estranged from it. True it is, and I am thankful for it, that they have seen how difficult and perilous might be this repeal, and they proposed to us a plan which, while it meets their reasonable wishes, entirely avoids the dangers of that repeal; but to the Union itself, for every year for which it has lasted, they have become more and more irreconcilably opposed; and therein their course is diametrically opposed to that which has been taken by the people of Scotland. You cannot take from the satisfaction of Scotland with its Union, which it has adopted and made its

Glasgow, June 22.

own—you cannot from that draw an argument to show that the Irish ought to be equally satisfied with their Union, which was born in disgrace and dishonour, and which, having violated all their national traditions and recollections, has utterly failed to meet their political and their social wants.

The Scottish Union has on the whole been beneficial to Scotland.

Now, gentlemen, one thing more perhaps I ought to say of the Union. I have said that Scotland was satisfied with her Union after a time, and I think as an historical fact that is undeniable. I assume, for it is the almost universal belief, that its advantages have greatly outweighed its disadvantages; and that may be a rational, and is probably the proper conclusion. I confess I think this not altogether a subject on which the whole weight is on one side of the argument. I view with some regret the almost total displacement, not of the Scottish nobility and the great families since the Union—for they have held their ground—but the almost entire displacement of the old Scottish gentry. The land of Scotland, as far as the gentry are concerned, apart from the very great families, has nearly all of it changed hands, and I am afraid that much of that was due to the temptation which the Union offered to the Scottish gentry to enter into competition—social competition—with their wealthier brethren in the south. Well, gentlemen, in your magnificent capital of Edinburgh I confess myself to be weak enough to have a lingering regret, when I see the gradual disappearance of one and another family of high rank from the practice of residing in Edinburgh; that the attractions of London govern everything; that one nobleman only, I believe, at this moment has a house and mansion in Edinburgh, and I am credibly informed that that mansion is for sale. I am not going to dwell upon these points, for I don't doubt that your judgment has been right, and that upon the whole you have greatly prospered under, and prospered in a large degree from the Union; but I wish to put this to you, that if you should change your minds, if in the course of time you should arrive at the conclusion that there

Glasgow, June 22.

might be a better system—that you might with advantage manage your own local affairs within your own borders —well, gentlemen, do you think, if you had arrived at a clear conclusion to that effect, and if out of your seventy-two members sixty were united as one man to demand that change in your name—do you think that England would either dare or wish to refuse you? No, gentlemen, she would not dare it, but she would not wish to dare it. She would wish your wishes to prevail, and prevail they would.

National Radical Union.

Well, then, that brings me to another proposition that has been made,—in my opinion one of the most foolish propositions ever imported into a great subject. I must read you three lines. There has been lately founded—perhaps you have not heard of it, it is new—but three or four days ago a meeting was held in Birmingham to found a National Radical Union, and the basis of this great institution is, "that it is desirable to establish an organization to be called the National Radical Union, for the purpose of promoting a system of local government applicable to England, Scotland, and Ireland"—poor Wales is left out, but for my part I will put in a word for Wales—" and under the supreme authority of one Parliament of the United Kingdom." Well, these are very good words; these last are very good words; and everything we are now doing is under the supreme authority of the Parliament of the United Kingdom. And now, gentlemen, is this or is this not a wise proposition? Well, just consider the enormous difference between the Irish and the Scottish questions. What is the Scottish question? Look at it. If I had my friend Professor Blackie at my elbow, and on every social ground I wish that I had, he would admit that the question of Home Rule in Scotland, even as viewed by him, is a question of making an improvement in a country already happy and well governed. Is that the case of Ireland? Are we dealing with a country well governed? We are dealing with a country in which the

Glasgow, June 22.

Tories, on the 26th of January, told us that they found it their duty immediately to propose coercive measures, and in which Lord Salisbury has since pointed out to us that such measures ought to last for twenty years, and that then Ireland might perhaps be fit to see them remitted. But the whole difference lies between a question of political improvement and a question of ministering to the immediate necessities of social order; and the characteristic feature of these questions of social order is that you cannot delay your dealing with them. Under these circumstances it is quietly proposed by the National Radical Union that we should leave social order in Ireland to take care of itself, while we set to work, assembled round the Parliamentary table, to examine the conditions of Scotland, to examine the conditions of England, to examine the conditions of Wales, to examine the conditions of Ireland, to bring the whole of these into comparison, weld them into one mass, and have one measure for them all. How long is that process to take, and what is to become in the meantime of the moonlighter and the agrarian assassin, and what is to be done to restore confidence to Ireland, to give strength to its social system, or tolerable contentment and satisfaction to its people? A more absurd proposition, as applicable to the present state of things, and the crisis now demanding our attention, never proceeded from the mouths of rational men. You know perfectly well,—I think it was in this part of the assembly—(indicating a particular quarter)—that I heard warm cheers when I spoke of the hope that Scotland might manage her own affairs,—but those gentlemen who cheer me know as well as I do that the question is not ripe. It has not been discussed. It is new to Scotland—to a great part of Scotland. It has received no thorough examination; and the wisdom of statesmen and of Parliaments is to refuse to discuss any question until it is ripe, and when it is ripe then to refuse to delay the discussion. But this National Radical Association exactly inverts that law. It wants to force us

Glasgow, June 22.

to discuss and to settle the question for Scotland, and the question for England, and I hope for Wales, which are not ripe; and it wants us to refuse to discuss and to settle the question of Ireland, which, God knows, is ripe, and over-ripe, until you have settled these other questions, to which you cannot, as practical men, as yet attempt to address yourselves. Now, gentlemen, do not be afraid; you have got a little mouthful of Home Rule; you have got the Scottish Office in London. The Scottish Office is not a matter of very primary importance. But why was it founded? Do you suppose it was founded because all the gentlemen in England were satisfied that it was necessary and desirable to found it? Nothing of the sort. It was founded because Scotland wished it; and the wish of Scotland—compatible always with the safety of the Empire, and compatible with those paramount considerations to which we have given the fullest weight in the Irish Bill—the wish of Scotland, within those limits, will, I venture to predict, without the least fear of being disappointed by the result, always govern the Parliamentary destiny of Scotland.

Home Rule in Scotland.

A general and uniform application of Home Rule a false principle.

But, gentlemen, I go further. I say this principle of cast-iron uniformity for England, Scotland, Ireland, and Wales—that they are all to have institutions cast in the same mould, and corresponding in every particular—is a bad, a false, and a vulgar principle. It has never been the principle upon which this country has been governed. The principle of this country has been largely varied and diversified. Even at this moment in the county of Kent there is a different law of succession to landed property from that which prevails in the generality of England. And you know how different your laws in Scotland are from the English laws. When we sent our colonists to America, gentlemen, the thirteen States, whose revolt against us we can now look back upon with delight, because we say, "These were the children of our loins, and see what manhood they exhibited in the day of difficulty"—these thirteen States and their

Glasgow, June 22.

inhabitants did not spring from this bastard and emasculated notion of uniformity. Why, there were hardly two of those States that had the same constitution. In some of them there were two legislative chambers; in some of them there was one. In one of them the Governor was not appointed by the Crown. In one or two of them the Acts of the Assembly were not ratified by the Crown. It was out of all that variety, gentlemen, that substantial harmony sprang. And so it is that, if you want to provide well for the settlement of this great question of the subject of local government in any part of the country, you must have regard to the special wants of that part of the country, and the special history and traditions of that part of the country, and the special wishes of that part of the country. So much for the question of Home Rule in Scotland.

The main issue: Ireland's claim to free self-government.

Let me call your attention now before I close, which I am about to do soon, to this, What is the main question? The main question is, whether Ireland is to have a free government, or whether Ireland is to be overridden by England and Scotland, whether she is to be made an exception in this great Empire — an Empire of many States; an Empire comprising one-fifth of the human race; an Empire on which, as has been truly said, the sun never sets; an Empire in which separate political societies and constitutions are to be counted by the score, and of which there is not one, sprung from the same source as ourselves, that does not enjoy a free government. But what, gentlemen, is meant by a free government? That is a question that does not seem to be understood by all persons. Will you allow me to read three or four words from one whom I am never wearied of quoting on this subject, whose works it seems not to consist with the views of our opponents to consult. I mean the great Edmund Burke, whom your own countryman, Sir James Mackintosh, in his later years declared to be the greatest among the masters of civil wisdom. What said Mr. Burke about free

Glasgow, June 22.

government in one of his invaluable compositions on the subject of America, when he was in the same position, in the face of a majority, as we are now,—in the face, I mean, of that majority of thirty, but I hope and trust not in the face of a majority of the nation? Mr. Burke said this—"The disposition of America is wholly averse to any other than a free government. If any ask me what a free government is"—Now, mark the reply. Mr. Burke was no revolutionist; I doubt whether he would have been admitted into this National Association that I have been talking about, because they would have said to him—"You cannot come in. You are not a Radical." But Mr. Burke, who was not a Radical, but boasted of the name of Whig according to the fashion of the Whigs of those days, Mr. Burke said, "If you ask me what a free government is, I answer that for any practical purpose it is what the people think so, and that they, not I, are the natural, lawful, and competent judges of this matter." That, gentlemen, was the opinion of Mr. Burke. He did not, if you observe, there interpose—for he was writing to the Sheriffs of Bristol: he was not framing a detailed plan—therefore he did not interpose the condition which we have always carefully interposed, namely, that the local freedom of every portion of the Empire must be subject to the general laws which bind together the whole. Gentlemen, that is the principle which Ireland, through the mouth of her representatives, has freely and cheerfully admitted. You know that such was their confidence in the Imperial Parliament that they were willing that all Imperial concerns should be settled without their direct authoritative intervention. You know that it is not their movement, but rather your movement on their behalf, which has caused the modifications in our Bill, not to be introduced—for introduced they could not be until the Committee on the Bills—but to be promised by the Government. You know that we have engaged that no tax shall be passed by the Imperial Parliament, so far as we are concerned, without giving an opportunity, if it affects the Irish people,

Glasgow, June 22.

without giving an opportunity to Ireland to be heard and to vote upon that tax. You know likewise that at the meeting held at the Foreign Office, of which much was said at the time, the Government took an engagement to introduce into the Bill an important provision, which would require the reconstruction or abandonment—one of the two—of the 24th clause of the Bill, and which would recognize the continuing claim of Ireland to be heard, and to take part through her representatives in the discussion of Imperial affairs. I say that must be done so as not to interfere with the freedom of the Irish Legislature, nor with the dignity, and order, and independence of the English one, but under those conditions the Government would undertake to satisfy that desire. Let no man, therefore, say that there is danger on that score. And then I call you back—having reminded you of the manner in which Imperial obligations are recognized—I call you back to the definition of Mr. Burke, and I ask you to give to Ireland, when you have disposed of this question of Imperial obligation, that which you have asked for yourselves. She does not demand an innovation; she does not require you to call up from the deep something that never appeared on earth before. She had a Parliament of her own till the year 1800. We took it from her by fraud and by force,—by a mixture of fraud and force as disgraceful, gentlemen, as has ever been recorded in history. She abates her claim for the restoration of that Parliament, in order that she may show her fidelity to Imperial obligation; but she says, subject to Imperial obligation, allow us in God's name, as you have failed in the management, to see what we can do for ourselves in the conduct of our own affairs.

Scotland's position towards Ireland as distinct from England's.

The remaining word which I have to speak to you I speak to you as Scotchmen. I have told you that I would speak on this subject to-day especially in the aspects interesting to Scotchmen; and there are some consolatory topics which Scotchmen can appropriate to themselves in which England has no share. Scotland had no relations with Ireland before

Glasgow, June 22.

the Union in 1707, and is totally free from responsibility for those terrific confiscations of the land which have had so much to do with the present difficulty. Since 1707 Scotland has nominally shared the responsibility of England, but I make bold to say that from 1707 to 1832 the responsibility of Scotland was only nominal. What share, gentlemen, had you, the vast community of Glasgow, in the government of this Empire before the Reform Bill of Lord Grey? You had none whatever. What was the case of Edinburgh, and of in general all the burghs in Scotland,—and the counties were no better? The case was, that the member for Parliament was elected by the municipality, and the municipality was elected by itself. See, gentlemen, what are the blessings of free government which we ask you and entreat you to give to Ireland. Was the Scotland of the last century and of the early part of this century the same as the Scotland of to-day? No, she was not. Having no voice and no vent for her feelings in political affairs, nothing remained to her but force. She is not to-day the Scotland of the Porteous mob. She is not to-day the Scotland of those times in Edinburgh, when the people of that city, having no suffrage, no function to perform, no recognized political existence, brooded over their wrongs as well as they could, until some famine or some special exigency made these for the time intolerable, and then matters usually took the form of a project for laying hold of the Lord Provost and casting him over the North Bridge.

Salutary effect of political responsibility.

That, gentlemen, was the only remaining resource. You have got rid of these things now, but why do I refer to them? why do I point out to you that, when the suffrage was new in Scotland, the very first of your elections were in several cases dishonoured by outbursts of popular violence, such as now most of those who hear me have in their whole lifetime never witnessed? Why was it that politics, coming to them as a novelty, brought the temptations of novelty; that political freedom, coming to them as a cure, has brought that cure, and has made of Scotland one of the most loyal and one of the most law-abiding, as well as one of the most liberty-loving countries on the face of the globe? Rely upon it, gentlemen, that the same salutary effects will be produced in Ireland through bringing into operation the same wholesome and healthful causes.

Glasgow, June 22.

Appeal to the people of Scotland.

But what I wish to point out to you is this: You, the people of Scotland, had from 1800 to 1832 virtually no responsibility, no share in that miserable record of transactions with Ireland which have disgraced England and Great Britain in the eyes of the civilized world. It is not so now. Since 1832 there has been, I think, but one election in which the people of Scotland were solicited to give their votes mainly with respect to Ireland, and that was the election of 1868. An appeal was made to them. They answered that appeal. They voted in favour of political justice and freedom, and they contributed their fair and full share of that majority which disestablished the Irish Church, perhaps the most unfortunate and the most perverse system that ever was introduced into the machinery of civilized and organized life. That was in 1868; but, gentlemen, you are now even more fully an enfranchised people. You have now made upon you an even greater call. Thirteen reformed Parliaments there have been. They measure the years of your political life. To every one of these reformed Parliaments you have sent a majority of reformers. What will you do now? Will you do the like again? Or will you in Glasgow and elsewhere have a Parliament made of Tories, or made of gentlemen who, without meaning to be Tories, and without calling themselves Tories, nevertheless speak with Tories, act with Tories, and vote with Tories? If you will have that Parliament, yours be the responsibility and not mine. I have done, gentlemen, what I could to open the case and to lay it before you. I have the utmost confidence in the decision at which you will arrive. As yet you are virtually free from all the sad responsibility connected with the former history of relations between Great Britain and Ireland. I beseech you to

Glasgow, June 22.

claim no share in that miserable and dishonourable inheritance. Do not associate yourselves with it. Do not touch it in any of its parts. Recoil from it, and fly from it, and seek for something else, and give your voice and your suffrage in favour of the work of peace and justice.

After Mr. Gladstone had resumed his seat, Mr. Thomas Wilson proposed a vote of thanks to the right hon. gentleman for his address, which was seconded by Mr. Thomas Glen Coats, and unanimously adopted.

A resolution approving of the Irish policy of the Government, proposed by the Rev. George Gladstone, Glasgow, seconded by Mr. John Battersby, was also carried amid great enthusiasm.

Mr. Gladstone acknowledged both resolutions, and the meeting separated.

XI.

SPEECH AT MANCHESTER.

FRIDAY, JUNE 25, 1886.

Delivered in the Free Trade Hall, Manchester, before an immense audience.

MR. GLADSTONE'S appearance was the signal for a unanimous and enthusiastic outburst of cheering from the vast assemblage, and it was some time before quiet was restored. Mr. Thomas Ashton, president of the Manchester Liberal Union, took the chair, and amongst those on the platform, in addition to Mr. and Mrs. Gladstone, were Sir Henry Roscoe, M.P., Sir U. Kay-Shuttleworth, M.P., Mr. J. T. Hibbert, M.P., Mr. William Agnew, M.P., Mr. B. Armitage, M.P., Mr. T. B. Potter, M.P., Mr. W. Mather, M.P., Sir Horace Davey, Mr. Isaac Hoyle, M.P., Mr. Robert Leake, M.P., Mr. R. Peacock, M.P., Mr. Abel Buckley, M.P., Mr. E. Crossley, M.P., Mr. T. G. Ashton, M.P., Mr. J. T. Brunner, M.P., Mr. Caleb Wright, M.P., Mr. T. P. O'Connor, M.P., Dr. Pilkington, M.P., Colonel Schwabe, M.P., Mr. George Newnes, M.P., Mr. C. E. Schwann, Mr. Henry Lee, Mr. and Mrs. Jacob Bright, Mr. W. H. Gladstone, Rev. Mr. Drew, Mrs. Drew, Mr. Arthur Arnold.

The chairman, in a short speech, introduced Mr. Gladstone to the meeting, after which the right hon. gentleman, rising, spoke as follows :—

Mr. Chairman, Ladies, and Gentlemen,—I have come from the railway station to this hall in a great triumphal procession, *Introduction.*

Manchester, June 25.

which, if we may judge by an external sign, appears to indicate pretty clearly the sense of the inhabitants of Manchester on this occasion. It was distinguished, let me add, by that magnificent order which I have always observed to be a peculiar characteristic, even in this orderly country, of the city in which I have the honour to speak. It tempts me to compare the House of Commons, where I have lately been an actor, with the people among whom I now find myself. I deplore, gentlemen, as I need not tell you, the recent action of the House of Commons, which has given you—I might say given me—a good deal of trouble. But though I deplore, I do not complain. For in surveying what has passed I must take into view many extenuating circumstances. Irish questions, unfortunately, have been too much associated with doubt and with controversy to make it easy at once to extricate them from that fatal association. It is only fair to admit that it takes some time for many persons fully to embrace all the aspects of a question so large as this. There has been a great deal of unnecessary and pretended difficulty, but there has been a great deal of true and honest difficulty. Above all, I do not complain of the House of Commons on this account, that at any rate it mustered 313 men to vote in favour of a proposition such that their support of it, if there could have been a doubt, renders the success of that proposition in its substance and its main outlines absolutely certain. Still there is something satisfactory in a question of this kind in getting into free contact with the people of this country. Somehow there appears to be an instinctive sense of what is just and true, when it is presented in very broad aspects and outlines, that enables the nation to outstrip the few in the rapidity as well as in the justice of its perceptions.

Mr. Bright.

Gentlemen, I do not disguise from you our position. We have suffered heavy losses. Of all the losses we have suffered there is none, I think, that causes me such acute pain as the loss of Mr. Bright. Mr. Bright, although his conscience has unfortunately led him, for the first time in his life, to place

Manchester June 25.

himself in opposition to what I think is the sentiment of the nation, yet has shown no eagerness to be in the first rank of the battle. He has shown that tenderness of feeling towards old friends and associates that I should have expected from a man of his stamp. Of course our opponents would not let him alone. He was too valuable for that; but he has avoided speaking, and even in the writing of letters he has been very sparing. I wish he could have kept off that ground altogether. He has felt himself obliged to deliver a strong testimonial of honesty and wisdom on behalf of Mr. Caine, the candidate at Barrow, who, I feel bound to say, in professing to give an account of what he calls a solemn declaration of mine, has deplorably misrepresented it. And Mr. Bright has likewise said a party cannot be expected to follow the sudden changes of its leader; but Mr. Bright knows as well as any man that since the time, fifteen years ago, when Home Rule came up above the surface, and long before it was at the front, I never once on any occasion have in principle condemned it. I have required to know its meaning; I have required to see that it was asked and sought for by the bulk of the Irish nation; but never in its principle has it been condemned by me. Mr. Bright also ought to know, and you know, that in the last election I told my constituents in a published speech, and through them, as well as I could, I told the country, that in all likelihood the new Parliament would have to face a great Irish question, which went down to the very root and foundation of our civil and political constitution. But though I make these remarks, you will hear from me no criticism upon Mr. Bright. One resolution I have taken to myself, I will never be his critic. I will never utter one word of disparagement in reference to a man whose integrity I revere, whose characteristics I love, and who has conferred upon his country inestimable services which cannot be cancelled and cannot be forgotten.

The seceding Liberals in the House of Commons.

We have lost, among what may be called the upper ten thousand of our party, a good many friends. But happily it is a party that depends less than some other parties

Manchester, June 25.

on its upper ten thousand. I must, however, make a remark upon those who have left us in the House of Commons particularly, much as I respect the general body of that section of seceders. They claim to be the Liberal party, and they say that we are the seceders. Well, I happen to recollect the fraction that they formed of the party in the House of Commons, and I remember it, because they formed just the same fraction in the House of Commons as in the constituency of Midlothian those did who supported my last opponent. They were about two out of seven. It is very disagreeable to have such a defection; but still I look upon the five as constituting the party rather than the two. When we go out of doors, how does the case stand? It is not one in three, nor one in ten or twenty among Liberals, nor one in fifty, who assumes the name and acts the part of a seceder; and when these gentlemen claim to be the Liberal party, it reminds me a little of the old legal story of the juryman who dissented from the verdict that the rest of the jury were disposed to give, and who complained that he had never in his whole life met with eleven such obstinate fellows as the men on that jury, whom, although all reason was on his side, he had found it impossible to convince. Gentlemen, the Liberal seceders were ninety-three in that great division. I ask you how many they will be after the election. (A voice: "Three.") It is dangerous to prophesy; and I am bound to say many of them, some of them certainly, will be glad to rejoin our ranks, because they voted against us from doubt whether they had sufficient authority from their constituents to vote in our favour. But with regard to those who are determined paper Unionists, I have very great doubt indeed whether mishap will not befall a good many of them. I remember a case which I may compare with theirs, except as to the wisdom and rectitude of the course taken. In 1846, when Sir Robert Peel proposed the repeal of the Corn Laws, 109 of the Conservative party voted with him,—voted right, as we think, and as nobody now dare deny. Dissolution came in 1847, and that body of 109 was cut down to about 40. They got crushed between the masses of the two opposing parties; and if they got so crushed when they were obviously right, I am very doubtful whether those who have been, we think, as obviously wrong will come better out of the next election.

Manchester, June 25.

Now, gentlemen, this I must say, as I constantly see myself reproached with having lost the assistance of many valued members of old Liberal Cabinets—this I must say, that, though we have had heavy losses, yet such have been the resources of the party with which I have the honour to be connected that I feel I have no reason at all to be ashamed of the present Cabinet and the present Government. I have never known a Government—and I have naturally watched the working of the several departments in the House of Commons—I have never known a Government which was, I will say, better manned for conducting the business of the country. But I will quit the House of Commons and go to the House of Lords, where a body of able Ministers fill many important departments, with every one of whom I think it an honour to be associated; and among them in this rash, wild enterprise of ours whom do I find? I find Lord Granville, a man who has sat as many years in Cabinets as pretty nearly the whole of the Tories put together, a man who is known to represent, perhaps better than any other, a Liberalism which is genuine and thorough, and which is not ostentatious, and which is not rash. I find Lord Spencer, a man who, during nearly nine years of the most critical part of the history of Ireland, has administered with unquestioned courage the affairs of that country, who knows more of that country, has had a more living experience of it, than all of our opponents put together; and who, as he is among the most valuable, so he is among the most determined supporters of the Government policy. I will name one more—a man of whom you will hear even more than you have yet heard; and I pass to the youngest member of

Members of the present Government.

Lord Granville.

Lord Spencer.

Manchester, June 25.

Lord Rosebery.

the Cabinet, Lord Rosebery, of whom I will say to the Liberal party of this country, and I say it not without reflection, for if I said it lightly I should be doing injustice not less to him than to them—of whom I say to the Liberal party of this country that in him they see the man of the future. While that is so, I say to you what I said in the House of Commons on introducing this Bill, that my main reliance is on the nation, and all the signs which crowd in upon me from day to day tend more and more to convince me that we shall not rely upon it in vain.

Gentlemen, there are two points of a practical character which are made to do good service by our opponents. One is with regard to the representation of Ireland in Parliament, on which I will say one very brief word. It appeared to me to be a great act of self-denial on the part of the Irish members that they should show such a confidence in the working of the British Parliament as to be content to leave the whole of their Imperial interests in our hands. But undoubtedly a very strong desire has been shown in England and Scotland that Ireland should not be severed from the transaction of Imperial concerns; and I wish to remind you that we have undertaken two things. We have, indeed, already in the Bill provided for a certain contingency; but, besides that, we have undertaken that the fiscal interests of Ireland shall not be affected without giving her members an opportunity of being heard; and we have also undertaken to propose a plan for recognizing permanently the concern of Ireland in the transaction of Imperial as distinct from Irish business. That is the first point; and the second point is the question of Land Purchase, upon which I would request you to give me an attention as close and as tranquil as, in the extreme crowding of this vast assembly, it may be possible for you to afford.

Irish Members at Westminster.

The Land Purchase Bill.

With regard to this subject of Land Purchase, some persons have spoken as if it were some novel fancy of Her Majesty's Government. They appear to forget that there is in Ireland at this moment in operation, at the expense of the British taxpayer, who does not seem to be aware of it, a system of Land Purchase, under which land may be transferred upon his responsibility, under a system which I consider dangerous, and which undoubtedly I never will engage not to make some effort to amend. Now, I should like you to know what views have been taken upon this subject. I hold in my hand an extract from an article published only in February last in the *Fortnightly Review.* This article says: "The materials exist for a great transaction which, without inordinate risk to the Imperial taxpayer, would place the Irish people in full possession of the land of their birth on terms involving a real and considerable relief from present burdens." The article then goes on to speak with criticism, but upon the whole with commendation, of a gigantic plan that had been propounded by a great statistical authority, Mr. Giffen, involving the issue of 160 millions of consols. It proceeds: "In any case, the fact remains that our grants are made to Ireland annually to a very large extent, and represent a capital sum which affords the basis for an immense operation in the way of Land Purchase and of the municipalization of the land of Ireland by its transfer to local authorities. Such an offer to the whole of the 600,000 cultivating tenants of Ireland would be entitled to very serious consideration, and would not be lightly rejected." Gentlemen, by the side of this magnificent scheme the plan of the Government in regard to Land Purchase dwindles into utter insignificance. And yet it is commonly said that even this magnificent scheme, declared to deserve attention, and spoken of in general terms of praise in this article, had the countenance, as the author of the article had the countenance, of Mr. Chamberlain. Of course I cannot tell you; the article is signed "A Radical," but I am told Mr. Chamberlain owned to it at the time. It would be interesting to know whether he owns to it now. He has been of all others the severest critic of the plans of the Government. Now I will tell you what I propose to him on this subject of

Manchester, June 25.

Manchester, June 25.

Land Purchase. I propose to him that he should produce to the country the plan he himself prepared in February last, and which was printed on my proposal, made in the regular course and in accordance, as I was careful to ascertain, with his wish, for the consideration of the Government. I think that is a fair demand to make; and I think I can venture to assure you that, if you have the opportunity of becoming acquainted with that plan, which was not a mere suggestion, but a plan formally drawn out, you will think that it stands in curious contrast with the latest views of Mr. Chamberlain on Land Purchase. But let that matter pass for the moment. I speak now of the Land Purchase Bill. There cannot be a doubt that the Land Purchase Bill has been ill received by the country. That I admit. It has been ill received by those who were supposed to be likely to receive it well; by Lord Hartington, who said it was a Bill which nobody seemed to approve, and even by Mr. Goschen. Mr. Goschen, finding, I imagine, that he is totally out of sympathy with the country upon every possible point of politics except this, lays his hand on the Land Purchase Bill and tears it in pieces in order to find one point of contact at least with the feelings of the country. However, I admit the fact, and I remind you of what is really the position of the Land Purchase Bill. The Land Purchase Bill ought to be considered as if it were so many clauses of the Irish Government Bill. It is not the end of the scheme. It is part of the machinery of the scheme. I stated in introducing it that I would have introduced it as part of the Government of Ireland Bill, had it not been for the vastness of the entire subject. Being substantially part of the clauses of the Government Bill, of course it is liable in the first place to disapproval by all those friends of Home Rule in Ireland who do not like the clauses of the Bill; and in the second place, it is open to review, and even to reconstruction, if better methods can be produced; or, if it can be shown that there is no call in honour or duty or policy for persevering in such a plan, it is open to reconstruction or even rejection by the people. It will be our duty to review and reconsider it upon the principles that we have already laid down.

Manchester, June 25.

Reconstructing the Irish Government Bill.

You have been told, I must say with considerable audacity, that I stated in the House of Commons with iteration that I would never, never reconstruct the Irish Government Bill. It is an absolute fiction. I stated I had never promised to reconstruct it. People say, or some people say, that is a refined distinction. A very refined distinction indeed! You may intend to give £100 to an object, and yet may totally deny that you have ever promised to give it. But why was I bound to deny, and with vehemence, that I had given such a promise? Because a statesman, a Minister, is guilty of the highest offence against his country in promising anything, even small, much more anything great, before he is completely satisfied that he can redeem that promise. Plans of Irish government do not spring up like mushrooms in an evening. They require great thought and the deliberation of months, and perhaps more than months; and it would have been wicked on my part had I allowed it for a moment to be supposed that I had entered into an engagement as to the fulfilment of which I was totally uncertain. It is our duty to review the whole of the plan we have put forward. But to the principle itself, of an effective government in Ireland, to be secured by giving Irishmen the control of Irish affairs, we are immovably attached. With regard to the means, we are perfectly free, after the vote of the House of Commons. I am not ashamed at all of the disposition of the engagement we have taken, which is simply an engagement to consider suggestions and to devise any improvements we can.

Lord Hartington's recent proposal.

I will not trouble you any more upon the details of the Bill, but I will refer to an important proposal that has lately been made by Lord Hartington. I see that it is not intended by the Liberals of Rossendale to oppose the return of Lord Hartington—(A voice, "Renegade")—No, I do not use any

Manchester, June 25.

such expression—although they may feel they are making a great sacrifice; and Lord Hartington will have to pay a severe penalty, if he, being, as he is, a man of the highest honour and a most conscientious Liberal, for the first time has to sit in Parliament for the purpose of contravening the wishes of the great bulk of his Liberal constituents and of giving effect to the wishes of the Tories. But there is one great advantage to the Government in Lord Hartington's return to Parliament, and it is this, that we have in him a perfectly open and straightforward adversary, who knows what he means, who says what he means, and who will do what he says he will do. Next to a friend, it is better to have an adversary such as that. But, gentlemen, he is an adversary. Do not conceal that from yourselves. I see that he has stated last night that if a Bill were introduced of a totally different character from that which has lately been before Parliament, he might be found haply to support it. But I am grateful to Lord Hartington for not so much as breathing a whisper of expectation that I should be a party to bringing in such a Bill. Lord Hartington has published in his election address the conditions which he thinks necessary to be observed in legislating for Ireland; and, moreover, he has said that, in his opinion, they might form the basis of a measure. His conditions are these. First, if I understand it right, that the Irish representation in Parliament shall remain just as it now is. Now, gentlemen, I will not be a party to giving to Ireland a legislative body to manage Irish concerns, and at the same time to having Irish members in London acting and voting on English and Scotch concerns. The second of Lord Hartington's conditions is that the powers shall be delegated, but not surrendered. With that I have no quarrel. It is the exact thing that we are doing. We are constituting certain powers by Act of Parliament, and all powers so constituted are powers delegated, and not surrendered. Thirdly, Lord Hartington says you ought not to give them power over Irish affairs, but to give them

His four conditions.

power over certain Irish affairs. Again I am obliged to part company with Lord Hartington. We have never introduced that degrading distinction in dealing with the smallest of our colonies, as far as I am aware. We certainly have not introduced it in the case of Canada, as to which I have lately consulted the Act, and I will not put upon Ireland a disability which I have thought would be dishonouring to the Colonial subjects of the Queen. Lastly, the fourth of Lord Hartington's conditions is that we must retain in our own hands the administration of justice. **Manchester, June 25.**

Administration of justice in Ireland.

Now, of all subjects, the administration of justice is that which excites the sorest memories in the minds and hearts of the Irish people, and, I am sorry to say, with too much reason. How does this matter stand? The administration of justice is in three branches. First, there is the case of the judges; secondly, the case of the magistrates; and thirdly, the case of the constabulary. Lord Hartington requires that the whole of these matters are to be kept out of the hands of the Irish authority. You are to refuse to give to the Irish authority the control of police which you give to every municipality in this country, and you are to refuse it to the Irish nation. I will do nothing of the sort. Now, with regard to the magistracy, it is proposed to keep that in the same hands as have hitherto regulated it. And how do you think the magistracy is at present managed? I see it stated, and I believe it to be true, that in the county of Fermanagh, for example, where the Roman Catholics form a considerable majority of the population, there are sixty-seven or seventy-seven magistrates, of whom every one, with a single exception, is a Protestant. Do not suppose that the administration of justice by the magistrates in Ireland means the same thing as it does in this country. I heard myself in the House of Commons, and I believe some of my friends near me heard, in this very year, one of the Northern Nationalist members give an account of the mode in which a particular case was handled before a bench of justices, a case in which, I think, the stipendiary magistrate

Manchester, June 25.

was so shocked with the proceedings that he retired and would have nothing to do with it. If that case had occurred in England, there would have been a thrill of indignation from one end of the country to the other; but it was in Ireland, and the statement remained uncontradicted, and nobody seemed to think it required the least notice or the least anxiety to consider how justice was administered to a parcel of Irish labourers. As to the judges, perhaps you know that we have surrounded all the existing judges with every security that the wit of man can devise; and I will tell you this, that it will be a long time before they get rid of these existing judges. There are just twice as many of them as are needed, therefore they will not die of hard work; and, being so numerous, it will be a good while before they die down below the limit necessary to transact all the business of the country. Most of those judges are very worthy and excellent men, whose great fault it is to have been appointed under a system the most wasteful and extravagant that ever was devised in the world, because it has been devised in order to prop up a bad political system. All these judges will, I believe, without a single exception, give perfect satisfaction to the Irish people; and, long before they become too few for their work, you will know by practical experience whether this scheme of local self-government in Ireland is working well or ill.

I cannot accept the four conditions of Lord Hartington, and Lord Hartington knows that perfectly well; and, if you observe, like a man of honour as he is, he makes no attempt to gild his four conditions; he makes no attempt to say that he is friendly to Home Rule, but he does not like the Government Bill. Such shifts are beneath Lord Hartington. He comes out as an opponent. He will not adopt, I will venture to say, Lord Carnarvon's language. We wish above all things to conciliate, if we can, and to meet our opponents, where it is possible. And I will tell you this: I for one will adopt the language of Lord Carnarvon. Lord Carnarvon says that in his opinion measures ought to

Manchester, June 25.

be passed which would completely meet the local wants of Ireland, and which would satisfy to some extent her national aspirations. There, gentlemen, is the dividing line. On one side of that line, I am sorry to say, stands my friend Lord Hartington. On the other side stands my opponent Lord Carnarvon. We want to meet the wants of Ireland, considered as a matter of business. We want also to give reasonable satisfaction to her national aspirations. And why? Because experience has shown, if we wanted the lesson, that nationality is one of the most powerful and useful factors in human affairs, so that you may enlist it in the service of law and order with infinite advantage; whereas if it is not your friend, it will be your enemy, and will teach you by sorrowful and painful lessons that it cannot be defied with impunity.

The Carnarvon conversation.

There is another point I must notice in passing. You have heard of the interview between Lord Carnarvon and Mr. Parnell. Since I have come out into this election contest, I have made great efforts to discover what it was that Lord Carnarvon admits that he did say to Mr. Parnell. Mr. Parnell has given us his account of it, and there is no use in appealing to him. Lord Carnarvon refuses to admit Mr. Parnell's account. I appeal to Lord Carnarvon, and I ask two questions. What did Lord Carnarvon say to Mr. Parnell? Did Lord Carnarvon tell to Lord Salisbury, the head of his Government, as he was bound to tell him, and as, I firmly believe, he did tell him, the whole substance of what he had said to Mr. Parnell? Now, gentlemen, I have been at some pains to get at the bottom of this matter, and I do not intend to leave it. I spoke of it on Thursday last week on going northwards at Carlisle. Lord Salisbury has all the hundred eyes of Argus, and he answered me in four-and-twenty hours; that is, he professed to answer me, and he said a number of things I did not want to know, but he answered neither of my questions, and I am just as ignorant now as I was then. What did Lord Carnarvon say to Mr. Parnell? Did Lord Carnarvon, as he was bound, tell Lord

Manchester, June 25. Salisbury what he had said to Mr. Parnell? For, gentlemen, you know what it is that our opponents, and Lord Salisbury in particular, now think of our plan. They say we are dismemberers, disintegrators, and separatists. Very well. Last July, Lord Carnarvon, as it appears, indicated to Mr. Parnell that he was in substance a dismemberer, a disintegrator, and a separatist. If he told that to Lord Salisbury, it follows that Lord Salisbury kept a man in the position of Viceroy of Ireland for six months, from July to January, without saying one word of reproof, without withdrawing one tittle of his confidence, and that man a dismemberer, a disintegrator, and a separatist. Lord Salisbury has shown a great disinclination to be questioned on this subject, but that is no reason why we should not question him. The people of England are entitled to know what took place. I have made every effort, I will make every effort, and I trust my friends here who are near me will also make every effort, for the purpose of getting to the bottom of this really important matter.

Now, gentlemen, we have acted upon two rules—one to conciliate our adversaries as much as possible; the other to conciliate Ireland as much as possible, and to conciliate Ireland by offering her only what is right and just. I own to you that, considering the language held of late years, when I began in the autumn to weigh deeply this question, I entertained very great misgivings and very great apprehension for fear the Irish, after the manner in which the Tories had dallied and coquetted with them, should make unreasonable demands. And, gentlemen, rely upon it that if such a thing were to come about—were Ireland, in virtue of her own nationality, to demand anything that was perilous or inconvenient to the great Empire to which she belongs—we, as the representatives of the Liberal party, and the Liberal party throughout the country, would be the first, and the sternest, and the firmest in resistance to those demands. But what is the actual demand? Ireland has wisely restricted her demand. She has not asked for the repeal of the Union. She has not asked for the revival of that Grattan Parliament, which would have been undoubtedly, had it been revived, an independent and not a statutory power. It would have had, if it had the will, it would have had the power of inconvenient interference at every point with the proceedings of the Imperial Parliament. Ireland has in that respect wisely abated her demand, and asks for a statutory Parliament. On the other hand, at the time of the Grattan Parliament, Ireland did not enjoy the advantage of a responsible Executive. I do not know whether at that time the world afforded any example of a country, united with another country under the same crown, yet having a different Legislature, and likewise a separate responsible Executive. But experience has made us wiser. The experience of our colonies, and of many foreign countries, has shown us that you can have with perfect safety different Parliamentary institutions with responsible Executives working together in harmony for the common good. That is the case in Canada, all through Australia, and that generally is part of the British system. Ireland has gladly accepted the boon of the responsible Executive, which is perfectly safe. The Irish have wisely foregone the demand for an unlimited Parliament, like the Parliament of Grattan, which, if not dangerous, yet certainly would have been open to some suspicion that in possible circumstances it might become inconvenient. So then, with regard to our two rules, the Irish have given us every assistance in going forward with our plan by confining their demands within the limits of reason and moderation. Has it been the same on the other side of the House? How have our efforts to conciliate been met? You know we have filled our Bill with every kind of provision in the way of safeguards for the minority. Have those safeguards been frankly and generously welcomed, not perhaps as sufficient, but, at any rate, as well meant? No. I never hear them referred to by opponents in Parliament except as proofs that we mistrust

Manchester, June 25.

Manchester, June 25.

the legislature we are calling into existence, and that therefore it ought not to be allowed to exist. Again, we have said, It is not our mistrust, it is your mistrust that has made us use these safeguards. But in vain, gentlemen. You well know the proverb, "There are none so deaf as those who will not hear." Where there is a resolute disposition to turn every proposition to a wrong account, all attempts to conciliate are idle.

Lord Hartington's plan condemned by Lord Salisbury.

Well, now, I must give you a very conclusive judgment upon Lord Hartington's plan; because there is now a feeling, even in the Tory party, that twenty years' coercion or repression is not a very safe thing to defend in the face of a British electorate, and some Tory candidates apparently are beginning a little to draw back, and therefore Lord Hartington is to have an intermediate plan. There is to be a body in Ireland subject to continued interference and overhauling of all its proceedings from London. This body is not to look after Irish affairs generally, but after certain affairs which are to be specially given as a matter of grace and favour; and, finally, the police and the powers that you give to your ordinary municipalities in towns of 10,000 inhabitants are not to be granted to the legislative body of Ireland. I will read you, gentlemen, a judgment upon a plan of that kind. It is worth your hearing. It is a passage from a speech of Lord Salisbury: "This policy of Home Rule, if rumour is correct, will be ingeniously veiled"—he means what is commonly called local government, county government, in a restricted sense—and then he goes on to say: "If the power of taxation and of local government is conceded to those who are hostile to the connection with England, it requires no great foresight to predict that the time must come when the pressure of their action, as against those with whom they differ in their own country, and as against the Government of England, will make the relations between the two countries almost intolerable, and at all events will give enormous advantage to the clamour for Home Rule."

Therefore I leave it to Lord Salisbury, according to his speech at Reading on the 13th October 1883, to answer Lord Hartington; and I say that of all the courses proposed there is none more unwise than to give to the Irish people, with the pretended expectation of finality, the concessions which they tell you they will use from the first day onward simply for the purpose of a leverage to get the whole of the rest of their demands.

Manchester, June 25.

The teaching of History.

Before I can release you, gentlemen, there is one more subject upon which I must briefly touch. I referred to it in a few words at Glasgow, and it is this: that a vow or self-denying ordinance seems to have been taken by our opponents never in this discussion to have any regard to history, or to learn anything from experience in other nations of the world, or to observe the lessons derived from the history of our own Colonies. I think they are very wise in not touching history. At every point it condemns them. At every point it shows that when Ireland was comparatively independent, I do not say she was a happy country in herself, but I say she interfered infinitely less than she has done of late years, and than she will do, unless we wisely deal with her, with the happiness of England. Moreover, she would have remained so, had it not been for our wanton, and I must almost say wicked interference to prevent her. It is no wonder that they do not like referring to history. A learned gentleman on the Tory side of the House called out, "There was no Irish Parliament in 1703." So much for that gentleman's historical knowledge. Well, another gentleman on the Liberal side—I am sorry to say he was one of the seceding Liberals—referred to something having been said or done in the Grattan Parliament in 1779 or 1769, whereas that was years before the Grattan Parliament existed. A clever gentleman, Mr. Jephson, in the *Contemporary Review*, gives a history of the Grattan Parliament which professes to present the whole of the merits of the case, and in that history he has omitted what is infinitely the most important period of the history of

Manchester, June 25.

the Grattan Parliament, namely, the administration of Lord Fitzwilliam and the fatal consequences of his recall. Mr. Jephson does not think that worthy of mention. I want you to bear in mind that here is a great portion of our strength. It is a great feature of sound politics, ay, of Conservative politics in the true sense of the word, to have regard to history; and the history of the past as well as the hopes of the future, in this great controversy are wholly on our side. Europe is full of countries the political difficulties of which have been mitigated or solved by means of granting local autonomy to separate portions of those countries. The case of Austria and Hungary, the case of Austria in particular in Galicia; the case of Norway and Sweden; the case of Denmark and Iceland; the case even of Russia, which has set us a good example in the case of Finland—one which it seems we have not the pluck to follow—all of these show the wisdom of this policy. I have challenged our opponents in the House of Commons to produce to us one single case in the whole world where the free grant of local autonomy has been followed by the separation which they are always making a bugbear of for us, and not one instance can they produce, have they produced, or will they produce.

European experience.

Colonial experience.

Now, gentlemen, with regard to the experience of our Colonies, surely this is rather a sad case and rather a hard case. What have we done all over the world? We have given this great boon, sometimes freely and with dignity, sometimes late and under pressure, but invariably with the greatest benefit. And then, says Lord Salisbury, Oh yes, but we do not give free local government to Hottentots. Such is the illustration which a late Prime Minister of this country thinks not unseemly for the discussion of the affairs of his Irish fellow-subjects. No, gentlemen, I have not much to say about Hottentots; but then I will say this, that we have not confined the gift of local government to men of the British race. We have given the gift of local government to Frenchmen in Canada; we have given the gift of free autonomy to Dutchmen at the

Cape. We have gone further. We had Australian colonies; we had one in particular, the colony of Tasmania, in which the absolute majority of the population were either convicts or the descendants of convicts. We gave them this free local government; and with them, as well as all over the world, it has acted like a blessing and a charm. With the case of Frenchmen in mind, with the case of Dutchmen on record, ay, with the case of convicts on record, we are to stand in the face of our Irish fellow-countrymen and to say, "No, you are not worthy; we do not give local autonomy to Hottentots." **Manchester, June 25.**

The Irishman's appeal.

Let me now for a few minutes just bring the Irishman before you, and let him make his appeal to this country. What has he to say? He addresses you as a free people, and he says, "You believe in representative institutions. You believe in them not only as a power but as a virtue. You believe not only that they are wrung by necessity from the upper orders and sovereigns, but you believe they strengthen the position of every class in the community, that they consolidate the foundations of the throne, and that they add, above all, efficiency to the law by giving it a place in the affections of the people. Why will you not do this for us? Why are we disabled and disqualified for receiving the boon which you have so largely given?" And why, gentlemen? What is the difficulty in Ireland? Are you aware, probably many may not be aware, that of the Irish nation the great, by far the greater part are of British extraction? In the reign of James I., Sir John Davis, the Attorney-General, a most able authority, said, in the year 1612, that at that period much the largest number of the Irish population were descended from the British race. But that was before the great migration of Scotchmen into Ulster, and before the great migration of Cromwellians into Tipperary, and, if it was true then, it is much more true now; but, gentlemen, I ask you to go a little further, and I tell you this, that your difficulties in governing Ireland have been chiefly in those parts of the

Manchester, June 25.

country where the British blood was strongest and the Celtic blood of Ireland the weakest. Who does not know the name of Tipperary as a synonym of the focus and the centre of violent and unwarrantable but still natural and inevitable resistance to unjust law? But Tipperary is the place where the old blood of the country has been deeply pervaded by an infusion of the strongest Englishmen, settled there 250 years ago, and assimilated in language and manners to the Irish type. So that really what we ought to admit is this, that these powerful elements of resistance that we have had to deal with in Ireland have been British; and it is notorious that, until within the last few years, when the cup overflowed, counties like Kerry and Cork, which were purely Celtic and Irish, produced the smallest proportionate number of outrages or of acts of resistance to the law. Well, I think that is a very strong appeal to make to us, if we are really in earnest when we say that we think representative government a good thing, and when we hold that there is a fair title to enjoy its benefits among all the people of the Empire—not its European inhabitants alone, but among Africans, Australians, and Americans, not less than Europeans.

His appeal to Manchester in particular.

One word more. The Irishman may make an appeal to England. May he not make a special appeal to Manchester? It is impossible to forget at this moment in what noble hall I am addressing you. Do not the walls and roof of this hall speak to us of the past? They speak to us of triumphs in the cause of peace, justice, and national prosperity. They speak of campaigns which were fought, and of victories which were won, and victories in which Manchester, as the metropolis of the greatest manufacturing district of the country, proudly and nobly took the lead. That was her position then. What is her position now? How far does the present state of the representation of Manchester correspond with the place she took in the battle of free trade, and in the execution of the purpose which you have commemorated by the erection of this lofty building? Gentlemen, beware lest you lay yourselves open to severe reproach. Beware lest you leave to the adversary the opportunity of saying, "Oh yes, Manchester was very wise when wisdom went directly to fill her own pocket, when her sight was sharpened by self-interest. Then she led the country to free trade, in spite of and in contempt of all the prophecies of universal ruin which were showered upon her from every quarter. Now Manchester is no longer awake, no longer awakens others. She goes quietly to sleep, and allows herself to be led mainly by the Tory party." At a time when it is no longer a question of opening works, enlargement of warehouses, and filling pockets, when the only objects that we have in view are the honour of Great Britain and the peace and happiness of a sister nation, do not let it be said, gentlemen, do not let it be whispered, here or elsewhere, that you are less alive, less determined in such a cause, than you were when you gallantly led England in the great battle of free trade, and achieved inestimable benefit to your country. I stand here surrounded by political friends. I see among them Mr. Agnew and Mr. Lee; and for a moment I will allude to the seat which Mr. Agnew holds, and the seat sought by Mr. Lee, under the similitude of a fortress. Mr. Agnew holds a fortress, and it is your business to make that fortress impregnable. Mr. Lee does not hold a fortress; he assaults it. I call upon you for your own honour, in the most Tory quarter of Manchester, to scale the walls and take possession of the citadel, and make Mr. Lee a member of the coming Parliament. These I only take as instances. They do not exhaust the catalogue. They are but instances, cases in which I hope an example will be set; and one to be followed, as I trust it will, by the whole of Lancashire and throughout the land.

Manchester, June 25.

Conclusion.

And what, gentlemen, will be the end? I don't think that even our opponents believe it is possible for them to win. They do believe, or they think they believe, that they can delay the triumph of the cause. They know they cannot prevent it. They can delay it; and by that means perhaps

Manchester, June 25.

they may destroy something of its grace, something of its dignity, something of its freedom. They may produce further controversy, further exasperation. What is the good of results like these? Is it desirable that you should now give this boon, of your own spontaneous will, to Ireland, thankful and grateful, in the anticipation of a future of loyalty and joy, or that you should wait until difficulty gathers around you, and it is extorted from your hands, as Roman Catholic emancipation was dragged from out of the hands of the Duke of Wellington in order to avert civil war? Now, gentlemen, be wise, and be wise in time. Rekindle the ancient fire which was the beacon from Manchester thirty or forty years ago, and went blazing throughout the land. Again set the example to England and lead us to victory: to a bloodless victory; to a victory without tears, without shame; to a victory where, after a short time of happy retrospect, the conquered will join with the conquerors in the rejoicings it brings about, and will recognize what has been done as, for the whole Empire, a common triumph and a common joy.

Mr. Gladstone resumed his seat amid the renewed and long-continued cheers of the audience.

Sir Henry Roscoe, M.P., moved a resolution of cordial thanks to Mr. Gladstone for his address, asking the meeting to pledge itself to support Mr. Gladstone's policy of self-government for Ireland. This was seconded by Mr. B. Armitage, M.P., supported by Mr. Jacob Bright, and unanimously carried by the meeting.

Mr. Gladstone briefly acknowledged the resolution, and the meeting dispersed after passing a vote of thanks to the chairman.

On Saturday the 26th June Mr. Gladstone received an address from a small deputation, introduced by Mr. B.

Armitage, M.P., from the borough of Salford, within which is Summer Hill, the residence of Mr. Agnew, with whom Mr. Gladstone was staying, and where the address was presented. **Manchester, June 26.**

Mr. Gladstone replied as follows:—I was very much struck with this address, especially the last sentence of it.[1] It surely ought to teach us a lesson by the wisdom there is in it. Here is this vast Empire, reaching all over the world, consisting of a multitude of states, countries, and provinces, embracing one-fifth part, some say a fourth part, of the human race; and within all that Empire there is not a discontented province except one, and that is the one at our door, and that is one with which we have been dealing by methods of force for 700 years, and that is the one in respect to which the whole civilized world cries out with one voice, "Ireland is the disgrace of England." Well, gentlemen, is it or is it not time to put an end to that disgrace? It is in vain that you struggle against that sentence of mankind. The judgment of the whole world, continued and prolonged through generations, is never wrong. As the great Mr. Burke has said, that judgment of the world anticipates the judgment of posterity, and records for the instruction of mankind what comes as near to absolute truth as it is permitted to the human race to attain. Well, gentlemen, we are associated together in this endeavour, and we appeal to the whole nation to assist us. Under God, we put our trust in the sound heart and sound mind of the nation. And I rejoice to see around me here men who have been labouring with us in this cause. I am a good deal exhausted with the work of yesterday, and it will be better that I should not attempt to say further words to you beyond

The world's sentence against England.

[1] The sentence referred to was as follows:—"We would remind you that our gracious and beloved Queen has entered upon her jubilee year of a reign distinguished by the addition to her empire of many valuable possessions: but we hope that on the occasion of Her Majesty completing the fiftieth year of her sovereignty, it will be celebrated by adding the brightest jewel to her crown, a peaceful, law-abiding, loyal and contented Ireland, in consequence of your wise and generous statesmanship."

Manchester, June 26.

gratefully and affectionately thanking you for your kindness. In these beautiful grounds I can hardly believe I am in a borough, but I will take it upon your assurance; and I take it also upon your assurance that this borough will do its duty. I am tempted to say one thing—merely to narrate to you a little anecdote, not without interest to the people of Salford. It is very slight, but it is a gracious and graceful saying of your old and esteemed representative, Mr. Brotherton. It was the custom of the Tories in his time to reproach all men who came from the manufacturing districts as bloated millionaires, and as tyrannical factory owners; and one night, poor Mr. Brotherton was pointed out as one of these millionaires. He said in a very kind and quiet tone that that was quite a mistake, that he had himself worked in a mill or factory, I forget which, as a boy, that he had never attained to the position which was so described by opponents; and he added these simple words, which I recollect exactly: "My riches consist in the fewness of my wants." Gentlemen, that was a golden saying. I leave it to abide in your memories, as it has abided for fifty years in mine.

The deputation thanked Mr. Gladstone and retired.

XII.

SPEECH AT LIVERPOOL.

MONDAY, JUNE 28, 1886.

Delivered in Hengler's Circus, Liverpool.

Mr. Gladstone received a most enthusiastic welcome. Among those who accompanied him to the platform were:—Mrs. Gladstone, Mr. W. H. Gladstone, Mr. A. R. Gladstone, Mr. W. L. Gladstone, Mr. R. F. Gladstone, the Rev. Harry Drew and Mrs. Drew, Mrs. Tomkinson, Sir Thomas Brassey, Mr. Serjeant Hemphill, West Derby; Mr. Ralph Neville, Kirkdale; Mr. T. P. O'Connor, Scotland; Sir George Errington, Bart., Newton; Mr. Augustine Birrell, Widnes.

The chair was occupied by Mr. R. D. Holt, who made a few introductory remarks, after which Mr. Gladstone was presented with the following address of welcome:—

TO THE RIGHT HON. WILLIAM EWART GLADSTONE.

Sir,—In offering you a cordial welcome to the city of your birth and earliest recollections, the Liberal Associations of over

Liverpool, June 28.

twenty constituencies in Liverpool and the surrounding district desire to tender you their warmest thanks for coming among them in the present crisis.

At an age, sir, when you might have sought, in the bosom of your family, and among your scholarly and peaceful surroundings at Hawarden, the repose to which you have earned so just a title by your long life of conflict in the cause of justice, of freedom, and of humanity, you have, at the imperative call of duty, courageously undertaken an enterprise, more arduous than any in which you have previously engaged, on behalf of a nationality whose wrongs, though they have been always present to your thoughts, opportunity has not hitherto enabled you to redress.

Your presence among us under these circumstances imparts to our old men some touch of your own marvellous vigour, both of mind and of body, and inspires our young men with renewed enthusiasm for the noble cause which, in common with yourself, we all have at heart.

We witness with pain—as much on their account as on yours or on our own—the defection of some who have fought shoulder to shoulder with you in the battles of the past against privilege and class interests for broadening the liberties and promoting the welfare of the masses of the people; but in you, sir, we recognize the true exponent of those unchangeable principles of Liberalism to which, in all ages and under every clime, the pioneers of progress have consecrated their fortunes and their lives.

It is for this reason that, in the face of open enemies and failing friends, we again respond to your call. We follow the standard which you have raised aloft, not because we are slaves to a great name, or have fallen under the enchantment of transcendent gifts, but because you have had the insight to perceive, and the magnetic sympathy to draw out those sentiments of justice and of generosity which, however they may be overlaid for the time being by prejudice or by selfishness, are latent in every human breast.

Liverpool, June 28.

We look in vain through the addresses of those who would tempt us from our allegiance for one word of sympathy, one expression of kindly feeling towards Ireland in her hour of trial. This is our test. We feel that if it had fallen to you even to refuse to Ireland her prayer, you would have pronounced her doom with sorrow and not with cold indifference.

We are devoutly thankful, sir, that you have been so long spared to undertake, on behalf of your country, a task in the discharge of which even your great abilities and high moral qualities demand the support of that ripened wisdom and extensive and varied experience which age alone can give; and that you may be still endowed with the requisite measure of health and strength to carry your beneficent work of reconciliation to completion, and receive the blessings of a grateful people amid the applause of civilized mankind, is the earnest prayer of, sir, your faithful and devoted servants.—[Here follow the signatures of the chairmen of the Abercromby, Walton, Everton, Kirkdale, Scotland, Exchange, West Derby, West Toxteth, East Toxteth (Liverpool); Birkenhead, Wirral, Bootle, Southport, Widnes, Chester, Warrington, Ormskirk, Wigan, Ince, Leigh, Northwich, Newton, St. Helens, and Crewe Liberal Associations.]

In reply, Mr. Gladstone addressed the meeting in the following words:—

Introduction.

Mr. Chairman, Mr. Lovell, and Gentlemen,—It is, I can assure you, in reliance very much more upon your patience and indulgence than upon my own physical or moral force that I undertake before this vast assembly to signify my acceptance of the address which has been presented to me. And, gentlemen, what I have to say to you will really be little more than an expansion of the admirable ideas, so far as they are public and political ideas, contained in that address, and in the short but excellent speech delivered from the chair by our friend Mr. Holt.

I would ask you, in a contest of this kind, and at an early

Liverpool, June 28.

The weapons on our side and those against us.

stage of it, to remember what are the different means by which it is carried on. One of them is argument; one of them is numbers; one of them is enthusiasm; and there are other means besides these, the whole of which I look upon as perfectly legitimate. But there is a different set of means. One of them is the long purse; another is the display, the imposing display of rank and station; another is the power of political organization, and the command of positions of advantage. Gentlemen, do not let us conceal from ourselves that as regards this second class of weapons we are I may almost say nowhere in comparison with our antagonists. But I turn to the first. I will not now speak of numbers, because that has yet to be put to the proof; but I will speak of enthusiasm, and I will speak of it by reference only to experience. It was by and with enthusiasm throughout the country that in 1880 we carried a great cause, and overthrew a strong Government; and this I will say, without too confident prediction, that the enthusiasm on this occasion has surpassed anything that I ever witnessed either in 1880 or at any period of my life. So, gentlemen, I look forward without being disheartened. But will you forgive me when I say that it is on the first head, on the weapon of argument, that I rely most; and it is here that I am most astonished at the weakness of our antagonists. Allow me to give you one illustration. I am not able, neither eyesight nor time permits me, to read all that is said, but I sometimes look at the speeches. I sometimes look at those speeches where I think I am most likely to find strength of argument, and you will not wonder when I say that I look to the speeches of Lord Hartington. And I am going to give you an illustration of his arguments, from which I infer, not the weakness of the man, but the poverty of the cause. Why, what do you think, gentlemen, is this argument that he makes, and seems to think a very fine thing? He finds that in 1881, in the town of Leeds, I denounced the action at that time of the Nationalist party. It is not the question now whether I was right or whether I was wrong. But what Lord Hartington argues is this—"Is it not monstrous? Here is the very man that denounced them in 1881, and supports them now." It is true, gentlemen. Why did I denounce them? Because I thought they were wrong. And why do I support them? Because I think and know they are right. Gentlemen, it has never been the rule of my life to denounce all men at all times. I endeavour, very imperfectly, to regulate praise and blame by conduct to which it is attached. Let me give you an illustration. No man ever attacked other men more—well, I won't say violently, but at any rate more earnestly and eagerly than I attacked Lord Salisbury in the years 1878, 1879, and 1880, when he was engaged in conduct which I thought to be, not only adverse to the interests, but above all destructive of the honour and character of my country. Therefore I did my best to denounce him, and denounced him and those with whom he acted as strongly as I ever denounced the Nationalists of Ireland. But what did I do last winter? I found that Lord Salisbury had, so far as I could judge, in the important affairs of the Balkan Peninsula, been doing well and justly, and I praised him and supported him to the best of my power. Can you conceive anything more ridiculous than that Lord Hartington should suppose that he has got hold of a good argument, when he shows that I did denounce and condemn what I thought wrong in 1881, and that I am supporting and assisting what I think right in 1886?

Liverpool, June 28.

But that is not the only instance upon which I have to remark. Coming to Liverpool, naturally I have been learning something of what is going on in Liverpool. I have learnt something about the state of your local representation, and I need not say that I find with delight that you are about to make a formidable attack upon the monopoly of the Tories, and I need hardly assure you how warm are my good wishes on the part of all those candidates who are to be engaged in breaking down that monopoly. Let me speak of one whom

The representation of Liverpool.

Liverpool, June 28.

I know best, my friend Sir Thomas Brassey. I make no doubt you will send him back to Parliament, with a goodly company around him; and if you do, you will send there one of the best of English gentlemen, a tried servant of the Crown, an experienced member of Parliament, and one who is loved and admired wherever he is known. And perhaps I may remind you that, if at any time you should happen to fall short in Liverpool of skilled mariners, he is a man who will take one of your liners across the Atlantic.

A hostile handbill.

But, gentlemen, though I was greatly pleased to find him here, it is not all good that I find going on. I hold in my hand a sheet of paper, which may have been in some of your hands, and upon which I am about to make free comment, especially because I believe that the authors and propounders of this wonderful sheet of paper, whom we call paper Unionists, and who call themselves Liberals, are about to meet in this very place to-morrow night. Then I hope they will direct their attention to supporting the statements that I am about to challenge.

The position of the "loyal" Irish.

I find it stated in this paper that the loyal Irish are about to be thrust out of their allegiance to the Imperial Parliament. Now the loyal Irish—those who call themselves so, and who, I hope, are so—are not going to be thrust out of any allegiance whatever. The whole Irish people is going to remain in its allegiance to the Crown, and its allegiance to the Imperial Parliament, at whose hands it asks, and is prepared thankfully to receive, the gift of a legislative body, sitting under statutory authority, for the control of properly and exclusively Irish affairs. But I tell you this. Do not suppose that I mean that no difference is about to be made. A great difference is about to be made. The allegiance now rendered to the Imperial Parliament is rendered, has been rendered, feebly, doubtfully, grudgingly, variably, half-heartedly, and sometimes not at all. We want, if we can, not to thrust, but to draw men out of that kind of allegiance; and we want to provide that hereafter they shall render in Ireland exactly the same kind of allegiance as you render in England and in Scotland—an allegiance coming from the heart, rooted in the mind, governing the conduct, famous in history, and constituting the strength and basis of the State.

Liverpool, June 28.

The privileges of the men of Ulster.

Well, then, the next statement in this most inaccurate—I had almost said, forgive me, this most blundering paper,—the next statement is that we are going to deny to Ulster the privileges which we give elsewhere. I am afraid, gentlemen, you have not read this paper as carefully as I have, and I cannot say it will repay you if you do; but I will tell you what I pick out of it, and just venture to make a remark here and there. It is stated that we deny to Ulster the privileges that we are going to give to others in Ireland. Why, this is doubly untrue. First of all, it is untrue because Ulster, under our plan, has just the same privileges as everybody else; and further, it is untrue because it refers not so much to the whole of Ulster, but to portions of Ulster. We have gone out of our way to say that if a good and rational plan, with general approval, can be contrived under which a part of Ulster can be separately dealt with, we are willing to take up that point in a friendly spirit. What they call denying to Ulster what we give to others, is that we offer to Ulster an option that we do not offer to others, and, in fact, that we are giving more to Ulster in that shape than we give to anybody else. So much for this wonderful paper that I hold in my hand.

The Land Purchase Bill.

Once more this paper states that it is not a question of Home Rule only, but it is a question of a Bill that must necessarily and in justice be accompanied by another Bill, involving the expenditure of many millions of the hard-earned money of the taxpayer. That means the Land Purchase Bill; and I tell you this, that if those who signed this paper will prove to me what they have said, that that Land Purchase Bill involves the expenditure of many millions, or of any millions of the money of the British taxpayer, I myself will be the man to throw the Land Purchase

Liverpool, June 28.

Bill behind the fire. To spend your money, gentlemen, is one thing, and to invest your money is another thing. When you buy £100 of consols, you don't spend the money, but you invest it. If consols were worthless, you would spend it while you thought you were investing it; but, as consols are good and sound, you don't spend, but you invest. I should have thought some of the gentlemen who have signed this paper, with Lord Derby at the head of them, knew pretty well the difference between spending and investing. But mark what I have said, that if it can be shown that this is not an investment, but an expenditure, I shall not ask you to spend your money for such a purpose as we have proposed. Moreover, I wish you to understand that the whole of that question must necessarily be considered afresh from the new starting-point which, if you return us as a Ministry, we shall have to set out from when we enter upon the new Parliament. I have said it, and I say it again, the end we have in view is, consistently with justice, honour, and Imperial unity, to give self-government to Ireland. Everything compatible with these principles it is open to us to adopt, and it is our duty to adopt. Nothing can be adopted by us excepting what is within those principles.

Are our two Bills inseparable?

And, I must say, I complain of the authors of this paper, who ought to have known better what they were talking about, for they say, or seem to say, that we have inseparably joined together these two plans. That is not the fact, and any one who takes the trouble to refer to the speech in which I introduced the Land Purchase Bill will find these words, that "the two Bills are in our minds inseparable at the present moment;" and that I went on to say that a refusal of the offer which we then made must necessarily have most important consequences on the future course of the question. Well, I think you are not likely to fall into a trap with respect either to the Irish Government Bill, the Land Purchase Bill, or anything else. He would be a very clever man indeed who passed a Land Purchase Act in the teeth of

Liverpool, June 28.

the national sentiment, after the subject had been considered at a general election. But this you ought to know, although the paper Unionists conceal it from you, and take no notice of it, that you have got at present in operation a land purchase system in Ireland which, in my opinion, is a bad and a dangerous system. It is a system under which the British Treasury is made the creditor of a multitude of dispersed individuals all over Ireland; and although I believe that the Irish debtor pays his debts quite as well and as honourably as any other debtor, yet it is not a good or a safe system under which the Treasury is at innumerable points to be placed in contact with the private individual in the relation of creditor and debtor; and to reform that system, and substitute for it something better, is a most important part, if not an obligatory part, of the Irish legislation, which we hope that we have now in prospect.

Individual and collective responsibility.

So much, gentlemen, for those three points; but I must make a general remark upon this paper. You see the looseness of the assertions it contains. Well, but when I look at the paper and at the signatures, I find seven most respectable signatures, and at the head of them Lord Derby, who is known to me, as well as to you, as being a most cautious, careful, and accurate man. I tell you fairly I do not believe that Lord Derby would have put his hand to that paper if it had been a paper to be signed by him alone. But gentlemen will put their hands to a great many things when they do not sign them alone but in company with others, to which they would on no account put their hands if they had to sign them alone. I will tell you what it reminds me of. It sometimes, unfortunately, happens that a soldier, for some great offence, is condemned to be shot. How is it done? Not by setting up the soldier there where that gentleman stands under the gallery, and asking me, for example, at this moderate distance to take a shot at him. It is not a difficult thing to hit him; still they would not ask me to do it alone, because they know it is a rather painful operation; but they ask ten or twenty

Liverpool, June 28.

men, they put out a file of ten or twenty men, and these all shoot at the unfortunate man, who falls pierced by balls, and nobody knows whose balls they are. And just in the same way it is that none of those gentlemen would like to be wholly responsible for these assertions; yet, clubbing themselves together, like the soldiers who have to fire, they venture it, and put their signatures to it.

The classes against the masses.

This is an illustration of a very great and important fact, namely, the fact that you are opposed throughout the country by a compact army, and that army is a combination of the classes against the masses. I am thankful to say that there are among the classes many happy exceptions still. I am thankful to say that there are men wearing coronets on their heads who are as good and as sound and as genuine Liberals as any working man that hears me at this moment. But, as a general rule, it cannot be pretended that we are supported by the dukes, or by the squires, or by the Established clergy, or by the officers of the army, or by a number of other bodies of very respectable people. What I observe is this: wherever a profession is highly privileged, wherever a profession is publicly endowed, it is there that you will find that almost the whole of the class and the profession are against us. But if I go to more open professions, if I take the Bar, where, though it is endowed in its higher regions, yet in its lower regions every member fares according to his merits; if I take the medical profession, where that invaluable body of men minister to your wants, each of them perfectly contented to stand or fall by his capacity for performing his great work —in these open professions I am thankful to say that we make a very good show, and pass a very respectable muster indeed. For a good many years past, if you had taken the dividing line in the House of Commons—and I think such members of the House of Commons as are here will bear me out in this—you would have found that the majority of the able and distinguished lawyers have sat on the Liberal side of the House. But still, in the main, gentlemen, this is a question,

Liverpool, June 2d.

I am sorry to say, of class against mass, of classes against the nation; and the question for us is, Will the nation show enough of unity and determination to overbear, constitutionally, at the polls, the resistance of the classes? It is very material that we should consider which of them is likely to be right. Do not let us look at our forces alone; let us look at that without which force is worthless, mischievous, and contemptible. Are we likely to be right? Are the classes ever right when they differ from the nation? ("No.") Well, wait a moment. I draw this distinction. I am not about to assert that the masses of the people, who do not and cannot give their leisure to politics, are necessarily, on all subjects, better judges than the leisured men and the instructed men who have great advantages for forming political judgments that the others have not; but this I will venture to say, that upon one great class of subjects, the largest and the most weighty of them all, where the leading and determining considerations that ought to lead to a conclusion are truth, justice, and humanity, there, gentlemen, all the world over, I will back the masses against the classes.

Are the classes or the masses most likely to be in the right?

We pride ourselves very much in this great controversy on having regard to history, and we assert—and I wish the paper Unionists of Liverpool would pay a little attention to this—we assert they shut their eyes against history. But let me apply a little history to this question, and see whether the proposition I have just delivered is an idle dream and the invention of an enthusiastic brain, or whether it is the lesson taught us eminently and indisputably by the history of the last half century. I will read you rapidly a list of ten subjects,—the greatest subjects of the last half century. First, abolition of slavery; second, reform of Parliament, lasting from 1831 to 1885, at intervals; third, abolition of the Corn Laws and abolition of twelve hundred customs and excise duties, which has set your trade free instead of its being enslaved; fourthly, the navigation laws, which we were always solemnly told were the absolute condition of maintaining the strength of this country and of this

The test of history.

Ten cases in which the masses have been right and the classes have been wrong.

Liverpool, June 28.

empire; fifthly, the reform of the most barbarous and shameful criminal code that ever disgraced a civilized country; sixthly, the reform of the laws of combination and contract, which compelled the British workmen to work, as I may say, in chains; seventhly, the change of foreign policy. Gentlemen, you may recollect—I am speaking of sixty years ago—you have heard of the Holy Alliance. You may know that for a considerable time the policy of this country was subordinated in a great degree to that of the Holy Alliance. Mr. Canning, an old representative of Liverpool, whom I rejoice to say my father brought to Liverpool, emancipated this country from its servitude to the Holy Alliance; and for so doing he was more detested by the upper classes of this country than any man has been during the present century. Eighthly—I take another piece of foreign policy—there was what we call the Jingo policy. That was put down. Who put it down? It was not put down by the classes; it was put down by the hearty response to an appeal made to the people. Ninthly, the abolition of religious distinctions; and tenthly, I take the matter in which I had a hand myself, the disestablishment of the Irish Church. These ten subjects—many of them are really not single subjects, but groups of subjects—are the greatest that have formed the staple employment and food of our political life for the last sixty years. On every one of them, without exception, the masses have been right and the classes have been wrong. Nor will it do, gentlemen, to tell me that I am holding the language of agitation; I am speaking the plain dictates of fact, for nobody can deny that on all these ten subjects the masses were on one side and the classes were on the other, and nobody can deny that the side of the masses, and not the side of the classes, is the one which now the whole nation confesses to have been right.

Pray recollect that I have not gone so far as to say that the masses will always be right and the classes wrong. On a great many subjects I think it may very likely be otherwise. I have given you what I think is the test. But there is an authority which goes a great deal beyond me. You will be shocked almost when I read to you what he says. He said these words only a year and a half ago at Blackpool: "Governments will go wrong." (A voice: "Lord Randolph.") That is rather hard upon me, gentlemen. I was preparing what I thought a very good theatrical effect, and my friend over there has prematurely let the cat out of the bag. I am quoting, or going to quote, from Lord Randolph Churchill. I am told he has said a good deal about me lately, but I cannot say whether that is true or not, for I have not been careful to inform myself. I have not named his name before in this election, and I do not think I shall name it again. He is a very difficult person to give an impartial and fair account of, but my own opinion of him—a very imperfect one—is that, if by any process you could cut out of him about one-half of the qualities he possesses, you might make out of the other half a valuable and distinguished public servant. Now, let me read my quotation from Lord Randolph about the masses and the classes, which runs as follows: "Governments will go wrong, Parliament will go wrong, classes will go wrong, Society and the Pall Mall clubs always go wrong, but the people don't go wrong." So you see, gentlemen, how Lord Randolph, in his brisk manner, sweeps away all the little reservations and securities and cautions which I, as an "old Parliamentary hand," had endeavoured to set up on behalf of the classes against the masses. He will admit no qualification at all; the masses are always right, and the classes are always wrong.

Liverpool June 28.

A threefold appeal—

Now I am going to make, if I may, and if you have patience to follow me, a threefold appeal to Englishmen, and not to Liberals alone. I appeal to their prudence; I appeal to their courage; and I appeal to their sense of honour.

(1) To prudence.

And first to their prudence. Have you considered, gentlemen, the present condition of your Parliament? Many and many a man of you has at heart some question closely associated with his interests in life, and many and many a

Liverpool, June 28.

man of you has perhaps still more nearly at heart many a question associated with the welfare of the community. Are you satisfied with the capacity which your Parliament has lately shown for dealing with these questions? You know as well as I do that for legislation generally your Parliament is in a state of paralysis. It has worked hard. Many a man has sacrificed his life to his public labours; but the difficulties are such that they cannot be overcome. And what is the cause of these difficulties? The cause of them has been Ireland. What has happened to the questions which we laid before the country last autumn? What has happened to the temperance legislation? What has happened to the legislation about the land laws? We want to reform the land laws, and one of the objects we have in view is to give the labouring man readier and easier access to a real interest in the land. And there is a certain Mr. Jesse Collings—I believe he is the man who promised three acres and a cow; I have never shared in that promise, and whether he made it or not I do not know; I rather believe it is so—but that gentleman, who is so extremely anxious on behalf of the labourer, is now in the field as a candidate to prevent Parliament doing its work. He stands for a Division in Birmingham, and his action is directed to blocking the way to all useful legislation, by leaving the Irish question in a position in which every man of sense knows, whatever his inclination may be, that no real work can be done until that question is got out of the way.

The block of Parliamentary business.

The Nationalists and the work of the British Parliament.

I see here a man of great ability, Mr. T. P. O'Connor, who has been an important member of the body of Nationalists. I suppose no delicacy need prevent me from stating before him what is, I take it, quite indisputable, that this body of Nationalists have considered that the interest of their country, in the condition in which she stood, was primary, and that it was for them to urge it under all circumstances and at all times, irrespective of the effect it might have in blocking the business and paralysing the action of Parliament. I cannot be surprised at it. I do

Liverpool, June 28.

not complain of it. I refer to it as a fact. But you have had a specimen of it for the last six years. I know pretty well what it is. Is it likely to be better—mind, I am now only on the argument of prudence—is it likely to be better in the next six years? Gentlemen, I can tell you what the difference will be; and I say that what has been done by Irishmen in the last six years is but a trifling miniature and specimen of what will result in the next six years, unless you take thought and counsel, not from the mere will of these gentlemen, but from the necessities of the position. Why, gentlemen, in the last six years the Irish Nationalist party has consisted of somewhere about forty or forty-five men. (Mr. O'Connor: Forty-five at the highest.) Forty-five was the highest. They have had no backing from England or from Scotland. One or two men have given them qualified and occasional assistance, but you may fairly say that they have had no backing on the whole, and being forty-five members out of 103, pray observe that, whatever conviction they might feel that they were speaking the true sense of Ireland, yet they have never been in a position to assert that with authority. No forty-five men representing a country which returns 103 members can possibly say, "We are the nation speaking for itself." How does the matter stand now? They are no longer forty-five, but eighty-five. They are no longer something more than one-third of the Irish representation; they approach five-sixths of it. They now are virtually, I do not hesitate to say, if there be such a thing as constitutional principle, if we really believe in representative institutions—and we think we hold them dearer than our lives—if we really believe in them, then I say that these eighty-five gentlemen, say what you will and what you like, speak for the Irish nation, and are virtually the Irish nation speaking for itself in Parliament, just as much as a corresponding proportion of English members or of Scotch members would be the English or the Scotch nation speaking for itself in Parliament.

Liverpool, June 28.

Ireland mistress of the situation.

And then, as I told you before, hitherto they have had no backing. Will that be so now? Why, gentlemen, take the most sanguine estimate that any paper Unionist can form, let him indulge all the flights of his imagination, let him defeat Liberal candidates right and left and send to Parliament mock Liberal candidates in their places—it will all come to nothing. There will be and must be—it is as certain as if it had come about—in every coming Parliament a powerful body of English and of Scotch representatives who are attached, heart and soul, to the cause of self-government for Ireland, and whom nothing will induce to surrender or betray that cause. In fact—do not conceal it from yourselves; I will exhibit it in a more amusing point of view if I can, though the matter is a serious one—Ireland is the mistress of the situation. Ireland is mounted on the back of England, as the old man in the *Arabian Nights* was mounted on the back of Sinbad the Sailor. You recollect that incident. I hope you have not all of you given up reading the *Arabian Nights.* It is a great pity if you have. I will read the passage. Sinbad, upon one of his islands, sees a venerable-looking old man. He invites him to get on his back. The old man mounts accordingly. He takes him wherever he wishes to go. But at last he begins to wish that the old gentleman would dismount. "I said to him, 'Dismount'"—he made the demand a very modest one—"'dismount at thy leisure.' But he would not get off my back, and wound his legs about my neck. I was affrighted and would have cast him off, but he clung to me and gripped my neck with his legs, till I was well-nigh choked. The world grew black in my sight, and I fell senseless to the ground like one dead." Gentlemen, Sinbad is the Parliament of England. The old man is Ireland, whom we by our foolish initiative invited and almost compelled to place herself upon our back; and she rides you, and she will ride you until, listening to her reasonable demand, you shall consent to some arrangement that justice

Liverpool, June 28.

and policy alike recommend. So much for the appeal to prudence. I want to see the Parliament go to work, and I know it cannot go to work. Let it struggle as it will, the legs are gripping the neck, it is well-nigh throttled, the world grows black in its sight, and virtually it falls to the ground; and at the end of each session a beggarly account is presented to the world of the good it has not been able to do, of the laws it has been incompetent to make.

(2) *To courage.*

Again, gentlemen, I appeal to the courage of this nation. How is the English nation for courage? I will give you my opinion. For real dangers the people of England and Scotland form perhaps the bravest people in the world. At any rate, there is no people in the world to whom they are prepared to surrender, or to whom I, for one, would ask them to surrender the palm of bravery. But I am sorry to say there is another aspect of the case; and for imaginary dangers there is no people in the world which in a degree anything like the English is the victim of absurd and idle panics. It is notorious, gentlemen, all over the world. The French we think an excitable nation, but the French stand by in amazement at the passion of fear and fury into which an Englishman will get himself when he is dealing with an imaginary danger. Now we have got before us one of the best cases that I ever knew for an imaginary danger. The imaginary danger is this, that if, from a high sense of justice, as well as of policy, we make to Ireland a great and inestimable boon, first of all, the Irish are such a set of fools that they will not see that their own interest is to receive that boon in a becoming manner; secondly, they are such a set of monsters that our good actions towards them will be simply a basis and incentive to the worst actions on their part towards us. That is what we are to set out with. Oh, gentlemen, I have not done yet. That is what we are to set out with—the cool assumption that God Almighty has made these people monsters or idiots in human shape.

English courage and English panics.

Liverpool, June 28.

The relative strength of England and Ireland.

But let us suppose that is true, and they come to a tussle with us, how do they stand, and how do we stand? Well, they are five millions of people, and I am sorry to say I am afraid that they are still a decreasing five millions of people. They hope that this change now meditated may lead to a growth of their population. I hope so too. And if there be any English labourer that is afraid of the competition of the Irish labourer—I don't know whether there are or not such in Liverpool—surely it is reasonable to suppose that the Irishman, who, whatever he is, certainly is a being that loves Ireland, will get back to Ireland as quick as he can, and will diminish the pressure of that competition upon the English labourer. But that is a by-point. The Irish are five millions of people, decreasing, poor, without public establishments, without army, without navy, without any title or any power, under the Bill that we propose, to create either an army or a navy. Such are the formidable antagonists that you have to look in the face. Now let us see how you stand. On this side of the Channel a body already exceeding thirty millions of people, a population constantly increasing, a population knit and welded together in heart as much as any population in the world, a population with a powerful army and with a powerful navy, and a population to which you are about to add a strength that in its relations with Ireland it never yet has fully enjoyed—the strength of a just cause. And it is in that extraordinary inequality that you are exhorted by the paper Unionists and by the Tories to shrink back from this frightful danger, and from a conflict which can never come, with a people which could never resist you. Gentlemen, allow me to illustrate this by a very short and simple tale of Dean Swift, who had the power of conveying truths in the form of wit such as no man who ever lived enjoyed. Only recollect that what we are speaking of is this portentous battle, after Home Rule has been conceded, between England and Ireland. Dean Swift has said somewhere that there are upon record various well-authenticated

Liverpool, June 28.

cases where it is historically clear that ten men well armed have fought with one man in his shirt and have beaten him.

How do we hold Ireland at present?

Well now can you bear with me a moment, while I give you yet one more specimen of your paper Unionists, who are to figure here to-morrow night? They say what a dreadful case it will be that, after all they predict has come to pass—it never will come to pass—but still after all that has come to pass, there will be no remedy against Ireland except that of armed force. These gentlemen are extremely shocked at the idea of holding Ireland by armed force. I want to know, gentlemen, how you hold it now? I want to know how you have held it for these six-and-eighty years? You have held it by armed force. Do not conceal from yourselves the fact; do not blind yourselves to the essential features of the case upon which you have to judge. By force you have held it; by force you are holding it. By love we ask you to hold it. And our opponents, who have been very patient indeed of the evils of force while they had it, who seem to have been perfectly content with continuing for ever a rule of force in Ireland, so, when we propose this very different and contradictory method of procedure, they are raised to a state of horror, because they think all will go wrong, owing to the monstrous, incurable wickedness of this Irish nation, and that they will have again to resort to the aid of force, which, if they did resort to it, would be exactly to put themselves where they are now, and where they have been for six-and-eighty years, and where to all appearance they are perfectly content to remain.

(3) *To honour.*

Gentlemen, one more appeal. I appeal to the honour of England: and it has been a matter of some surprise to me, and of pain much more than surprise, to see that in this controversy upon the side of our opponents the honour of England is never mentioned. Gentlemen, I have heard enough of honour in my lifetime to make a man sick, if it were possible, of the very word; but that has been always honour pleaded as an excuse

False honour and true.

Liverpool, June 28.

for bloodshed. We heard enough of honour in 1878, 1879, and 1880. We heard of peace with honour, at a time when the representatives of England, for the first occasion in our history, came back from an illustrious Congress of Europe, and had been in that Congress, from the beginning to the end of its proceedings, the foes of liberty and the champions of oppression. Then it was that they came back and said, "We bring you peace with honour." No, gentlemen, thank God, through your action in 1880, which I hope you will repeat in 1886, we were enabled to break down that system, to give liberties which had been denied, to put together again countries that had been broken to pieces, to establish peace and tranquillity, where nothing reigned but disorder, war, and cruelty. And now I make a plea to you for the honour of England; not for bloodshed, not for strife, but for the wiping away of those old and deep stains that are not yet obliterated, but deface and deform the character of an illustrious nation in the face of the world, against which condemnation has been recorded against you for generations past in every civilized country, and with which now at last, at this late moment, we seek effectually to deal. Oh, gentlemen, is there no honour except that which causes the sword to be drawn? Is there no honour in integrity, in justice, in humanity, in mercy, in equal rights, in purity of dealing, in horror of fraud, and hatred of falsehood? Honour, gentlemen, is the life and soul of civilization, and it is that honour to which I appeal, and which now we wish to relieve from the burden and the stains which encumber it.

The history of the Act of Union.

When I opened this question in the House of Commons on the 8th of April, I said very little about the Act of Union, for two reasons. First of all, because, looking at the facts, whatever that Act may have been in the beginning, I do not think that it could safely or wisely be blotted out of the Statute Book; but also for another reason—that I did not wish gratuitously to expose to the world the shame of my country. But this I must tell you, if we are compelled to

Liverpool, June 28.

go into it. The combination against us, the resolute banding together of the great, and the rich, and the noble, and I know not who, against the true genuine sense of the people compels us to unveil the truth; and I tell you this, that, so far as I can judge, and so far as my knowledge goes, I grieve to say, in the presence of a distinguished Irishman, that I know of no blacker or fouler transaction in the history of man than the making of the Union between England and Ireland. It is not possible to tell it fully, but in a few words I may give you some idea of what I mean. Fraud is bad, gentlemen, and force—violence as against right—is bad; but if there is one thing more detestable than another it is the careful, artful combination of the two. The carrying of the Irish Union was nothing in the world but an artful combination of fraud and force, applied in the basest manner to the attainment of an end which all Ireland—for the exceptions might almost be counted on your fingers—detested, Protestants even more than Roman Catholics. In the Irish Parliament there were 300 seats, and out of these 300 seats there were 116 placemen and pensioners. The Government of Mr. Pitt rewarded with places, which, if I remember aright, did not vacate the seats as they do in this country, those who voted for them, and took away the pensions of those who were disposed to vote against them. Notwithstanding that state of things, in 1799, in the month of June, the proposal of Union was rejected in the Irish Parliament. The Irish Parliament in 1795, under Lord Fitzwilliam, had been gallantly and patriotically exercised in amending the condition of the country. The monopolists of the Beresford and other families got the ear of Mr. Pitt, and made him recall Lord Fitzwilliam; and from that moment it was that the revolutionary action began among the Roman Catholics of Ireland. From that moment the word separation, never dreamt of before, by degrees insinuated itself into their councils, an uneasy state of things prevailed, undoubted disaffection was produced, and it could not but be

Liverpool, June 28.

produced, by abominable misgovernment. Being so produced, it was the excuse for all that followed. And what was done? Inside the walls of Parliament, the terror of withdrawing pensions, and wholesale bribery in the purchase of nomination boroughs, were carried on to such an extent as to turn the scale. Outside Parliament, martial law and the severest restrictions prevented the people from expressing their views and sentiments upon the Union; and again, as I have told you, that that detestable union of fraud and force might be consummated, the bribe was held out to the Roman Catholic bishops and clergy, in the hope of at any rate slackening their opposition, that if only they would consent to the Union it should be followed by full admission to civil privileges and by endowments which would, at any rate, have equalized the monstrous anomaly of the existence of an established Protestant Church.

Gentlemen, that was the state of things by which,—by the use of all those powers that this great and strong country could exert through its command over the Executive against the weakness of Ireland—by that means at last they got together a sufficient number of people, with 116 placemen and pensioners out of 300 persons, and, with a large number of borough proprietors bought at the cost of a million and a half of money, at last they succeeded in getting a majority of between forty-two and forty-six to pass the Union. I have heard of more bloody proceedings; the massacre of St. Bartholomew was a more cruel proceeding. But a more base proceeding, a more vile proceeding, is not recorded, in my judgment, upon any page of history than the process by which the Tory Government of that period brought about the union with Ireland in the teeth, and in despite of the protest, of every Liberal statesman from one end of the country to the other.

England's duty to Ireland after the Union.

Is it possible to atone for so great a wrong? Now, I will make one admission. The Union produced changes so enormous, the whole machinery of the Government had to be reconstituted to such an extent, and the alteration

Liverpool, June 28.

of system was so vast, that in my opinion it became the duty, at any rate of Englishmen, after the Union had once been passed and consolidated as a mere statute, to see whether it could be made to work compatibly with justice and with honour. Therefore I am not at all surprised when I find that men like Lord Grey, who had been one of the most illustrious and vehement opponents of the Union, in later years declined to be responsible for unsettling it. He said—and I think he might say with perfect truth—that there was a great deal to do, that Ireland had great grievances which Parliament might redress, and that, if it was possible it was certainly desirable to avoid the unsettling of so vast a piece of legislation. Yes: but have we atoned since the Union for what we did to bring about the Union?

Failure to perform that duty.

Now I am making my appeal to the honour of Englishmen, and I want to show to Englishmen who have a sense of honour that they have a debt of honour that remains to this hour not fully paid. The Union was followed by these six consequences:—firstly, broken promises; secondly, the passing of bad laws; thirdly, the putting down of liberty; fourthly, the withholding from Ireland benefits that we took to ourselves; fifthly, the giving to force, and to force only, what we ought to have given to honour and justice; and, sixthly, the shameful postponement of relief to the most crying grievances. I will give you the proof in no longer space than that in which I have read these words.

"Broken promises"—the promise to the Roman Catholics of emancipation and the promise of endowment. Emancipation was never given for twenty-nine years. It would have been given if the Irish Parliament had remained. It would have been given in the time of Lord Fitzwilliam. It was never given for twenty-nine years after the Union. "No endowment." Well, you will say, and I should say, that was not a thing to be desired. I cannot wish that the Roman Catholic clergy should have received endowment. But, on the other hand, it was a base thing to break your promise to them.

Liverpool, June 28.

"Passing bad laws." Yes, slow as it was to pass good laws, the Parliament could pass bad laws quick enough. In 1815 they passed a law most oppressive to the Irish tenant, and it was the only measure relating to Irish land of serious consequence that ever received its attention until the year 1870.

"Restraint of liberty." What happened after the Union? In 1810 the people met largely in Dublin. Almost all the Roman Catholic wealth and influence of the country, and a great deal of the Protestant power too, met in Dublin for the purpose of protesting against the Union. Not the slightest heed was given to their protest. In 1820 there was a county meeting of the shire of Dublin for the purpose of paying compliments to George IV. The people moved a counter resolution, and this counter resolution complained of the Act of Union. The sheriff refused to hear them, refused to put their motion, left the room, and sent in the soldiers to break them up—a peaceful county meeting!

Fourthly, we withheld from Ireland what we took to ourselves. Take the case of the franchise. The franchise in Ireland remained a very restricted franchise until last year; in England it had been largely extended, as you know, by the Acts of 1867 and 1868. In England you thoroughly reformed your municipalities, and you have true popular bodies. In Ireland the number of them was cut down to twelve, and after a battle of six years, during which Parliament had to spend the chief part of its time upon the work, I think about twelve municipalities were constituted in Ireland, with highly restricted powers. Inequality was branded upon Ireland at every step. We established in this country denominational education right and left, according as the people desired it; but in Ireland denominational education was condemned, and until within the last few years it was not possible for any Roman Catholic to obtain a degree in Ireland, if he had received his education in a denominational college. Such is the system of inequality under which Ireland was governed.

Fifthly, we have given only to fear what we ought to have given to justice. I refer to the Duke of Wellington, who, in 1829, himself said with manly candour that the fear of civil war, and nothing else, was his motive for coercing, I might almost say, the House of Lords, certainly for bringing the House of Lords to vote a change which it is well known that the large majority of them utterly detested. **Liverpool, June 28.**

Sixthly, "the shameful postponement of the relief of crying grievances." Yes, we shamefully postponed it. In 1815 we passed an Act to make infinitely more dependent and assailable the position of the Irish tenant. Not till 1843 did we inquire into his condition. Sir Robert Peel has the honour of having appointed the Devon Commission. That Commission reported that a large number of the population of Ireland were submitting with exemplary and marvellous patience—these people whom we are told you cannot possibly trust—were submitting with marvellous and unintelligible patience to a lot more bitter and deplorable than the lot of any people in the civilized world. Sir James Graham in the House of Commons admitted that the description applied to three and a half millions of the people of Ireland. And yet, with all that, we went on, certainly doing a great deal of good, improving the legislation of this country in a wonderful manner, especially by the great struggle of free trade; but not till 1870 was the first effort made, seventy years after the Union, to administer in any serious degree to the wants of the Irish tenant, the Irish occupier—in fact, to the wants and necessities of the mass of the people of Ireland.

Even measures of relief denounced by Conservatives.

Now I say that that is a deplorable narrative. It is a narrative which cannot be shaken. I have been treading upon ground that our antagonists carefully avoid. It is idle to say we have done some good to Ireland. Yes, we have. By the Land Acts of 1870 and 1881, and by the disestablishment of the Irish Church, we did some good to Ireland; and by the enlargement of the Maynooth grants Sir Robert Peel did some good to Ireland. Yes; but these very

Liverpool, June 28.

Acts, which class of Acts alone the paper Unionists can claim as showing that we have done good to Ireland—these very Acts are down to the present day denounced by the Tory party,—the Church Act as sacrilege, and the Land Acts as confiscation. I say it is time that we should bethink ourselves of this question of honour, and see how the matter stands, and set very seriously about the duty, the sacred duty, the indispensable and overpowering duty, of effacing from history, if efface them we can, these terrible stains, which the acts of England have left upon the fame of England, and which constitute a debt of honour to Ireland that it is high time to consider and to pay.

An appeal to Conservatives.

Now let me ask a question of our friends the Tories, or Conservatives, and I hope there are some of them here. Why should they oppose us in the great object upon which we are bent? I want to know why a man because he is a Conservative should oppose us? Why is it a Radical measure to give self-government to Ireland, unless it is Radical because it is just? I can understand that every Radical, and I have no doubt there are a great many Radicals here, will be well content to a certain extent with that view of the case. But what do my Conservative friends say to it? Is it Radical because it is just? No, unless they are to come to the conclusion that it is not Conservative because it is just, and could only be Conservative if it were unjust. That is where I want to persuade them that they are doing themselves an injustice. I do not appeal to the Conservatives here or elsewhere upon the ground that they will be beaten. They know that as well as I do. But they do not much care about that: and shall I tell you why? They are well accustomed to it. I read you out ten subjects. On every one of them they fought; on every one of them they were beaten. And now I am charitably endeavouring, by good-humoured attempts at persuasion, to save them from being beaten again; and I want to save them by showing them, if I can, without, I hope, offending even the best Radical that hears me, that Radicalism is in no way the special characteristic, the distinctive feature, of this measure. What are we doing? Are we inventing what is new? That is the device of Radicalism. No; we are doing what Tories always preach to us—restoring what is old. A statutory Parliament in Ireland is no novelty. Does the love of antiquity, to which a Tory lays claim, carry him no further back than the time of his own grandmother? For eighty-six years, and eighty-six years only, he has a reverence for the institutions of his country. But has he no reverence for anything that happened before 1800? (A voice: "Certainly.") Somebody says "Certainly." I hope that is true, and if it is true he must vote with us on this occasion. It is essentially, gentlemen, a work of restoration in which we are engaged. The Parliament of Ireland in 1800, when it was extinguished, was five hundred years old. It was not the gift of England; it had sprung from the soil. It had been an unhappy connection with us, but in 1782, by an act of late but of great wisdom, the Parliament of Ireland was placed upon a footing on which she would have worked out the regeneration of that country; and she was working it out patiently and steadily, had it not been for the evil fate which induced the British Government to interfere and to prevent that Parliament from consummating its beneficent purpose. Therefore I say we go back to that time. We ask you to reconstitute that Parliament, divested, with the free consent of Ireland, of whatever might have made it work inharmoniously with the rest of the institutions of the empire. But essentially we ask you to do a work of restoration, and, if Conservatives won't follow us in that work, they are opposing not only us, but they are opposing their own principles according to every enlightened sense and construction of such principles.

Liverpool, June 28.

A work of restoration

In conclusion I have only this one remark to make. I am much struck by a very important difference between the opposition offered us in this case and the opposition offered on all former occasions. I take the case of the Corn Laws.

Our opponents cannot coerce, and they will not conciliate.

Liverpool, June 28.

The opponents of the Corn Laws thought that they were doing, and they were doing, a very great good; but the friends of the Corn Laws were accustomed to say that it was by the Corn Laws that the people, and especially the peasantry, of this country were kept upon a much higher level of subsistence and comfort than the peasantry of the rest of Europe. That allegation entirely broke down in the long run; but all I wish you to see is that the opponents of abolition thought it necessary to have some allegation of the kind, and were obliged to say something satisfactory on their own side of the case. What is shown now by the Tories and paper Unionists? What is the redeeming feature to which they point in the case which we are trying to cure, and to which they will not allow us to apply a remedy? Why, gentlemen, there is no redeeming feature at all. They tell you that capital is driven from Ireland, that confidence is destroyed, that population is diminishing, that the law is not respected, that social order is sapped and undermined, and that it is necessary to have a prescription of twenty years of repression and coercion. It is under these circumstances that your paper Unionists are to meet to-morrow night in this building, and to devise means for upholding a cause so miserable that it is destitute even of the thin pretexts that have made opposition in other cases respectable, have enabled men to blind their own understandings and to play with their own consciences, whereas here the facts are glaring and stare us in the face. Coerce you cannot. By coercion you could not advance, even if you could coerce. Conciliate they will not; but we ask the people of England and of Scotland to override them, and in the name of justice to say it shall not be so.

Conclusion.

In that touching address which was presented to me at the beginning of our proceedings I was reminded that in this city I first drew breath. I have drawn it now for seventy-six years, and the time cannot be far distant when I must submit to the universal law, and pay the debt of nature. It may be these words I speak to you are the last that I shall ever have the opportunity of speaking in Liverpool. (A voice: "We hope not.") That is in higher hands than ours. I say that to you to show you that I am conscious of the deep solemnity of the occasion, of the great controversy which has been raised between nation and nation. I wish we could expand our minds and raise our visions to a point necessary to understand what these controversies really are, how deep their roots go down, what incalculable results they produce, and through what immense periods of time, upon the peace and happiness of mankind. Many of you will recollect, in that spirited old ballad of "Chevy Chase," the lines—

Liverpool, June 28.

"'The child that is unborn shall rue
The hunting of that day.'

And so, should you fail in your duties on this occasion, should the idle, hollow, and shallow pretexts that are used against us bewilder the mind of the people of England or of Scotland, or should the power of the purse, of wealth, of title, of station—should all these powers overbear the national sense, I fear it may again be true that

The child that is unborn shall rue
The *voting* of that day.

Gentlemen, I entreat you—you require it little, but I entreat through you the people of this country, to bethink themselves well of the position in which they stand; to look back upon the history of the past, and forward into the prospects of the future; to determine that it shall be no longer said of England, as it is now habitually said thoughout the civilized world, that Ireland is the Poland of England. Let us determine not to have a Poland any longer. We have had it long enough. Listen to prudence; listen to courage; listen to honour; and speak the words of the poet—

"'Ring out the old,
Ring in the new.'

Liverpool, June 28.

Ring out the notes and the memory of discord, and ring in the blessed reign and time of peace.

The right honourable gentleman sat down, after speaking one hour and forty-five minutes, amid loud and long-continued applause.

The meeting, on the motion of Sir Thomas Brassey, seconded by Mr. A. Birrell, accorded the chairman a hearty vote of thanks and then slowly dispersed.

APPENDICES.

APPENDIX I.

THE GOVERNMENT OF IRELAND BILL.

THE following is the full text of Mr. Gladstone's Home Rule Bill :—

PART I.

LEGISLATIVE AUTHORITY.

1.—On and after the appointed day, there shall be established in Ireland a Legislature consisting of Her Majesty the Queen and an Irish Legislative Body. *A free Parliament.*

2.—With the exceptions and subject to the restrictions in this Act mentioned, it shall be lawful for Her Majesty the Queen, by and with the advice of the Irish Legislative Body, to make laws for the peace, order, and good government of Ireland, and by any such law to alter and repeal any law in Ireland. *Powers.*

3.*—The Legislature of Ireland shall not make laws relating to the following matters or any of them :— *Limitations.*

(1) The status or dignity of the Crown, or the succession to the Crown or a Regency.

(2) The making of peace or war.

(3) The army, navy, militia, volunteers, or other military or naval forces ; or the defence of the realm.

(4) Treaties and other relations with foreign States, or the relations between the various parts of Her Majesty's dominions.

(5) Dignities or titles of honour.

(6) Prize or booty of war.

* Clause 19, sub-section 2, was framed with reference to this Clause exclusively, and not to Clause 4, which was inserted in the draft at a later date. It was intended to limit the sub-section so as to preserve the intention of the framers.—W. E. G., August 12, 1886.

(7) Offences against the law of nations, or offences committed in violation of any treaty made or hereafter to be made between Her Majesty and any foreign State; or offences committed on the high seas.

(8) Treason, alienage, or naturalization.

(9) Trade, navigation, or quarantine.

(10) The postal and telegraph service, except as hereafter in this Act mentioned with respect to the transmission of letters and telegrams in Ireland.

(11) Beacons, lighthouses, or sea marks.

(12) The coinage, the value of foreign money, legal tender, or weights and measures; or

(13) Copyright, patent rights, or other exclusive rights to the use or profits of any works or inventions.

Any law made in contravention of this section shall be void.

Further limitations.

4.—The Irish Legislature shall not make any law—

(1) Respecting the establishment or endowment of religion, or prohibiting the free exercise thereof; or

(2) Imposing any disability or conferring any privilege on account of religious belief; or

(3) Abrogating or derogating from the right to establish or maintain any place of denominational education, or any denominational institution or charity; or

(4) Prejudicially affecting the right of any child to attend a school receiving public money, without attending the religious instruction at that school; or

(5) Impairing, without either the leave of Her Majesty in Council first obtained, on an address presented by the Legislative Body of Ireland, or the consent of the corporation interested, the rights, property, or privileges of any existing corporation, incorporated by Royal Charter or local or general Act of Parliament; or

(6) Imposing or relating to duties of Customs and duties of Excise, as defined by this Act, or either of such duties, or affecting any Act relating to such duties, or either of them; or

(7) Affecting this Act except in so far as it is declared to be alterable by the Irish Legislature.

Queen's prerogative.

5.—Her Majesty the Queen shall have the same prerogatives with respect to summoning, proroguing, and dissolving the Irish Legislative Body as Her Majesty has with respect to summoning, proroguing, and dissolving the Imperial Parliament.

A five years' Parliament.

6.—The Irish Legislative Body, whenever summoned, may have continuance for five years and no longer, to be reckoned from the day on which any such Legislative Body is appointed to meet.

EXECUTIVE AUTHORITY.

7.—(1) The Executive Government of Ireland shall continue vested in Her Majesty, and shall be carried on by the Lord-Lieutenant on behalf of Her Majesty, with the aid of such officers and such Council as to Her Majesty may from time to time seem fit. *Lord-Lieutenant's powers.*

(2) Subject to any instructions which may from time to time be given by Her Majesty, the Lord-Lieutenant shall give or withhold the assent of Her Majesty to bills passed by the Irish Legislative Body, and shall exercise the prerogatives of Her Majesty in respect of the summoning, proroguing, and dissolving of the Irish Legislative Body, and any prerogatives the exercise of which may be delegated to him by Her Majesty.

8.—Her Majesty may, by Order in Council, from time to time, place under the control of the Irish Government, for the purposes of that Government, any such lands and buildings in Ireland as may be vested in, or held in trust for, Her Majesty. *Royal lands.*

CONSTITUTION OF LEGISLATIVE BODY.

9.—(1) The Irish Legislative Body shall consist of a First and Second Order. *First and Second Orders.*

(2) The two Orders shall deliberate together, and shall vote together, except that if any question arises in relation to legislation, or to the standing orders, or rules of procedure, or to any other matter in that behalf in this Act specified, and such question is to be determined by vote, each Order shall, if a majority of the members present of either Order demand a separate vote, give their votes in like manner as if they were separate legislative bodies, and if the result of the voting of the two Orders does not agree, the question shall be resolved in the negative.

10.—(1) The First Order of the Irish Legislative Body shall consist of one hundred and three members, of whom seventy-five shall be elective members, and twenty-eight peerage members. Each elective member shall, at the date of his election, and during his period of membership, be *bona fide* possessed of property which, *Election and powers of First Order.*

(a) If realty, or partly realty and partly personalty, yields two hundred pounds a year or upwards, free of all charges; or

(b) If personalty, yields the same income, or is of the capital value of £4000 or upwards, free of all charges.

(2) For the purpose of electing the elective members of the First Order of the Legislative Body, Ireland shall be divided into the electoral districts specified in the first schedule to this Act, and each such district shall return the number of members in that behalf specified in that schedule.

(3) The elective members shall be elected by the registered electors of

each electoral district, and for that purpose a register of electors shall be made annually.

£25 franchise. (4) An elector in each electoral district shall be qualified as follows, that is to say:—He shall be of full age, and not subject to any legal incapacity, and shall have been during the twelve months next preceding the twentieth day of July in any year the owner or occupier of some land or tenement within the district of a nett annual value of twenty-five pounds or upwards.

(5) The term of office of an elective member shall be ten years.

(6) In every fifth year thirty-seven or thirty-eight of the elective members, as the case requires, shall retire from office, and their places shall be filled by election. The members to retire shall be those who have been members for the longest time without re-election.

(7) The offices of the peerage members shall be filled as follows, that is to say:—

(a) Each of the Irish peers who on the appointed day is one of the twenty-eight Irish representative peers shall, on giving his written assent to the Lord-Lieutenant, become a peerage member of the First Order of the Irish Legislative Body, and if at any time within thirty years after the appointed day any such peer vacates his office by death or resignation, the vacancy shall be filled by the election to that office by the Irish peers of one of their number in manner heretofore in use respecting the election of Irish representative peers, subject to adaptation as provided by this Act; and if the vacancy is not so filled within the proper time it shall be filled by the election of an elective member.

(b) If any of the twenty-eight peers aforesaid does not within one month after the appointed day give such assent to be a peerage member of the First Order, the vacancy so created shall be filled up as if he had assented and vacated his office by resignation.

(8) A peerage member shall be entitled to hold office during his life or until the expiry of thirty years from the appointed day, whichever period is the shortest. At the expiration of such thirty years the offices of all the peerage members shall be vacated, as if they were dead; and their places shall be filled by elective members qualified and elected in manner provided by this Act with respect to elective members of the First Order, and such elective members may be distributed by the Irish Legislature among the electoral districts, so, however, that care shall be taken to give additional members to the most populous places.

(9) The offices of members of the First Order shall not be vacated by the dissolution of the Legislative Body.

(10) The provisions in the second schedule to this Act relating to members of the First Order of the Legislative Body shall be of the same force as if they were enacted in the body of this Act.

11.—(1) Subject as in this section hereafter mentioned, the Second Order of the Legislative Body shall consist of two hundred and four members. *Election and powers of Second Order.*

(2) The members of the Second Order shall be chosen by the existing constituencies of Ireland—two by each constituency, with the exception of the city of Cork, which shall be divided into two divisions, in manner set forth in the third schedule to this Act, and two members shall be chosen by each of such divisions.

(3) Any person who on the appointed day is a member representing an existing Irish constituency in the House of Commons shall, on giving his written assent to the Lord-Lieutenant, become a member of the Second Order of the Irish Legislative Body as if he had been elected by the constituency which he was representing in the House of Commons. Each of the members for the city of Cork, on the said day, may elect for which of the divisions of that city he wishes to be deemed to have been elected.

(4) If any member does not give such written assent within one month after the appointed day, his place shall be filled by election in the same manner and at the same time as if he had assented and vacated his office by death.

(5) If the same person is elected to both Orders, he shall within seven days after the meeting of the Legislative Body, or if the body is not sitting at the time of the election within seven days after the election, elect in which Order he will serve, and his membership of the other Order shall be void, and be filled by a fresh election.

(6) Notwithstanding anything in this Act, it shall be lawful for the Legislature of Ireland at any time to pass an Act enabling the Royal University of Ireland to return not more than two members to the Second Order of the Irish Legislative Body, in addition to the number of members above mentioned.

(7) Notwithstanding anything in this Act, it shall be lawful for the Irish Legislature, after the first dissolution of the Legislative Body which occurs, to alter the constitution or election of the Second Order of that body, due regard being had in the distribution of members to the population of the constituencies, provided that no alteration shall be made in the number of such Order.

FINANCE.

12.—(1) For the purpose of providing for the public service of Ireland, the Irish Legislature may impose taxes other than duties of Customs or Excise, as defined by this Act, which duties shall continue to be imposed and levied by and under the direction of the Imperial Parliament only. *Power to tax.*

(2) On and after the appointed day there shall be an Irish Consolidated Fund separate from the Consolidated Fund of the United Kingdom. *An Irish Consolidated Fund.*

Land Purchase Bill.

(3) All taxes imposed by the Legislature of Ireland, and all other public revenues under the control of the Government of Ireland, shall, subject to any provisions touching the disposal thereof contained in any Act passed in the present session respecting the sale and purchase of land in Ireland, be paid into the Irish Consolidated Fund, and be appropriated to the public service of Ireland according to law.

13.—(1) Subject to the provisions for the reduction or cesser thereof in this section mentioned, there shall be made, on the part of Ireland to the Consolidated Fund of the United Kingdom, the following annual contribution in every financial year, that is to say :—

Annual contribution to Britain.

(a) The sum of one million four hundred and sixty-six thousand pounds, on account of the interest on and management of the Irish share of the National Debt.

(b) The sum of one million six hundred and sixty-six thousand pounds on account of the expenditure on the army and navy of the United Kingdom.

(c) The sum of one hundred and ten thousand pounds on account of the Imperial Civil expenditure of the United Kingdom.

(d) The sum of one million pounds on account of the Royal Irish Constabulary and the Dublin Metropolitan Police.

(2) During the period of thirty years from this section taking effect, the said annual contributions shall not be increased, but may be reduced or cease, as hereinafter mentioned. After the expiration of the said thirty years, the said contribution shall, save as otherwise provided by this section, continue until altered in manner provided with respect to the alteration of this Act.

The National Debt.

(3) The Irish share of the National Debt shall be reckoned at forty-eight million pounds Bank annuities, and there shall be paid in every financial year on behalf of Ireland to the Commissioners for the Reduction of the National Debt an annual sum of three hundred and sixty thousand pounds, and the permanent annual charge for the National Debt on the Consolidated Fund of the United Kingdom shall be reduced by that amount, and the said annual sum shall be applied by the said Commissioners as a sinking fund for the redemption of the National Debt, and the Irish share of the National Debt shall be reduced by the amount of the National Debt so redeemed, and the said annual contribution on account of the interest on and management of the Irish share of the National Debt shall from time to time be reduced by a sum equal to the interest upon the amount of the National Debt from time to time so redeemed, but that last-mentioned sum shall be paid annually to the Commissioners for the Reduction of the National Debt in addition to the above-mentioned annual sinking fund, and shall be so paid and be applied as if it were part of that sinking fund.

(4) As soon as an amount of the National Debt equal to the said Irish share thereof has been redeemed under the provisions of this section,

the said annual contribution on account of the interest on and management of the Irish share of the National Debt and the said annual sum for a sinking fund shall cease.

5) If it appears to Her Majesty that the expenditure in respect of the army and navy of the United Kingdom, or in respect of Imperial Civil expenditure of the United Kingdom for any financial year has been less than fifteen times the amount of the contributions above named on account of the same matter, a sum equal to one-fifteenth part of the diminution shall be deducted from the current annual contribution for the same matter.

6) The sum paid from time to time by the Commissioners of Her Majesty's Woods, Forests, and Land Revenues to the Consolidated Fund of the United Kingdom, on account of the hereditary revenues of the Crown in Ireland, shall be credited to the Irish Government, and go in reduction of the said annual contribution payable on account of the Imperial Civil expenditure of the United Kingdom, but shall not be taken into account in calculating whether such diminution, as above mentioned, has or has not taken place in such expenditure.

(7) If it appears to Her Majesty that the expenditure in respect of the Royal Irish Constabulary and the Dublin Metropolitan Police for any financial year has been less than the contribution above named on account of such constabulary and police, the current contribution shall be diminished by the amount of such difference.

(8) This section shall take effect from and after the thirty-first day of March, one thousand eight hundred and eighty-seven.

14.—(1) On and after such day as the Treasury may direct, all moneys from time to time collected in Ireland on account of the duties of Customs or the duties of Excise, as defined by this Act, shall, under such regulations as the Treasury from time to time make, be carried to a separate account (in this Act referred to as the Customs and Excise Account), and applied in the payment of the following sums in priority, as mentioned in this section, that is to say:— *Customs and Excise duties.*

First, of such sum as is from time to time directed by the Treasury in respect of the costs, charges, and expenses of and incident to the collection and management of the said duties in Ireland, not exceeding four per cent. of the amount collected there.

Secondly, of the annual contributions required by this Act to be made to the Consolidated Fund of the United Kingdom.

Thirdly, of the annual sums required by this Act to be paid to the Commissioners for the Reduction of the National Debt.

Fourthly, of all sums by this Act declared to be payable out of the moneys carried to the Customs and Excise Account.

Fifthly, of all sums due to the Consolidated Fund of the United Kingdom for interest or sinking fund in respect of any loans made by the issue of Bank annuities or otherwise to the Government of Ireland under *Land Purchase Act.*

any Act passed in the present session relating to the purchase and sale of land in Ireland, so far as such sums are not defrayed out of the moneys received under such Act.

(2) So much of the moneys carried to a separate account under this section as the Treasury consider are not, or are not likely to be, required to meet the above-mentioned payments, shall from time to time be paid over, and applied as part of the public revenues under the control of the Irish Government.

15.—(1) There shall be charged on the Irish Consolidated Fund in priority, as mentioned in this section—

First, such portion of the sums directed by this Act to be paid out of the moneys carried to the Customs and Excise Account in priority to any payment for the public revenues of Ireland as those moneys are insufficient to pay.

Secondly, all sums due in respect of any debt incurred by the Government of Ireland, whether for interest, management, or sinking fund.

Thirdly, all sums which at the passing of this Act are charged on the Consolidated Fund of the United Kingdom in respect of Irish services of other than the salary of the Lord-Lieutenant.

Fourthly, the salaries of all Judges of the Supreme Court of Judicature or other superior Court in Ireland, or of any county or other like Court who are appointed after the passing of this Act, and the pension of such Judges.

Fifthly, any other sums charged by this Act on the Irish Consolidated Fund.

Power to tax. (2) It shall be the duty of the Legislature of Ireland to impose all such taxes, duties, or imposts as will raise a sufficient revenue to meet all sums charged for the time being on the Irish Consolidated Fund.

Irish Church property. 16.—(1) Until all charges which are payable out of the Church property in Ireland, and are guaranteed by the Treasury, have been fully paid, the Irish Land Commission shall continue as heretofore to exist, with such commissioners and officers receiving such salaries as the Treasury may from time to time appoint, and to administer the Church property and apply the income and other money receivable therefrom; and so much of the salaries of such commissioners and officers and expenses of the office as is not paid out of the Church property shall be paid out of moneys carried to the Customs and Excise Account under this Act, and, if these moneys are insufficient, out of the Consolidated Fund of Ireland, and if not so paid shall be paid out of moneys provided by Parliament—

Provided as follows:—

(a) All charges on the Church property for which a guarantee has been given by the Treasury before the passing of this Act shall, so far as they are not paid out of such property, be paid out of the moneys carried to the Customs and Excise Account under this Act, and, if such moneys are insufficient, the Consolidated Fund of Ireland, without prejudice, nevertheless, to the guarantee of the Treasury.

(b) All charges on the Church property for which no guarantee has been given by the Treasury before the passing of this Act shall be charged on the Consolidated Fund of Ireland, but shall not be guaranteed by the Treasury nor charged on the Consolidated Fund of the United Kingdom.

(2) Subject to any existing charges on the Church property, such property shall belong to the Irish Government, and any portion of the annual revenue thereof as the Treasury on the application of the Irish Government certify at the end of any financial year not to be required for meeting charges, and shall be paid over and applied as part of the public revenues under the control of the Irish Government.

(3) As soon as all charges on the Church property guaranteed by the Treasury have been paid, such property may be managed and administered and, subject to existing charges thereon, disposed of, and the income or proceeds thereby applied in such manner as the Irish Legislature may from time to time direct.

(4) "Church property" in this section means all property accruing under the Irish Church Act, 1869, and transferred to the Irish Land Commission by the Irish Church Act Amendment Act, 1881.

17.—(1) All sums due for principal or interest to the Public Works Loan Commissioners or to the Commissioners of Public Works in Ireland in respect of existing loans advanced on any security in Ireland, shall on and after the day appointed be due to the Government of Ireland instead of the said Commissioners, and such body of persons as the Government of Ireland may appoint for the purpose shall have all the powers of the said Commissioners or their secretary for enforcing payment of such sums, and all securities for such sums given to such Commissioners or their secretary shall have effect as if the said body were therein substituted for those Commissioners or their secretary. *Public loans.*

(2) For the repayment of the said loans to the Consolidated Fund of the United Kingdom the Irish Government shall pay annually into that fund, by half-yearly payments on the first day of January and the first day of July, or on such other days as may be agreed on, such instalments of the principal of the said loans as will discharge all the loans within thirty years from the appointed day, and shall also pay interest, half-yearly, on so much of the said principal as from time to time remains unpaid at the rate of three per cent. per annum, and such instalments of principal and interest shall be paid out of the moneys carried to the Customs and Excise Account under this Act, and, if those are insufficient, out of the Consolidated Fund of Ireland.

18.—If Her Majesty declares that a state of war exists, and is pleased to signify such declaration to the Irish Legislative Body by speech or *War vote* message, it shall be lawful for the Irish Legislature to appropriate a further sum out of the Consolidated Fund of Ireland in aid of the army, or navy, or other measures which Her Majesty may take for the prosecution of the war and defence of the realm, and to provide and raise money for that purpose ; and all moneys so provided and raised, whether by loan, taxation, or otherwise, shall be paid into the Consolidated Fund of the United Kingdom.

Limitations in taxation.

19.—(1) It shall not be lawful for the Irish Legislative Body to adopt or pass any vote, resolution, address, or bill for the raising or appropriation for any purpose of any part of the public revenue of Ireland, or of any tax, duty, or impost, except in pursuance of a recommendation from Her Majesty signified through the Lord-Lieutenant in the session in which such vote, resolution, address, or bill is proposed.

Power to vote money.

(2) Notwithstanding that the Irish Legislature is prohibited by this Act from making laws relating to certain subjects, that Legislature may, with the assent of Her Majesty in Council first obtained, appropriate any part of the Irish public revenue, or any tax, duty, or impost imposed by such Legislature, for the purpose of or in connection with such subjects.

Exchequer Court retained.

20.—(1) On and after the appointed day the Exchequer Division of the High Court of Justice shall continue to be a Court of Exchequer for revenue purposes under this Act, and whenever any vacancy occurs in the office of any Judge of such Exchequer Division his successor shall be appointed by Her Majesty, on the joint recommendation of the Lord-Lieutenant of Ireland and the Lord High Chancellor of Great Britain.

(2) The Judges of such Exchequer Division appointed after the passing of this Act shall be removable only by Her Majesty on address from the two Houses of the Imperial Parliament, and shall receive the same salaries and pensions as those payable at the passing of this Act to the existing Judges of such division, unless, with the assent of Her Majesty in Council first obtained, the Irish Legislature alters such salaries or pensions, and such salaries and pensions shall be paid out of the moneys carried to the Customs and Excise Account in pursuance of this Act, and, if the same are insufficient, shall be paid out of the Irish Consolidated Fund, and if not so paid shall be paid out of the Consolidated Fund of the United Kingdom.

(3) An alteration of any rules relating to the procedure in such legal proceedings mentioned in this section shall not be made except with the approval of the Lord High Chancellor of Great Britain, and the sittings of Exchequer Division and the Judges thereof shall be regulated with the like approval.

(4) *All legal proceedings instituted in Ireland by or against the

* It was the intention of this sub-section to place every force of Her Majesty in Ireland at the command of the Court of Exchequer for the enforcement of its

Commissioners or any officers of Customs or Excise or the Treasury shall, if so required by any party to such proceeding, be heard and determined before the Judges of such Exchequer Division, or some or one of them, and any appeal from the decision in any such legal proceeding, if by a Judge shall lie to the said division, and if by the Exchequer Division shall lie to the House of Lords, and not to any other tribunal; and if it is made to appear to such Judges, or any of them, that any decree or judgment in any such proceedings as aforesaid has not been duly enforced by the sheriff or other officer whose duty it is to enforce the same, such Judge or Judges shall appoint some officer to enforce such judgment or decree; and it shall be the duty of such officer to take proper steps to enforce the same, and for that purpose such officer and all persons employed by him shall be entitled to the same immunities, powers, and privileges as are by law conferred on a sheriff and his officers.

(5) All sums recovered in respect of duties of Customs and Excise, or under any Act relating thereto, or by an officer of Customs or Excise, shall, notwithstanding anything in any other Act, be paid to the Treasury, and carried to the Customs and Excise Account under this Act.

POLICE.

21.—The following regulations shall be made with respect to police in Ireland:—

(a) The Dublin Metropolitan Police shall continue and be subject as heretofore to the control of the Lord-Lieutenant, as representing Her Majesty, for a period of two years from the passing of this Act, and thereafter until any alteration is made by Act of the Legislature of Ireland, but such Act shall provide for the proper saving of all then existing interests, whether as regards pay, pensions, superannuation allowances, or otherwise. *Dublin police.*

(b) The Royal Irish Constabulary shall, while that force subsists, continue and be subject as heretofore to the control of the Lord-Lieutenant as representing Her Majesty. *Irish Constabulary.*

(c) The Irish Legislature may provide for the establishment and maintenance of a police force in counties and burghs in Ireland, under the control of local authorities, and arrangements may be made between the Treasury and the Irish Government for the establishment and maintenance of police reserves. *Burghs, etc.*

decrees in matters of revenue. It was argued by an opponent of the bill that the words of this sub-section were insufficient to the purpose. If this had been shown in the Committee, the framers of the bill would have proposed to enlarge them accordingly.—W. E. G., August 12, 1886.

PART II.

SUPPLEMENTAL PROVISIONS.

POWERS OF HER MAJESTY.

22.—On and after the appointed day there shall be reserved to Her Majesty—

Forts, magazines, etc.

(1) The power of erecting forts, magazines, arsenals, dockyards, and other buildings for military or naval purposes.

(2) The power of taking waste land and, on making due compensation, any other land for the purpose of erecting such forts, magazines, arsenals, dockyards, or other buildings as aforesaid, and for any other military or naval purpose or the defence of the nation.

LEGISLATIVE BODY.

Two Orders disagreeing.

23.—If a bill, or any provisions of a bill, is lost by disagreement between the two Orders of the Legislative Body, and after a period ending with a dissolution of the Legislative Body or the period of three years, whichever period is longest, such bill, or a bill containing the said provision, is again considered by the Legislative Body, and such bill or provision is adopted by the second Order and negatived by the first Order, the same shall be submitted to the whole Legislative Body, both Orders of which shall vote together on the bill or provision, and the same shall be adopted or rejected according to the decision of the majority of the members so voting together.

Irish representation to cease.

24.—On and after the appointed day Ireland shall cease, except in the event hereafter in this Act mentioned, to return representative peers to the House of Lords or members to the House of Commons, and the persons who on the said day are such representative peers and members shall cease as such to be members of the House of Lords and House of Commons respectively.

DECISION OF CONSTITUTIONAL QUESTIONS.

Arbitration of disputes.

25.—Questions arising as to the powers conferred on the Legislature of Ireland under this Act shall be determined as follows :—

(a) If any such question arises on any bill passed by the Legislative Body, the Lord-Lieutenant may refer such question to Her Majesty in Council.

(b) If in the course of any action or other legal proceedings such question arises on any Act of the Irish Legislature, any party to such action or other legal proceeding may, subject to the rules in this section mentioned, appeal for a decision on such question to Her Majesty in Council.

(c) If any such question arises otherwise than as aforesaid on any Act of the Irish Legislature, the Lord-Lieutenant or one of Her Majesty's principal Secretaries of State may refer such question to Her Majesty in Council.

(d) Any question referred or appeal brought under this section to Her Majesty in Council shall be referred for the consideration of the Judicial Committee of the Privy Council.

(e) The decision of Her Majesty in Council on any question referred or appeal brought under this section shall be final, and a bill which may be so decided to be or contain a provision in excess of the powers of the Irish Legislature shall not be assented to by the Lord-Lieutenant, and a provision of any Act which is so decided to be in excess of the powers of the Irish Legislature shall be void. *Rights of appeal.*

(f) There shall be added to the Judicial Committee, when sitting for the purpose of considering questions under this section, such members of Her Majesty's Privy Council being, or having been, Irish Judges as to Her Majesty may seem meet.

(g) Her Majesty may, by Order in Council, from time to time make rules as to the cases and mode in which, and the conditions under which, in pursuance of this section, questions may be referred and appeals be brought to Her Majesty in Council, and as to the consideration thereof by the Judicial Committee of the Privy Council, and any rules so made shall be of the same force as if they were enacted in this Act.

(h) An appeal shall not lie to the House of Lords in respect of any question, in respect to which an appeal can be had to Her Majesty in Council in pursuance of this section.

LORD-LIEUTENANT.

26.—(1) Notwithstanding anything to the contrary contained in any Act of Parliament, every subject of Her Majesty shall be eligible to hold and enjoy the office of Lord-Lieutenant of Ireland, without reference to his religious belief.

(2) The salary of the Lord-Lieutenant shall continue to be charged on the Consolidated Fund of the United Kingdom, and the expenses of his household and establishment shall continue to be defrayed out of the moneys to be provided by Parliament.

(3) All existing powers vested by Act of Parliament or otherwise in the Chief Secretary for Ireland may, if no such officer is appointed, be exercised by the Lord-Lieutenant until other provision is made by Act of the Irish Legislature. *Irish Secretary.*

(4) The Legislature of Ireland shall not pass any Act relating to the office or functions of the Lord-Lieutenant of Ireland.

JUDGES AND CIVIL SERVANTS.

Judges.

27.—A Judge of the Supreme Court of Judicature or other Superior Court of Ireland, or of any county Court or other Court with a like jurisdiction in Ireland, appointed after the passing of this Act, shall not be removed from his office except in pursuance of an address to Her Majesty from both Orders of the Legislative Body voting separately, nor shall his salary be diminished or right to pension altered during his continuance in office.

28.—(1) All persons who at the passing of this Act are Judges of the Supreme Court of Judicature, or County Court Judges, or hold any other judicial position in Ireland, shall, if they are removable at present on address to Her Majesty of both Houses of Parliament, continue to be removable only upon such address from both Houses of the Imperial Parliament, and if removable in any other manner shall continue to be removable in like manner as heretofore; and such persons, and also all persons at the passing of this Act in the permanent Civil Service of the Crown in Ireland, whose salaries are charged on the Consolidated Fund of the United Kingdom, shall continue to hold office and to be entitled to the same salaries, pensions, and superannuation allowances as heretofore, and to be liable to perform the same or analogous duties as heretofore, and the salaries of such persons shall be paid out of the moneys carried to the Customs and Excise Account under this Act, or, if these moneys are insufficient, out of the Irish Consolidated Fund, and, if the same are not so paid, shall continue charged on the Consolidated Fund of the United Kingdom.

Civil servants.

(2) If any of the said persons retire from office with the approbation of Her Majesty before he has completed the period of service entitling him to a pension, it shall be lawful for Her Majesty, if she thinks fit, to grant to that person such pension, not exceeding the pension to which he would have been entitled if he had completed the said period of service, as to Her Majesty seems meet.

29.—(1) All persons not above provided for, and at the passing of this Act serving in Ireland in the permanent Civil Service of the Crown, shall continue to hold their offices and receive the same salaries, and to be entitled to the same gratuities and superannuation allowances as heretofore, and shall be liable to perform the same duties as heretofore, or duties of similar rank, but any of such persons shall be entitled at the expiration of two years after the passing of this Act to retire from office, and at any time, if required by the Irish Government, shall retire from office, and on any such retirement shall be entitled to receive such payment as the Treasury may award to him in accordance with the provisions contained in the fourth schedule of this Act.

(2) The amount of such payment shall be paid to him out of the moneys

carried to the Customs and Excise Account under this Act, or, if those moneys are insufficient, out of the Irish Consolidated Fund, and, so far as the same are not so paid, shall be paid out of moneys provided by Parliament.

(3) The Pensions Commutation Act, 1871, shall apply to all persons who, having retired from office, are entitled to any annual payment under this section, in like manner as if they had retired in consequence of the abolition of their offices. *Pensions.*

(4) This section shall not apply to persons who are retained in the service of the Imperial Government.

30.—Where, before the passing of this Act, any pension or superannuation allowance has been granted to any person on account of services as a Judge of the Supreme Court of Judicature of Ireland, or of any Court consolidated into that Court, or as a County Court Judge, or in any other judicial position, or on account of services in the permanent Civil Service of the Crown in Ireland, otherwise than in some office, the holder of which is, after the passing of this Act, retained in the service of the Imperial Government, such pension or allowance, whether payable out of the Consolidated Fund or out of moneys provided by Parliament, shall continue to be paid to such person, and shall be so paid out of the moneys carried to the Customs and Excise Account under this Act, or if such moneys are insufficient, out of the Irish Consolidated Fund, and, so far as the same is not so paid, shall be paid, as heretofore, out of the Consolidated Fund of the United Kingdom, or moneys provided by Parliament.

TRANSITORY PROVISIONS.

31.—The provision contained in the fifth schedule to this Act relating to the mode in which arrangements are to be made for setting in motion the Irish Legislative Body and Government, and for the transfer to the Irish Government of the powers and duties to be transferred to them under this Act, or for otherwise bringing this Act into operation, shall be of the same effect as if they were enacted in the body of this Act. *Incorporation of schedule.*

MISCELLANEOUS.

32.—Whenever an Act of the Legislature of Ireland has provided for carrying on the postal and telegraphic services with respect to the transmission of letters and telegrams in Ireland, and the Post-Office and other Savings Banks in Ireland, for protecting the officers then in such service, and the existing depositors in such Post-Office Savings Banks, the Treasury shall make arrangements for the transfer of the said service and banks in accordance with the said Act, and shall give public notice of the transfer, and shall pay all depositors in such Post-Office Savings Banks who request payment within six months after the date fixed for such transfer, and after the expiration of such six months the said depositors shall cease to have any claim against the Postmaster-General, or the Consolidated Fund *Post-Office, Telegraph, and Savings Banks.*

of the United Kingdom, but shall have the like claim against the Consolidated Fund of Ireland; and the Treasury shall cause to be transferred, in accordance with the said Act, the securities representing the sums due to the said depositors in Post-Office Savings Banks, and the securities held for other Savings Banks.

33.—Save as otherwise provided by the Irish Legislature:

British Auditor, etc.

(a) The existing law relating to the Exchequer and Consolidated Fund of the United Kingdom shall apply to the Irish Exchequer and Consolidated Fund; and an officer shall from time to time be appointed by the Lord-Lieutenant to fill the office of the Comptroller-General of the Receipt and Issue of Her Majesty's Exchequer, and Auditor-General of Public Accounts, so far as respects Ireland; and

(b) The accounts of the Irish Consolidated Fund shall be audited as Appropriation Accounts in manner provided by the Exchequer and Audit Departments Act, 1866, by or under the direction of the holder of such office.

Privileges of Irish Members.

34.—(1) The privileges, immunities, and powers to be held, enjoyed, and exercised by the Irish Legislative Body and the members thereof, shall be such as are from time to time defined by Act of the Irish Legislature, but so that the same shall never exceed those at the passing of this Act, held, enjoyed, and exercised by the House of Commons, and by the members thereof.

(2) Subject as in this Act mentioned, all existing laws and customs relating to the members of the House of Commons and their election, including the enactments respecting the questioning of elections, corrupt and illegal practices, and registration of electors, shall, so far as applicable, extend to elective members of the First Order, and to members of the Second Order of the Irish Legislative Body.

Provided that—

(a) The law relating to the offices of profit enumerated in Schedule 2 to the Representation of the People Act, 1867, shall apply to such offices of profit in the Government of Ireland, not exceeding ten, as the Legislature of Ireland may from time to time direct.

Power to alter election laws.

(b) After the first dissolution of the Legislative Body, the Legislature of Ireland may, subject to the restrictions in this Act mentioned, alter the laws and customs in this section mentioned.

35.—(1) The Lord-Lieutenant of Ireland may make regulations for the following purposes:—

Lord-Lieutenant's powers.

(a) The summoning of the Legislative Body and the election of a Speaker, and such adaptation to the proceedings of the Legislative Body of the procedure of the House of Commons as appears to him expedient for facilitating the conduct of business by that body on their first meeting;

(b) The adaptation of any law relating to the election of representative peers;

(c) The adaptation of any laws and customs relating to the House of Commons, or the members thereof, to the elective members of the First Order and to members of the Second Order of the Legislative Body; and

(d) The mode of signifying their assent or election under this Act by representative peers or Irish members of the House of Commons as regards becoming members of the Irish Legislative Body in pursuance of this Act.

(2) Any regulations so made shall, in so far as they concern the procedure of the Legislative Body, be subject to alteration by standing orders of that body; and, so far as they concern other matters, be subject to alteration by the Legislature of Ireland, but shall, until alteration, have the same effect as if they were inserted in this Act.

Irish peerages.

36.—Save as is in this Act provided with respect to matters to be decided by Her Majesty in Council, nothing in this Act shall affect the appellate jurisdiction of the House of Lords in respect to actions and suits in Ireland, or the jurisdiction of the House of Lords to determine the claims to Irish peerages.

Power of Imperial Parliament.

37.—Save as herein expressly provided, all matters in relation to which it is not competent for the Irish Legislative Body to make or repeal laws shall remain in and be within the exclusive authority of the Imperial Parliament, save as aforesaid, whose power and authority in relation thereto shall in nowise be diminished or restrained by anything herein contained.

38.—(1) Except as otherwise provided by this Act, all existing laws in force in Ireland, and all existing courts of civil and criminal jurisdiction, and all existing legal commissions, powers, and authorities, and all existing officers, judicial, administrative, and ministerial, and all existing taxes, licence, and other duties, fees, and other receipts in Ireland, shall continue as if this Act had not been passed, subject nevertheless to be repealed, abolished, or altered in manner and to the extent provided by this Act, provided that, subject to the provisions of this Act, such taxes, duties, fees, and other receipts shall, after the appointed day, form part of the public revenues of Ireland.

(2) The Commissioners of Inland Revenue and the Commissioners of Customs, and the officers of such Commissioners respectively shall have the same powers in relation to any articles subject to any duty of Excise or Customs, manufactured, imported, kept for sale or sold, and any premises where the same may be, and to any machinery, apparatus, vessels, utensils or conveyance used in connection therewith, or the removal thereof, and in relation to the person manufacturing, importing, keeping for sale, selling, or having the custody or possession of the same, as they would have had if this Act had not been passed.

Act not to be altered.

39.—(1) On and after the appointed day this Act shall not, except such provisions thereof as are declared to be alterable by the Legislature of Ireland, be altered, except

(a) By Act of the Imperial Parliament, and with the consent of the Irish Legislative Body, testified by an address to Her Majesty, or

(b) By an Act of the Imperial Parliament, for the passing of which there shall be summoned to the House of Lords the peerage members of the First Order of the Irish Legislative Body; and if there are no such members, then twenty-eight Irish representative peers, elected by the Irish peers in manner heretofore in use, subject to adaptation as provided by this Act; and there shall be summoned to the House of Commons such one of the members of each constituency, or, in the case of a constituency returning four members, such two of those members, as the Legislative Body of Ireland may select; and such peers and members shall respectively be deemed, for the purpose of passing any such Act, to be members of the said Houses of Parliament respectively.

(2) For the purposes of this section it shall be lawful for Her Majesty, by Order in Council, to make such provisions for summoning the said peers of Ireland to the House of Lords, and the said members from Ireland to the House of Commons, as to Her Majesty may seem necessary or proper; and any provisions contained in such Order in Council shall have the same effect as if they had been enacted by Parliament.

Definition.

40.—In this section the expression "the appointed day" shall mean such day after thirty-first day of March, in the year one thousand eight hundred and eighty-seven, as may be determined by order of Her Majesty in Council.

The expression "Lord-Lieutenant" includes the Lords Justices, or any other chief governor or governors of Ireland for the time being.

The expression "Her Majesty the Queen," or "Her Majesty," or "The Queen," includes the heirs and successors of Her Majesty the Queen.

The expression "Treasury" means the Commissioners of Her Majesty's Treasury.

The expression "treaty" includes any convention or arrangement.

The expression "existing" means existing at the passing of this Act.

The expression "existing constituency" means any county or borough, or division of a county or borough, or a university, returning at the passing of this Act a member or members to serve in Parliament.

The expression "duties of Excise" does not include a duty received in respect of any licence, whether for the sale of intoxicating liquors or otherwise.

The expression "financial year" means the twelve months ending on the thirty-first day of March.

41.—This Act may be cited for all purposes as the Irish Government Act, 1886.

APPENDIX II.

THE LAND PURCHASE BILL.

THE following is the text of the Government Bill to make Amended Provision for the Sale and Purchase of Land in Ireland :—

Be it enacted by the Queen's Most Excellent Majesty, by and with the advice and consent of the Lords spiritual and temporal, and Commons, in this present Parliament assembled, and by the authority of the same, as follows : —

1.—This Act may be cited as the Land (Ireland) Act, 1886.

PART I.

SALES OF ESTATES.

2.—(1) On and after the appointed day and within the time limited by this Act the immediate landlord of any tenanted estate in Ireland to which this Act applies may apply to the State Authority to buy such tenanted estate at the statutory price, and the State Authority shall cause his application to be registered, and the applications so made shall be dealt with according to priority of time. *Landlord may claim purchase.*

(2) In the event of the purchase of the estate from the landlord being completed, the tenants of the several holdings of which such estate consists shall, except as in this Act mentioned, become, as soon as may be, in manner in this Act mentioned, the owners in fee-simple of their holdings for such consideration as is in this Act mentioned ; and where the tenants do not become the owners of their holdings under this Act, the State Authority shall become the owner thereof, and dispose of the same in such manner as the State Authority may think fit. *State to acquire the land.*

3.—(1) The statutory price of an estate shall be measured by the amount of the nett rent of the estate. *The price.*

(2) The nett rent of an estate equals the gross rent of the estate after deducting from that rent the tithe rent-charge, if any, payable to the Land Commission, and the average percentage for expenses in respect of bad debts, rates, or cess allowed or paid by the landlord, management, repairs, and other like outgoings, if any.

(3) Tithe rent-charges shall be ascertained by the books of the Land Commission, and the average percentage for such expenses as aforesaid shall be ascertained in the case of each estate by taking the average percentage on the rent for the time being of such estate to which such expenses have amounted, during each of the ten years immediately preceding the last gale day, in the year one thousand eight hundred and eighty-five, as ascertained by inspection of the rent rolls and books of the estate, and by other evidence if necessary.

Twenty years' purchase.

4.—(1) The amount of the statutory price of an estate shall, except as in this Act mentioned, be equal to twenty times the nett rent of the estate ascertained as aforesaid; and such price shall, subject to such option on the part of the person entitled to receive the same, or taking other annuities or debentures as is in this Act mentioned, be paid by three per cent. perpetual annuities issued under this Act at par.

(2) There shall be added to the statutory price of an estate a sum equal to the amount of any such arrears of rent coming due after the last gale day in the year 1885, and before the date of purchase, as the Land Commission may certify that the landlord has duly endeavoured, but has been unable to collect; and such sum shall, subject to the said option, be paid in permanent annuities to the person entitled to such arrears of rent.

5.—The consideration payable by a tenant for his acquisition of the fee-simple of his holding shall be the payment to the State Authority of a capital sum equal to twenty times the amount of the gross rent of the holding, and such sum may either be paid down in whole or in part, or may be paid by an annuity during a period of 49 years equal to four per centum per annum on such capital sum, or so much thereof as is not so paid down; but such annuity may be at any time redeemed as in this Act mentioned; provided that where the landlord is legally liable to pay for any repairs, or pays any county cess, or the whole of the poor-rate in respect of a holding, the average annual amount of such repairs and county cess, and half the average annual amount of such poor-rate during the ten years next preceding the last gale day in the year 1885, shall be deducted from the gross rent of the holding in calculating the consideration payable by a tenant in pursuance of this section.

PROCEDURE ON SALE OF ESTATE.

Applications for sale.

6.—(1) The application by an immediate landlord desirous of selling his estate to the State Authority shall be made in the prescribed manner to that Authority, who shall forthwith refer that application to the Land Commission.

(2) The Land Commission, on the applicant giving the prescribed security for costs, shall satisfy themselves as to his being authorized to make such application according to the Act.

(3) The Land Commission, if satisfied that the applicant is authorized to make the application, shall fix the price of the estate. *Fixing the price.*

(4) Where the landlord and State Authority have agreed on the price, the Land Commission shall fix that price as the price of the estate, if satisfied that it does not exceed the statutory price.

(5) In the absence of such agreement the Land Commission shall ascertain the statutory price, and notify the same to the landlord and the State Authority.

(6) If the landlord on receiving such notification does not accept the price, he may, within the prescribed time, withdraw his application on payment of such sum for costs as the Land Commission may order, but otherwise the Land Commission shall fix the price so notified as the price of the estate.

(7) As soon as the price is fixed the Land Commission shall, in the prescribed manner, cause to be carried to the account of the estate the amount of such price, after deducting one per cent. of such price for the costs of purchase and distribution, and the amount so carried to the account of the estate is hereafter referred to as the purchase-money.

(8) The Land Commission shall also make such orders or do such acts as may be prescribed—

(a) For vesting each tenanted holding on the estate, except as in this Act mentioned, in the tenant thereof for an estate in fee-simple free from incumbrances, but subject to any annuity due under this Act, for payment of the consideration payable by such tenant for the acquisition of the fee-simple, and with and subject to all rights and easements granted and reserved; provided that the interests so vested in the tenant shall, subject to any such annuity rights and easements as aforesaid, be a graft upon the previous interest of the tenant in the holding, and be subject to any rights or equities arising from its being such graft; and

(b) For vesting any holding of which the tenant does not, in pursuance of this Act, become the owner in the State Authority, for an estate in fee-simple, free from incumbrances, with and subject to all rights and easements granted or reserved.

DISTRIBUTION OF PURCHASE-MONEY.

7.—(1) As soon as the purchase-money is carried to the account of an estate sold under this Act, the claims of the immediate landlord of all other persons (except the tenant and persons claiming under him) who are interested in the estate, whether as incumbrancers or otherwise, shall attach to such purchase-money in like manner as immedi- *Incumbrances.*

ately before the sale they attached to the estate sold, and shall cease to be of any validity as against the estate, and, subject as in this Act mentioned, shall be discharged or redeemed out of such purchase-money, and the Land Commission shall determine the rights and priorities of the landlord and such other persons, and shall distribute the purchase-money in accordance with such rights and priorities.

Price—how paid.

(2) The distribution of the purchase-money shall be effected by the transfer or appropriation, in the prescribed manner, to or in trust for the person entitled to the same, or any part thereof, of a sum of three per cent. perpetual annuities at par, equal to the amount to which such person is entitled, subject to the option in this Act mentioned of taking other perpetual annuities or debentures or cash; and such distribution shall be made without cost to the persons so entitled, and a reasonable sum for costs may be allowed by the Land Commission to such persons for proving their title upon such distribution, and may be paid as part of the costs of the Land Commission; provided that this provision as to the payment of cost shall not extend to any expense which is caused by disputed titles or disputed priorities, or by unnecessary or unreasonable proceedings, or by the failure of any person to comply with the prescribed regulations, or by any other act or default of the parties which appears to the Land Commission to make it just that the parties, or any of them, should pay the costs, in which case they may order such parties to pay the costs caused as aforesaid, or such part thereof as to the Commission seems proper.

(3) Where the purchase-money, or any part thereof, so appropriated or transferred, is not immediately distributable, or the persons entitled thereto cannot be ascertained, or where from any other cause the Land Commission thinks it expedient for the protection of the rights of the persons interested, then, subject to prescribed regulations, the Land Commission shall, as the case requires, either retain the same under their control or deal with the same in manner provided by the Settled Land Act, 1882, with respect to capital money arising under that Act, and may by order declare the trusts affecting such money or share so far as the Land Commission has ascertained the same, or state the facts or matters found by it in relation to the rights and interests therein; and the Land Commission may from time to time make such orders in respect to any purchase-money or share, and the investment or application thereof, or the payment thereof, or the annual income thereof, to the persons interested, as the circumstances of the case may require.

RULES AS TO INCUMBRANCES.

Chief rents.

8.—(1) Where any estate in course of sale under this Act is subject to any chief rent as defined by this Act, the statutory price of such chief rents shall be ascertained by the Land Commission in manner in this section mentioned; and notice shall be given to the State Authority of the amount of such chief rent, and the statutory price thereof, and such Authority shall, within the prescribed time after receipt of the notice, signify to the Land Commission whether such Authority will continue to pay the chief rent, or redeem the same forthwith; but where such chief rent is a Crown rent, the same shall be redeemed forthwith.

(2) If the State Authority signify to the Land Commission their option to continue to pay the chief rent, such chief rent shall be paid out of the land revenues in this Act mentioned; but the State Authority may at any time redeem the chief rent by payment of the statutory price thereof, or of any less sum which may be agreed upon between such Authority and the owners of the chief rent.

(3) Where a chief rent is redeemed forthwith, the statutory price of the chief rent shall be added to the statutory price of the estate, and after the like deduction for costs shall be carried to the account of the estate and distributed in like manner as the statutory price.

(4) The statutory price of a chief rent shall be measured by the nett amount thereof; that is to say, by the sum receivable by the owner of the chief rent, after deducting therefrom the like deductions ascertained in like manner as in the case of an estate, and the statutory price of such chief rent shall be equal in the case of a Crown rent to twenty-four times, and in the case of any other chief rent to twenty-two times, the amount of such nett rent ascertained as aforesaid.

(5) In ascertaining for the purpose of this Act the nett rent of the estate subject to a chief rent, that chief rent shall be deducted from the gross rent.

9.—All such incumbrances other than chief rents as are not otherwise provided for in this Act shall be valued at such price as may be agreed upon between the parties interested, and, if there is no agreement, at such price as may be determined by the Land Commission to be the market value thereof, subject as follows:—

(1) Annual sums, such as jointures and other sums, the payment of which depends on a life or lives, shall be valued at the then present value of such sums, according to the tables in use by the Commissioners for the Reduction of the National Debt for the grant of life annuities, provided that— *Jointures.*

(a) If the person liable to pay such jointure requests that a portion of the purchase-money, sufficient to meet such annual sum, shall be set apart, and the annual sum shall continue to be paid, such request shall be complied with; and

(b) If such person is a tenant for life, provision may be made, in such manner as to the Land Commission seems equitable, for securing the remainder man against the loss which he might suffer by the redemption of such annual sum at the then present value.

Drainage charges. 2) Drainage charges and any charges payable only for a number of years, and not being chief rents, shall be valued at their then present value, interest being taken at the rate adopted in the creation thereof, or if none was so adopted, at three per cent. per annum.

(3) Capital sums shall be valued at the amount of the sums for the time being due.

10.—Where a chief rent, or head rent, or tithe rent-charge is charged on any other estate as well as on the estate sold, the Land Commission shall apportion the chief or head rent or tithe rent-charge between the estates sold and the other estate on which the rent or rent-charge is charged in such manner as to them seems equitable, and such portion of the rent or rent-charge as is apportioned to the estate in course of sale shall alone be deemed to be the chief or head rent or tithe rent chargeable on that estate.

RIGHTS OF COMMON AND OTHER RIGHTS.

Common rights. **11.**—(1) Where any beneficial rights of common pasturage, sporting, fishing, turbary, or cutting timber, or rights of way or other rights are exercisable over a tenanted estate sold under this Act, or exercisable over any other land as incident to the tenure by the landlord of such tenanted estate, or where the landlord of any such estate is the owner of any timber thereon, such rights, and the ownership of such timber, shall be dealt with in the manner provided by the first schedule to this Act.

Minerals. (2) Where there is reasonable cause to suppose that there are valuable minerals under a tenanted estate sold under this Act, there shall be added to the statutory price of the estate such sum as the Land Commissioners determine in respect to the value of such minerals, and such minerals shall vest in the State Authority, or in such local body as the Irish Legislature may provide, with full power to such Authority or body, or to persons authorized by them, to enter and do everything necessary for getting the same, paying, nevertheless, compensation for all damage done in so doing to the tenant or other person who suffered the same.

Pasturage. **12.**—(1) Where the tenants of any estate proposed for sale under this Act have been accustomed, whether of right or as incident to their tenancy or by permission, to exercise or enjoy any right or privilege of turbary, common pasturage, taking seaweed, or other right or privilege, the State Authority may refuse to purchase that estate unless such arrangements are made as satisfy the Land Commission that the tenants will enjoy the same right or privilege.

Bog. (2) Where the landlord of any tenanted estate proposed to be sold under this Act possesses any bog in the neighbourhood of such estate, the landlord may, and if the State Authority so require shall, also sell such bog to the State Authority, and this Act shall apply to such bog as if it were part of the tenanted estate, provided that such bog shall either be vested in the State Authority or in such local body as the Irish Legislature may provide, for the purpose of giving to the tenants of the estate or inhabitants of the neighbourhood rights or privileges of turbary, or, if the Land Commission think fit, may be apportioned among the tenants of the estate, inhabitants, or other persons, and in either case such payments shall be required from such tenants, inhabitants, or other persons as the Land Commission may consider sufficient to repay the State Authority for the price.

MODIFICATIONS OF GENERAL TERMS OF PURCHASE.

How price to be fixed.

13.—The Land Commission, in ascertaining the deductions to be made from the gross rent of any estate for the purpose of arriving at the nett rent, shall take into account any circumstances which make it inequitable to follow strictly the rules laid down by this Act for finding the nett rent, and shall deal with the case in such manner as they think most consistent with justice.

Leases.

14.—Where a tenant of a holding or an estate in course of sale under this Act holds a beneficial lease—that is to say, a lease the rent received by which is less than the rent which would be fixed as the judicial rent, the following provisions shall apply :—

(a) In ascertaining the statutory price of the estate, the gross and nett rental of such holding shall be ascertained in like manner as if there were no lease ; but a proper deduction shall be made from the statutory price in respect of the value of such beneficial lease, due regard being had to the additional security which the landlord has for the rent by reason of the existence of such lease.

(b) In determining the consideration to be paid by the tenant in respect of his acquisition of the fee-simple of his holding, an addition shall be made on account of increase of rent at the period corresponding with the end of his lease, and the terms of the annuity payable as the consideration for the purchase of his holding may be varied for that purpose, so, however, that he shall not be required to pay during a period corresponding with the term of his lease any sum in excess of the rent under the lease, after deducting the average sum allowed in respect of poor-rate or county cess during the ten years next before the last gale day in the year one thousand eight hundred and eighty-five.

Poor estates.

15.—Where it appears to the Land Commission that by reason of the character or impoverished condition of any estate, or the tenants thereof, the statutory price as ascertained under the Act is higher than the market value of the estate, or where for any other reason it appears to the Land Commission that it is inequitable that the State Authority should be required to buy an estate at the price ascertained under this Act, the Land Commission may make a declaration to that effect, and thereupon the State Authority shall not be required to purchase the same unless the landlord accept any lower price which the Land Commission declare to be equitable.

May give 22 years' purchase. 16.—Whereas in exceptional cases it may be just that the statutory price paid for an estate should be more than twenty times the nett rent of the estate, as ascertained in the manner provided by this Act, be it enacted that where it appears to the Land Commission that from the exceptionally good condition of an estate, or from the exceptional prosperity of the tenants, or from any other exceptional circumstances, the statutory price of twenty times the nett rent would be an insufficient price, the Land Commission may award, as the statutory price of such an estate, a sum not exceeding twenty-two times the nett rent of the estate, as ascertained in manner provided by this Act.

State to acquire estates. 17.—Where an estate sold under this Act is situate in any district mentioned in the second schedule hereto, the holdings thereon shall not vest in the tenants, and the State Authority on completion of the sale shall become the owner thereof, and the provisions of this Act respecting the vesting of holdings in the State Authority shall apply.

18.—A tenant of a holding valued under the Acts relating to the valuation of rateable property in Ireland at an annual value not exceeding £4 a year may, on application to the Land Commission, express his dissent from such holding vesting in him in the manner provided by this Act, and thereupon no such vesting shall take place, and the State Authority shall become the owner of such holding, and the provisions of this Act respecting the vesting of holdings in the State Authority shall apply.

PART II.

LAND COMMISSION.

A Land Commission. 19.—(1) The Land Commission for the purpose of this Act shall consist of the following persons, that is to say :—

(2) If any vacancy takes place in the office of any such Commissioner, Her Majesty may, by warrant under her Royal sign-manual, appoint a fit person to fill the vacancy.

(3) The Commissioners for the purposes of this Act shall continue in office during the pleasure of Her Majesty, and shall each be paid out of moneys carried to the Customs and Excise Account, under the Irish Government Act, 1886, such salaries as may be determined by the Treasury.

(4) Subject to any rules that may be made in pursuance of this Act, any matter authorized to be done by this Act may be done by any one or two of the Commissioners, but if any landlord, incumbrancer, or other person, or the State Authority, feels aggrieved by the decision of such Commissioner or Commissioners, such landlord, incumbrancer, person, or Authority may have his case reheard before a court consisting of not less than three Commissioners.

20.—(1) The Land Commission shall have such officers for the purpose of this Act and with such salaries as the Treasury may assign. Such officers may be appointed and removed in such manner as may be provided by the regulations of the Treasury. The salaries of such officers and the expenses of the office of the Land Commission shall, so far as they are not otherwise provided for by law, be paid out of moneys carried to the Customs and Excise Account under the Irish Government Act, 1886.

(2) Any officer attached to the Land Judges Branch of the Chancery Division of the High Court of Justice, or to the Court of either of the said judges, may, with his consent, be transferred to the office of the Land Commission, or discharge such duties under this Act as the Land Commission may assign to him, and in either case may be awarded such remuneration for his services as the Treasury may determine.

21.—The Land Commission shall be a superior Court of Record, and shall, for the purposes of this Act, have, in addition to the powers already possessed by them, all powers vested in or exercisable by the Land Judges, and may exercise such powers in relation to any person or matter within their jurisdiction.

22.—If the Land Commission desire to have a legal decision upon any point arising in the exercise of their powers under this Court, the Commission may submit a case to the Court of Appeal, and the Court shall hear the case as nearly as may be in like manner as if it were an appeal in an action between the persons interested in the matter, but with power for the Court to make such alterations in the course of the procedure as they may think expedient in the interests of justice; and the decision of such Court, or, if the decision is appealed against, the final decision on the appeal in such, shall be duly observed by the Land Commission, or by all persons concerned. *Appeals.*

The proceedings of the Land Commission under this Act shall not be questioned, save as provided by this section, and shall not be restrained by mandamus, prohibition, or otherwise howsoever.

23.—(1) Subject to any rules made in pursuance of this Act, where the purchase-money has been carried to the account of an estate the Land Commissioners may, in their discretion, distribute the same as funds are distributed on sales of estates in the Landed Estates Court; or may cause to be given notices calling on all persons to send in their claims against such purchase-money, which notices may be given in like manner as notices given by the High Court of Justice, in an administration suit for creditors and others to send in to the executors their claims against the estate of the testator.

(2) At the expiration of the time named in such notices for sending in claims, the Land Commission may proceed to distribute the purchase-money, having regard to the claims of which such Commission have

then given notice, and without regard to the claims of which they have not notice; but nothing in the foregoing provisions of this section shall prejudice any right of the claimant to recover the money from any person liable to pay the same, nor his right to establish a claim against any part of the purchase-money which remains under the control of the Land Commission, and has not been appropriated to any claimant.

(3) The Commission may also exclude any person who refuses or fails to produce such evidence of his claim as the Land Commission may reasonably require.

May make rules.

24.—The Land Commission may, with the approval of the Lord-Lieutenant, from time to time make, and when made alter and revoke, rules in respect of the following matters :—

(a) As to the mode in which the business is to be conducted by the Land Commission under this Act, and the procedure and forms to be observed and used in carrying into effect sales under this Act ;

(b) As to anything by this Act directed to be prescribed ; and

(c) For carrying into effect any provisions of this Act which require to be carried into effect by rule, with power to specify the manner in which the judicial business is to be separated from the administrative, but subject to the provisions of this Act as to the rehearing of cases and otherwise, and any such rules shall be of the same effect as if they were enacted in this Act.

PART III.

FINANCIAL ARRANGEMENTS.

A Receiver-General.

25.—(1) The Treasury shall from time to time appoint a Receiver-General of the Public Revenues of Ireland (in this Act referred to as the Irish Receiver-General), and such deputies or deputy to act under him in any part or parts of Ireland as to the Treasury may seem necessary for the execution of this Act.

(2) Such Receiver-General and deputies shall hold office as persons serving in an established capacity in the permanent Civil Service of the State, and shall be subject generally to the directions of the Treasury, and shall be paid out of money provided by the Imperial Parliament such salaries as the Treasury from time to time assign.

26.—All sums payable by tenants of holdings vested in them in pursuance of this Act, and all sums receivable by the State Authority in pursuance of this Act, whether as capital or income, from any estates which are vested in them, or over which they have any right, or from which they derive any profit (which sums are in this Act referred to as land revenues), shall be collected by such collectors as the Irish Government may from time to time appoint for that purpose.

27.—(1) There shall be paid to the Irish Receiver-General all sums collected by a collector in respect of any tax, duty, or impost imposed or levied by or under the direction of the Irish Legislature for the public service in Ireland, or collected by a collector in respect of the land revenues under this Act, and all sums other than those above mentioned, and payable on account or in respect of the public revenues of the Government of Ireland, whatever collector or person is liable to pay the same.

(2) There shall also be paid to the Irish Receiver-General all moneys directed by the Irish Government Act, 1886, to be carried to the Customs and Excise Account.

(3) If default is made in payment to the Irish Receiver-General of any sum by this section required to be paid to him by any person, the person who makes such default, and the person who receives such sum in respect of which such default is made, and every person, whether a member of a corporation or not, who is privy to such default, shall forfeit double such sum to Her Majesty, and the Irish Receiver-General or one of his deputies shall take proceedings to recover such sum, and the sums when recovered shall be paid into the Consolidated Fund of the United Kingdom. *Penalties.*

(4) If the Irish Receiver-General under this Act, or any of his deputies, is guilty of any malfeasance in his office, he shall forfeit to Her Majesty all sums lost by such malfeasance, and also such penal sum, not exceeding five hundred pounds, as the Court in which the forfeiture is sued for may determine, and such forfeiture and penal sum may be recovered by action on behalf of the Irish Government, and when recovered shall be paid to the Irish Consolidated Fund.

(5) Every action or legal proceeding by or against the Irish Receiver-General, or any of his deputies or deputy, shall, if either of the parties thereto so desire, be heard and determined by the Exchequer Division, or one of the Judges thereof, and the provisions of the Irish Government Act, 1886, with respect to legal proceedings by or against the Commissioners of Customs in the Exchequer Division shall apply in like manner as if those provisions were herein re-enacted, and in terms made applicable to the Irish Receiver-General; and such Exchequer Division shall have for such purpose the same powers as at the passing of this Act are vested in any division of the High Court of Justice.

28.—(1) The Irish Receiver-General shall apply all sums received by him—First, in paying all sums payable out of the moneys carried under the Irish Government Act, 1886, to the account therein called the Customs and Excise Account; and, secondly, in paying all sums directed by this Act to be paid out of the land revenues, or out of the moneys coming to the hands of such Receiver-General.

(2) The Receiver-General shall pay all sums which are not, or in his

opinion are not likely to be, required for making the above-mentioned payments, to the Irish Consolidated Fund.

50 millions to begin with.

29.—(1) There shall be issued and placed at the disposal of the Land Commission for the purposes of this Act, in such manner and under such regulations as the Treasury from time to time make, such sums of permanent annuities as are from time to time required for the said purposes, provided that the nominal capital amount of such annuities so issued shall not exceed—

(a) In respect of applications for purchase received from landlords during the financial year ending on the 31st day of March next after the appointed day, £10,000,000; and

(b) In respect of applications for purchase received from landlords during the said financial year and the succeeding financial year, £20,000,000, with the addition of so much of the above-mentioned £10,000,000 as is not required for the applications before mentioned; and

(c) In respect to applications for purchase received from landlords during the above-mentioned financial year and the financial year next following the same, the sum of £20,000,000, with the addition of so much of the above-mentioned £30,000,000 as is not required for the applications before mentioned, but so that not more than £20,000,000 permanent annuities shall be issued in any one financial year.

Annuities.

(2) The Treasury may, if they think fit, from time to time make regulations for the issue, in lieu of 3 per cent. permanent annuities, of annuities of the same class as existing permanent annuities of lower denomination; and if such regulations are made, any person entitled to the payment of any purchase-money or share of purchase-money under this Act may, instead of 3 per cent. permanent annuities, receive any of such annuities of lower denomination at such prices not less than those mentioned in the third schedule of this Act, and in accordance with such provision as may be made by the said regulations.

Scrip.

30.—Where the amount of permanent annuities authorized to be issued in any financial year is insufficient to meet the sums required in that year for the purchase-money of estates sold under this Act upon applications received from landlords, there shall be issued, under such regulations as the Treasury from time to time make, scrip representing the said sum for which the said annuities are so insufficient, so, however, that the aggregate capital amount of the annuities issued and the scrip shall not together exceed £50,000,000; and such scrip shall, in the next financial year, be exchanged, under such regulations as the Treasury may from time to time make, for the like nominal amount of permanent annuities, and until so exchanged shall bear interest at the rate of 3 per cent. per annum, which interest shall accrue from day to day, and be payable half-yearly on the days fixed by the Treasury by the Irish Receiver-General out of moneys coming into his hands next in priority after the annual sum for interest and sinking fund of the permanent annuities issued under this Act, and such scrip may be transferable to such extent and in such manner as may be from time to time provided by the regulations of the Treasury.

Bank of England Annuities.

31.—(1) For the purposes of this Act the Treasury may create £3 per cent. per annum permanent annuities, and £2, 15s. per cent. per annum permanent annuities, and £2, 10s. per cent. permanent annuities, and such annuities, and all interest from time to time due thereon shall be charged on and be payable out of the Consolidated Fund of the United Kingdom, or out of the growing produce thereof, at such times in each year as may be fixed by the Treasury.

(2) The said annuities shall be created by warrant from the Treasury to the Governor and Company of the Bank of England, by directing them to inscribe in their books the amount of such annuities in the names directed by the warrant.

(3) The said annuities shall, in manner directed by the warrant, be consolidated with annuities at the same rate of interest, and payable at the same date, and shall be transferable in the said books in like manner as the annuities with which they are consolidated, and shall be subject to the enactments relating to those annuities so far as consistent with the tenor of those enactments.

Payment of interest and sinking fund.

32.—(1) For the purpose of paying the interest and sinking fund on the permanent annuities issued under this Act, which annuities are in this Act referred to as the Land Purchase Debt, the Irish Receiver-General shall, out of moneys coming into his hands, pay to Her Majesty's Paymaster-General an annual sum of 4 per cent. on the nominal capital amount of the Land Purchase Debt.

(2) Such sums shall be applied under the direction of the Treasury in paying the interest on a portion of the National Debt equal to the amount of the Land Purchase Debt, or so much thereof as has not been redeemed, and the remainder shall be paid to the Commissioners for the Reduction of the National Debt, and shall be applied by them in the redemption of the National Debt, in like manner as if it were part of the new sinking fund.

(3) As soon as an amount of the National Debt equal to the Land Purchase Debt has been redeemed by payments under this section, the said annual sum shall cease to be payable.

(4) Where the consideration payable by a tenant in respect of the acquisition of the fee-simple of his holding under this Act is wholly or partly paid down, or any sum is paid for the redemption of the whole or part of any annuity payable on account of such consideration, or is paid on the sale of any estate, or holding, or minerals, or timber by the State Authority, or otherwise any sum in the nature of capital is paid in respect of any estates sold under this Act, the consideration or sum so paid shall be paid to the Irish Receiver-General, and shall be paid by him to the Commissioners for the Reduction of the

National Debt, and shall be applied by them as part of the sums received under this Act for the redemption of the National Debt, and the Treasury shall thereupon reduce proportionately the said annual sum.

Broken periods.

33.—The Treasury shall, from time to time, make such regulations to provide for broken periods, whether as regards the interest on annuities created under this Act, or as regards the annual sum payable by the Irish Receiver-General in respect of such annuities, or otherwise in connection with the financial arrangements under this Act, as they from time to time find most convenient for the public service.

Issue of land debentures.

34.—(1) Subject to the provisions of any Act passed by the Irish Legislature, the Irish Government may from time to time issue land debentures in such form and for such period, and payable off in such manner, and bearing such rate of interest, not exceeding the rate of 3 per cent. per annum, payable by coupons or otherwise, as the regulations of such Government may provide, so, however, that the total amount of such debentures shall not exceed five million pounds.

(2) Such debentures, or cash raised by such debentures, shall be placed at the disposal of the Land Commission for the purpose of paying to the persons interested the purchase-money of estates sold under this Act, and shall not be applied otherwise, and, subject to the prescribed regulations, any person entitled to payment of any such purchase-money or any share thereof may at his option take in lieu of permanent annuities any such debenture or cash which is available for such payment.

(3) The principal and interest of such debentures shall be charged on the sums coming into the hands of the Irish Receiver-General next after the charge of any other sums charged thereon under this Act.

(4) Subject to the provisions of any Act of the Irish Legislature, the provision of the Land Debts (Ireland) Act, 1865, shall, so far as consistent with the tenor thereof, apply to all debentures issued in pursuance of this Act.

Advances for costs of Land Commission.

35.—The Treasury, if the Irish Government so requires it, may from time to time make out of the Consolidated Fund of the United Kingdom, advances equal to the sums deducted by the Land Commission for the payment of costs from the statutory price of estates sold under this Act; and such advances shall be applied in payment of the costs of the Land Commission, and shall be repaid to the said Consolidated Fund within a period not exceeding ten years from the date of the advances out of moneys coming into the hands of the Irish Receiver-General, and interest at the rate of 3 per cent. per annum shall be paid out of the same moneys, on so much of the advances as is for the time being outstanding.

All other costs of the Land Commission incurred in the execution of this Act shall be defrayed out of the moneys coming into the hands of the Irish Receiver-General.

PART IV.

SUPPLEMENTARY PROVISIONS.

36.—The Irish Government shall establish a registry of title, and all estates and holdings purchased under this Act shall be entered on such register. *Registry of title.*

Subject to any Act of the Irish Legislature, stamp duty shall be payable on any order vesting an estate in any tenant on the State Authority under this Act, and shall be paid by such tenant or State Authority.

The rules in the fourth schedule hereto providing for the mode in which a registry is to be established and the effect of such registry shall apply to any registry of title established under this Act, and shall have the same effect as if they were enacted in the body of this Act.

The interest of a tenant in any holding which may be acquired under the provisions of this Act, or the fee-simple in which has been acquired under the provisions of the Irish Church Act, 1869, or the Land Law (Ireland) Act, 1881, or the Purchase of Land (Ireland) Act, 1885, shall be for all purposes personal estate without prejudice to any interest acquired by any dealing with, or devolution of, such holding before the passing of this Act. *Tenants without personal estate.*

37.—Every annuity payable by a tenant, in pursuance of this Act, shall be a charge on the holding subject thereto, having priority over all existing and future estates, interests, and encumbrances, and such sums shall be recoverable by the State Authority, or by any officer of that Authority, in such manner as may be provided by Act of the Irish Legislature, and until such provision is made in manner provided by Part III. of the Landlord and Tenant (Ireland) Act, 1870, as amended by the Landlord and Tenant (Ireland) Act, 1872, as if the annuity were such an advance as mentioned in those Acts, and the State Authority were the Board therein mentioned. *Annuity to have priority.*

A certificate, purporting to be under the seal of the State Authority, or of any officer of that Authority, shall be evidence that the amount of any annuity or arrears of annuity stated therein to be due under this Act, in respect of any holding named therein, is due to the Authority in respect of such holding. Any such annuity, as aforesaid, may be redeemed by the person for the time being liable for the same, in manner provided by section 51 of the Landlord and Tenant (Ireland) Act, 1870, or by section 28 of the Land Law (Ireland) Act, 1881, or by section 4 of the Purchase of Land (Ireland) Act, 1885, and the table in the schedule to that Act.

38.—So long as a holding is subject to any charge in respect of an annuity under this Act, the following conditions shall be imposed on such holdings—that is to say :— *Conditions as to an annuity.*

(a) The holding shall not be subdivided or let by the owner thereof without the consent of the State Authority.

(b) Where the owner subdivides or lets any holding or part of a holding in contravention of this section, the State Authority may cause the holding to be sold.

(c) Where the title to the holding is divested from the owner by bankruptcy, the State Authority may cause the holding to be sold.

(d) Where on the death of the owner the holding would by reason of any devise, bequest, intestacy, or otherwise become subdivided, the State Authority may require the holding to be sold within twelve months after the death of the owner, to some one person, and, if default is made in selling the same, the State Authority may cause the same to be sold.

With respect to any such sale, and the application of the proceeds thereof, the State Authority shall have the same power as is given to the Land Commission in relation to sales by section 30 of the Land Law (Ireland) Act, 1881, as amended by the Purchase of Land (Ireland) Act, 1885, and that section as so amended shall apply accordingly.

Landlord may require State to purchase.

39.—(1) Any immediate landlord who holds the estate on trust for any other person may without prejudice to any power conferred by the Conveyancing and Law of Property Act, 1881, or by the instrument creating the trust, or otherwise, require the State Authority to buy the estate under this Act, and may do all acts necessary for effecting such sale, and if the estate cannot otherwise be sold, may agree to accept a price lower than the statutory price.

Encumbrancer and landlord may agree.

(2) Without prejudice to any such power as aforesaid, any person holding on trust for any other person an encumbrance on an estate may, with a view to induce the landlord of such estate to exercise his option of selling the same under this Act, agree to reduce the amount due in respect of such encumbrance, or to commute or otherwise deal with the same in such manner as he may think expedient, having regard to the advantages to be derived from the conversion of the estate into annuities or money, or may purchase from the landlord the right to exercise his option.

(3) A person may exercise his discretion under this section in the same manner as if he was the absolute beneficial owner of the estate or the encumbrance, and he shall not be liable to have the discretion exercised by him in good faith reviewed in any court of law or equity, or be subjected to any liability in respect to the exercise thereof.

Rights of married women.

40.—Where a married woman entitled for her separate use, and not restrained from anticipation, is desirous of giving any consent, doing any act, or becoming party to any proceeding under this Act, she shall be deemed to be an unmarried woman; but when any other married woman, who is by law incapable of giving her consent, or of being a party under this Act, is desirous of making any application, giving any consent, or becoming party to any proceeding under this Act, she shall be examined in the prescribed manner; and if the Land Commissioners ascertain that she is acting freely and voluntarily, she may make such application, do such act, or give such consent as if she were unmarried, and the Land Commission may, where it sees fit, appoint a person to act as the next friend of a married woman, for the purpose of any proceeding under this Act, and may from time to time remove or change such next friend.

Rights of persons under disability.

41.—Where any person who (if not under disability) might have made any application, given any consent, done any act, or been party to any proceeding under this Act in relation to any land or encumbrance on land, is an infant, idiot, or lunatic, the guardian or committee of the estate respectively of such person may make such applications, give such consents, do such acts, and be party to such proceedings as such persons respectively, if free from disability, might have made, given, done, or been party to, and shall otherwise represent such person for the purposes of this Act. Where there is no guardian or committee of the estate of any such person as aforesaid, being infant, idiot, or lunatic, or where any person is of unsound mind, or incapable of managing his affairs, but has not been found lunatic under an inquisition, it shall be lawful for the Land Commission to appoint a guardian of such person for the purpose of any proceedings under this Act, and from time to time to change such guardian.

Punishment for certain offences.

42.—If in the course of any proceedings before the Land Commission, in pursuance of this Act, any person concerned in such proceedings, with intent to conceal the title or claim of any person, or to substantiate a false claim, suppresses, attempts to suppress, or is privy to the suppression of any document, or of any fact, the person suppressing, attempting to suppress, or privy to suppression shall be guilty of a misdemeanour, and upon conviction or indictment shall be liable to be imprisoned for a term not exceeding two years, with or without hard labour, or to be fined such sum, not exceeding £500, as the Court before which he is tried may award.

Payment of rent-charge.

43.—All tithe rent-charge payable to the Land Commission in respect of any estate sold under this Act shall be paid by the Irish Receiver-General out of the moneys coming into his hands for a period of 49 years from the date of the sale of such estate, unless the same is previously redeemed in manner provided by an Act of the Legislature of Ireland; but so long as any charge guaranteed by the Treasury on such tithe rent-charge is unpaid, the terms of such redemption shall be assented to by the Treasury before the passing of such Act.

PART V.

ESTATE.

Definitions.

44.—For the purposes of this Act "an estate" means any land which the Land Commission may by order declare to constitute an estate within the meaning of this Act.

"Tenanted estate" means any estate in the occupation of tenants, including any part of such estate which, though temporarily unlet, is ordinarily let to tenants, including also any part of an estate let for the purposes of agistment or temporary depasturage.

Town parks, houses in villages, and other houses which are held as part of or as incidental to any estate in the course of sale under this Act may be treated for the purposes of this Act as part of such estate.

45.—This Act shall not apply to

(1) Any estate which is not in the main agricultural or pastoral in its character, or partly agricultural and party pastoral, nor to

(2) Any estate which is within the limits of a town, nor to

(3) Any estate or part of an estate which is demesne land or is or forms part of a home farm, or is ordinarily occupied by a landlord ; nevertheless such estate or part may, on the request of the landlord, be purchased by the State Authority, if such Authority think fit, at a price not exceeding the agricultural value thereof, and shall be vested in the State Authority as owners thereof, and the proceedings of this Act with respect to the vesting of estates in the State Authority shall apply accordingly.

Where any holding let to be used wholly or mainly for the purposes of pasturage, and valued under the Acts relating to the valuation of rateable property in Ireland at an annual value of not less than fifty pounds, forms part of any estate proposed to be sold by the landlord, the landlord may, if he thinks fit, exclude such holding from the sale, and nevertheless require the State Authority to purchase the remainder of his estate. On the other hand, if the landlord wishes to include any such holding in the sale of his estate, the State Authority may, if they think it expedient so to do, refuse to purchase such holding.

LANDLORD.

Definition of landlord.

46.—"The immediate landlord of a tenanted estate" means the person, whatever his interest may be in the estate, who at the introduction of this Act into Parliament—that is to say, on the 17th day of April one thousand eight hundred and eighty-six—was the immediate landlord, or person entitled as landlord, and not as agent or receiver, to receive the rents or take possession of the holdings on such estate ; and that notwithstanding that a receiver has been appointed by a court or mortgagee, or otherwise.

47.—The option of sale conferred on the immediate landlord by this Act may be transferred by the immediate landlord to any other person, by deed or will, or if not bequeathed may pass by devolution on death, but, save as aforesaid, shall not be transferred to any person by law or otherwise without the voluntary act of the immediate landlord. Any person entitled to exercise an option derived from an immediate landlord in pursuance of this Act shall be deemed, for the purposes of this Act, to be the immediate landlord.

May transfer option of sale.

Subject to rules under this Act, where the immediate landlord, as defined by this Act, of any estate himself pays rent in respect of such estate to a superior landlord, he shall at the prescribed time give notice to such superior landlord of his intention to exercise the option of sale; and if such superior landlord objects to the exercise thereof by the inferior landlord, the superior and inferior landlords may agree as to the terms on which they or one of them may exercise such option, or, in the event of disagreement, the superior landlord may apply to the Land Commission to substitute him for the inferior landlord, and the Land Commission may substitute the superior landlord for the inferior landlord on the superior landlord purchasing the estate of the inferior landlord at such price as the Land Commission may think just; and so, if there are more superior landlords than one, each superior landlord may, by agreement, be substituted for the next inferior landlord, or may purchase his interest in manner hereinbefore mentioned, at a price to be determined by the Land Commission.

Landlord and his superior.

Where there is a succession of landlords deriving title from one another, the earlier in such succession is deemed to be the superior of the next below in succession, and the next below in succession to be the inferior landlord to the landlord next above.

Subject to rules under this Act, where the immediate landlord, on being applied to by a superior landlord to exercise the option of sale, refuses to do so, the landlord aggrieved by such refusal may apply to the Land Commission; and if it appears to such Commission that by reason of the smallness of the interest possessed by the immediate landlord, or for any just cause, it is inequitable that the immediate landlord should refuse to exercise his option, the Land Commission may substitute the landlord so applying for the immediate landlord on his paying or undertaking to pay out of the purchase-money to the immediate landlord such sum, if any, as to the Land Commission may seem just. Where, in the case of an estate sold under this Act, the gross rent received by a superior landlord from any inferior landlord under a lease granted to such inferior landlord is, or will when apportioned, be less than one-fifth part of the gross rent of the estate sold under this Act, and the interest of such inferior landlord in the estate is equal to or more than one hundred years in duration at the time of the sale, such rent shall be deemed to be a chief rent, and such superior landlord shall be dealt with as a person entitled to a chief rent, and not as a landlord.

When immediate landlord refuses to apply.

When there are several landlords.

Subject to the prescribed regulations, where there is a tenanted estate, the ultimate reversion of which belongs to one owner, but parcels of which are divided amongst divers immediate landlords, the State Authority may, on the application of several landlords entitled to exercise a landlord's option, purchase the whole of such estate, and the sale shall be conducted by such persons as the immediate landlords may agree upon, or may, in the event of dispute, be determined by the Land Commission.

Any question which may arise as to whether a person is a landlord or immediate landlord within the meaning of this Act, or with respect to the landlord entitled to exercise the option of sale under this Act, shall be determined by the Land Commission.

No application for sale after fixed date.

48.—A landlord shall not be entitled to make an application for the sale of his estate under this Act after the 31st day of March one thousand eight hundred and ninety, and any such application, if made, shall not be entertained by the State Authority.

The priority of applications made to the State Authority on the same day shall be determined by lot in the prescribed manner.

ENCUMBRANCES.

Definition of encumbrances, head rent, etc.

49.—In the construction of this Act, unless the context otherwise requires—

"Encumbrances" means and includes head rents, mortgages, jointures, annual charges, and all other pecuniary outgoings on land, whether capital sums or annual sums, with the exception of the rents payable by the tenants on the estate, of rates and cess, and of tithe rent-charge, payable to the Land Commission, but does not include rights of common way, water, sporting, fishing, or turbary, rights to timber and minerals, and other like rights or easements.

"Head rent" means any Crown rent, quit-rent, fee, farm rent, or other rent or rent-charge, but does not include tithe rent-charge payable to the Land Commission, and does not include the rent payable by a tenant as defined by this Act.

"Chief rent" means any head rent as so defined, the gross amount of which is, or when apportioned as in this Act provided, will be less than one-fifth of the gross rent of the estate in respect of which the same is paid.

"Crown rent" includes any quit-rent due to the Crown.

"Encumbrancer" includes all persons owing or interested in any incumbrance as herein defined.

TENANT.

Definition of tenancy.

50.—In the construction of this Act, unless the context otherwise requires—

"Contract of tenancy" means a letting or agreement for the letting of land for a term of years, or for lives, or for lives and years, or from year to year, or for a year certain, or for any less term.

"Tenant" means a person occupying land under a contract of tenancy, and includes the successors in title or occupancy to a tenant; but where the tenant sublets part of his holding with the consent of his landlord, he shall, notwithstanding such subletting, be deemed for the purposes of this Act to be still in occupation of the holding.

"Holding" means the land occupied by a tenant under a contract of tenancy. *Holding.*

Where any doubt exists as to who is the tenant in whom a holding forming part of an estate purchased under this Act should vest, the Land Commission shall decide such doubt in such manner, and upon such terms of payment or compensation, as they think just.

51.—In the construction of this Act, unless the context otherwise requires— *Gross rent.*

"Gross rent of an estate" means the aggregate of the gross rents of all the holdings on that estate, as the same were payable on the last gale day in the year one thousand eight hundred and eighty-five.

"Gross rent" of a holding means (1) the judicial rent of such holding, and (2) where a judicial rent has not been fixed in the case of any holding, then there may be found the average rate by which the rents previous to the date of the passing of this Act fixed by the Land Commission in the same electoral division exceed or are less than Griffith's valuation of the holding, and the gross rent of any holding may be deemed to be fixed at such average rate over or under Griffith's valuation, and this rule may be applied whether such holding is or is not a holding for which a judicial rent can be fixed;

Provided that, if a landlord selling an estate or the tenant of any holding is dissatisfied that the gross rent of a holding other than a judicial rent should be ascertained in manner above provided, he may apply to the Land Commission to fix a judicial rent for such holding; and the Commission, notwithstanding the Land Law (Ireland) Act, 1881, does not apply to such holding, shall fix, for the purposes of this Act, a judicial rent for such holding, and the cost of so fixing the judicial rent may, if the application appears to the Land Commission to have been groundless, be ordered to be paid by the applicant; *How gross rent ascertained.*

Provided that this Act shall not, nor shall any Act to be passed by the Irish Legislature, impair any obligations arising from contract or judicial decision under the Landlord and Tenant (Ireland) Act, 1870, and the Land Law (Ireland) Act, 1881, and any Acts amending the same, or any of such Acts

GENERAL DEFINITIONS.

52.—In the construction of this Act, unless the context otherwise requires—

"State Authority" means such person or body of persons or department of the Irish Government as the Irish Legislature may determine for the purposes of this Act, or, until such Legislature so determine, as may be appointed by the Irish Government; and, subject to any Act of the Irish Legislature, any such person or body of persons or department shall, until and unless otherwise provided by the Irish Legislature, be deemed to be incorporated and entitled to hold land for the purposes of this Act, and any Act of such State Authority may be testified in such a manner as the State Authority may from time to time determine.

"Treasury" means the Commissioners of Her Majesty's Treasury.

"Prescribed" means prescribed by rules made in pursuance of this Act.

Town. "Town" means any corporate town subject to the control of Commissioners appointed in pursuance of any Act of Parliament, or any town having a market or fair, or any town within the meaning of the Landlord and Tenant (Ireland) Act, 1870.

"Person" and "landlord" respectively include a body of persons corporate or unincorporate; also the Crown, and any Commissioners or persons holding, or having the management of, property on behalf of the Crown.

"Expenses of management" means agents', receivers', or stewards' fees or salary, and expenses allowed to them in their accounts for travelling, valuations, maps, scrivenery, stamps, bailiff's salary, and costs in legal proceedings against tenants for recovery of rent.

COMMENCEMENT AND APPLICATION OF ACT.

35.—This Act shall come into operation on the day determined by order of Her Majesty in Council made in pursuance of the Irish Government Act, 1886, to be the day on and after which the Irish Legislature is declared to be established; and such day is in this Act referred to as the appointed day.

This Act shall apply to Ireland only.

APPENDIX III.

ADDRESS FROM CALTON HILL MEETING.

On the evening of June 21, a deputation waited on Mr. Gladstone at the Royal Hotel, Edinburgh, to present an address which had been adopted at a meeting held on the Calton Hill immediately after his arrival in the city. In acknowledging the address, which was presented by Mr. Walter Thorburn,

Mr. Gladstone said—I have never received any address in the course of a long life with greater pleasure than the address you now present to me; for these reasons. In the first place, I very much doubt whether at any time we have had in view a purpose of such vast and unmeasured importance. In the second place, because I doubt very much whether we have ever had a cause in our hands where the good that we sought for was more unmixed, and where the evils that we desire to avoid were more palpable and the menaces more formidable, gentlemen, to you and to your children. In the third place, I am sure by the character of this meeting, and by the words which have just been read in my hearing, that you, who are better judges, concur with me in the opinion that the enthusiasm of the nation, of the nation as distinguished from minor portions and sections of the nation, never was so great as on the present occasion. That was my experience in London, where I am much in the sight of the people, and have considerable means of judging of the state of feeling. That was my experience all along the route. That has been my crowning experience in Edinburgh. I echo fervently the prayer which has been uttered, that we may by the blessing of God be enabled to conduct this enterprise of ours to a speedy termination. A speedy termination, gentlemen, will be an honourable termination, a termination accompanied with mutual respect on the other side of the Channel and on this. A slow termination will be a painful termination, and probably a shameful termination. For I call it a shameful termination when, as in 1829, an act of justice is done, not because it is an act of justice, but in order to avoid the terrors of civil war. It is a speedy termination, gentlemen, that I desire. I feel certain what will be the end of this controversy; but I feel that on the action of the nation at this crisis depends whether it shall be a termination of honour and satisfaction to all parties, or whether it shall be mixed all along with painful and dishonoured anxieties, leaving behind it rankling sores that will tend for a long time to qualify the good that it will do, and diminish the satisfaction with which you all wish to see it followed.

APPENDIX IV.

MR. GLADSTONE AND THE LONDON CONSTITUENCIES.

MR. SYDNEY BUXTON, the Liberal candidate for Poplar, has received the following letter from Mr. Gladstone:—

HAWARDEN CASTLE, *June* 29, 1886.

DEAR MR. SYDNEY BUXTON,—I regret that, after the labours through which I have been passing among my late constituents and elsewhere, I cannot appear personally before the electors of any of the numerous divisions of London, in whose welfare I feel a cordial interest, and on whose wise or unwise use of the present opportunity so much depends. Through the channel of a letter to you I venture to offer them a few words intended to sum up the question that is before them.

A great cause now lies for decision between England and Ireland. A hundred years ago we gave to Ireland a free Parliament of her own, with which she was satisfied. Its constitution was faulty, but it made many and great improvements, and was beginning to make more and greater, when in 1795 the Tory Government of England stopped the work by recalling Lord Fitzwilliam, to the horror of every Liberal statesman of the day, and against the wish of the whole Irish people. This tyranny begat discontent. Discontent was met by arbitrary government. Then came resistance in 1798, and frightful bloodshed. These mischiefs, of which the Tory Government was the author, were made a pretext for the Union. Against the sense of Ireland and her Parliament every engine of force and fraud, bribery and intimidation within doors, arbitrary government and reckless promises in the country at large, were profusely employed, and by these shameful means, and no others, Ireland was partly entrapped, and partly coerced, into the Union.

The promises made were disgracefully broken. The sufferings of the people, declared by the Devon Commission to surpass those of any other Christian country, were shamefully neglected, but laws were passed to coerce them, and laws were passed to increase the power of their landlords over them, and to enhance for the advantage of those landlords the prices of their food. An alien State Church was maintained among them; and men professing the religion of the country were forbidden to sit in Parliament, until they became too strong to be resisted, and emancipation was granted by the Duke of Wellington, only to avoid civil war. Meanwhile, when in 1820 the county of Dublin wished to make a peaceful demonstration at a meeting regularly called, soldiers were sent to break it up.

This is a revolting record, but it is only a small part of the truth. Can you wonder that a cry, long and loud, was heard from Ireland against this Union so foully brought about? But, like many bad laws, it was a great law, difficult to change, and it had one good thing in it, namely, that it established the supremacy of Parliament. What does Ireland now say? By the mouth of 85 out of 101 of her popular representatives, she declares herself content with this supremacy. She leaves you what is good in the Union, and asks to be rid of what is bad. She asks you to do for her what you did with such advantage for Frenchmen in Canada, for Dutchmen at the Cape, for the children of convicts in Tasmania, to give her the management, not of English or of Scotch or of Imperial, but of simply Irish affairs.

There is a long record of disgraceful deeds against us, and the question is about wiping it away. They were done mostly before the first Reform Act. Since that time matters have improved. Good has been done (almost wholly in defiance of the Tories), but evil has also been done, and the good that should have been done has largely been left undone. The long course of evil belongs to the time before the nation was enfranchised; the partial good to the time since. Now for the first time the question is put whole and clear to an enfranchised nation, and the people of England and of Scotland have either to purge out the old shame of their country by listening to reason, or, by refusing to listen, to make that shame their own, with all the wretched consequences which it will increasingly entail.

I tell the people of London, *this* is the question they have to deal with; and for his own share of dealing with it by his vote each one of them will be responsible.

I need hardly tell you, my dear Mr. Buxton, what faith I have from former experience in the strong sympathies and upright sense of the people, or how fervently I desire the success of every one of those who are labouring together with you to consolidate the real, the hearty union of the countries, and the real and I trust immortal strength of the Empire.

Hoping that my wife, who often visits the East-end for other purposes, may very shortly appear there, I remain, my dear Mr. Buxton, sincerely yours,

W. E. GLADSTONE.

www.ingramcontent.com/pod-product-compliance
Lightning Source LLC
Chambersburg PA
CBHW030916270326
41929CB00008B/719

* 9 7 8 3 7 4 4 7 1 7 2 1 2 *